Special Children, Challenged Parents

Special Children, Challenged Parents

The Struggles and Rewards of Raising a Child With a Disability

Robert A. Naseef, Ph.D.

A Birch Lane Press Book
Published by Carol Publishing Group

A Birch Lane Press Book
Published by Carol Publishing Group
Birch Lane Press is a registered trademark of Carol Communications, Inc.

Editorial, sales and distribution, rights and permissions inquiries should be addressed to Carol Publishing Group, 120 Enterprise Avenue, Secaucus, N.J. 07094

In Canada: Canadian Manda Group, One Atlantic Avenue, Suite 105, Toronto, Ontario, M6K 3E7

Carol Publishing Group books may be purchased in bulk at special discounts for sales promotion, fund-raising, or educational purposes. Special editions can be created to specifications. For details, contact Special Sales Department, 120 Enterprise Avenue, Secaucus, N.J. 07094.

Manufactured in the United States of America
10   9   8   7   6   5   4   3   2   1

DAY IS DONE, by Peter Yarrow. © 1969 Pepamar Music Corp. All Rights Reserved. Used by Permission. WARNER BROS. PUBLICATIONS U.S. INC. Miami, FL. 33014

LIBRARY OF CONGRESS CATALOGING-IN-PUBLICATION DATA

Naseef, Robert A.
    Special children, challenged parents : the struggles and
rewards of parenting a child with a disability / Robert A. Naseef.
        p.   cm.
    "A Birch Lane Press book."
    ISBN 1-55972-377-7
    1. Parents of handicapped children—United States—Psychology.
    2. Parents of handicapped children—United States—Attitudes.
    3. Handicapped children—United States—Family relationships.
    4. Handicapped children—United States—Psychology.   I. Title.
HQ759.913.N37   1997
649'.151—dc21
                                                    96-49752
                                                        CIP

To my future,
Tariq,
Antoinette,
Kara, and
Zoë

Contents

Prologue

A Letter to My Son

Your joy is your sorrow unmasked....
The deeper that sorrow carves into your being,
the more joy you can contain.

—KAHLIL GIBRAN

February 19, 1993

Dear Tariq,

I'll never forget the night you were born. It was more than incredible; indeed it was magical. It had been a long labor—over twenty-four hours. When you came out of your mother's belly, you seemed to look all around the delivery room, even before your body was completely out. Without thinking about it, I jumped from my position behind the delivery table and wound up right there beside the doctor—my knees wobbling, my heart pounding with excitement. The doctor, an older man who had delivered many babies, commented on how alert you looked.

Right away I could tell that your head was the same shape as mine. The skin on my face tightened as I beamed at you. I counted your fingers and your toes and breathed more easily knowing that every-thing was okay. The nurse cleaned you up while I watched eagerly, and she wrapped you in a flannel blanket. You looked so cute. You were a perfect newborn. I had dreamed of having a boy, and I love retelling this story. I love reliving those moments filled with ecstasy. Your birth is one of my warmest memories.

When the nurse put you in my arms, I felt the electricity of that instant. You felt so soft and delicate to my fingertips. I cradled you next to my heart. Our eyes met and locked on to each other's for the first time. Your eyes looked so big and round. It was one of the most exciting moments of my life. From that moment I have looked at the world differently.

Ever since then, I have held a special respect for a woman's ability to give birth—for every woman's special partnership in the miracle of life. I thought of my mother, who gave birth to eight healthy children. It was a new beginning in my consciousness. Through you, the wonder of life began to be revealed to me in a way that I could never have imagined. Now I know firsthand what Kahlil Gibran means about how inextricably woven together are our moments of joy and sorrow!

You were born in the wee hours of the morning of November 29, 1979. Jimmy Carter was the president; American hostages were being held in Tehran; Frank Rizzo was the mayor of Philadelphia. I saved the newspaper from that day for you to have when you were older, so you could read about what was happening in the world on the day you got here. You were born at the Medical College of Pennsylvania, formerly Women's Medical College, the first medical school for women in our country, high on the banks of the Schuylkill River in Philadelphia.

When I left you and your mom in the hospital that night, I looked up at the sky. The stars were shining brightly. There were a few clouds, but they didn't stop the nearly full moon from casting a warm glow over the earth near the river. It was a perfect moment frozen in time, in my memory, and in my heart. The cool night air filled my lungs and refreshed me, and even though it was winter, it reminded me of the words of a poem by Robert Browning that I had learned in grade school:

> *The year's at the spring,*
> *And day's at the morn;*
> *Morning's at seven;*
> *The hillside's dew-pearled;*
> *The lark's on the wing:*
> *The snail's on the thorn;*
> *God's in his heaven—*
> *All's right with the world.*

Telling people about you was so exciting. You were the second grandchild and the first grandson my parents had. I remember my dad saying how lucky I was to live when fathers could be present at the birth of their children. He never saw any of his children being born, and listening to his reaction to your birth brought me closer to him, knowing the excitement he, too, must have felt and hearing his wish to have been more involved.

I wish you could read this someday, Tariq. I wish you could know what you have meant to me. If anyone had told me when you were born that you would never read, never write, never carry on a normal conversation, I wouldn't have been able to handle it. In truth, I was crushed for a long, long time after I found out that you were autistic. The weight of my broken dreams was so heavy. It was as if a house had collapsed on me, but I stayed alive at the bottom of the heap of rubble. I have fought through it, and over time, the weight has lessened.

I want you to know that you have never lost your place in my heart. I still save that yellowed newspaper from November 29, 1979. Some of my greatest joys and some of my deepest sorrows have been in the moments you and I have shared. In many respects, your life is limited. But your life is priceless to me, and even to the world beyond us.

Pearl Buck, the writer and humanitarian, had only one biological child, and that child was retarded. Buck wrote a book about her daughter called *The Child Who Never Grew*. The title reminds me of how you will always be a little boy inside. Buck concluded that we can learn as much from illness as from health, that disability can have as much meaning as ability and sometimes even more, when we learn to find the treasures there.

There is one thing you have done and continue to do uniquely for me. Without speaking a word, you have taught the little boy in me to speak. In this way you are with me at every moment. You have all the positive emotions as well as the negative. You taught me to see them readily. When you feel good, you show interest and excitement. You show pride when you accomplish something you set out to do, and you have a refreshing sense of humor. When you're startled, you let me know by raising your eyebrows, opening your eyes wide, and opening your mouth.

Because of you, I have learned how to tune in to signals I used to miss. You don't recognize danger and you seldom experience fear, so I have to be extra vigilant. When you're in distress, you let people know it, although it's often hard to tell what's bothering you. Because you can't connect with others, we can only use empathy to try to understand you....But what power lies there! In a world that values reason and intellect above emotion, nonverbal children like you teach us to look inside ourselves.

Nature gave me a fair amount of intelligence and ability, but I was a shy child. Before you came, I didn't know much about my feelings or what they meant. When someone would ask me how I felt, I usually went blank. There was a confusing numbness deep inside my soul and a sense of frustration and inadequacy when I could not answer.

Unable to connect my thoughts and feelings, my abilities were locked in. Now I am aware of all the shades and colors of the emotions in my inner life—both positive and negative. You have revealed this great treasure to me. The need to translate our experiences together has made me more articulate about feelings, and I've been able to help others as a psychologist.

I've been keeping journals about you and our experiences for many years, and now I'm making a book from them, Tariq. I am going to share what you have meant to me because there are millions of other children like you—some with more ability, some with less. These "imperfect" children are usually born to loving parents who must struggle to rise from disappointment to find a stronger love—an unconditional love that lies on the other side of sorrow.

Not long ago, Tariq, I bought an old Peter, Paul, and Mary tape at a flea market for fifty cents. On it is a beautiful song called "Day is Done." As I was listening, Cindy, your stepmom, called my attention to a particular verse. She said it was about you.

> *Tell me why you're crying my son,*
> *I know you're frightened like everyone.*
> *Is it the thunder in the distance you fear?*
> *Will it help if I stay very near?*
> *I am here....*
>
> *And if you take my hand my son,*
> *All will be well when the day is done....*
>
> *Tell me why you're smiling my son.*
> *Is there a secret you can tell everyone?*
> *Do you know more than men who are wise?*
> *Can you see what we all must disguise,*
> *With your loving eyes?*

Of course you do, son. That's why the song speaks so directly to me. I think we have a lot to share with people about the meaning of our lives together, Tariq. It can be so full and rich amid all the difficulties. It will never fit completely in any book. It's a matter of the heart.

Take my hand....I am near....I love you,
Dad

God grant me the serenity
    to accept the things
    I cannot change,
Courage to change the things
    I can, and the
Wisdom to know the difference.

Living one day at a time;
Enjoying one moment at a time;
Accepting hardship as the
    pathway to peace.

— REINHOLD NIEBUHR

ONE

My Story

When you are a parent of a child who is developing more slowly than average, you may feel alone, but you are not. Knowing that you are not alone is a big part of the cure for the worry and pain. There is a great benefit for all parents whose children are not developing typically in understanding the similarities between themselves and others. Much healing can occur in exchanging stories with others in similar circumstances. This is why I am including some of the details of Tariq's early days here to explain more about the life I've lived. Readers will be able to relate to the material in this book better if they know my story.

My perspective has come from a journey through the grief of broken dreams. This is a passage that redefines the meaning of life for all who must travel through it. Its successful completion is guided by hope and leads to deeper love for your child and the other people in your life. This book provides the key to a way of thinking that has evolved from my personal life, my education, and my experiences as a professional guide to many others.

Sixteen years ago my only son and oldest child, Tariq, was a seemingly normal, happy toddler. He was all that I had imagined him to be and more. There was something new in our life every day. When he was four months old, for example, he began to lift up his head and look around. I took a picture of him then that I still prize. There is an amazing resemblance to an old picture of me that my mother had taken when I was the same age.

A month later he began to crawl. It was so much fun to see and feel his excitement. There was a gleam in his eye as he motored at will around the house, pulling himself along with the help of furniture and walls to get where he wanted to be.

1

By his eighth month and beaming with pride, Tariq could pull himself up to a standing position. He would glance around smiling, planning his route to whatever looked like fun. A few weeks later he began to "cruise," holding on to furniture and getting around upright whenever he could. I would frequently hold his hands above his head and walk behind him, full of anticipation for his next achievement.

Before long it was Tariq's first birthday, and his first baby steps came on that big day. I recall his initial look of apprehension and then the smile that expressed the thrill of achievement as he took his awkward, wobbly steps. I was so proud of him. What an amazing accomplishment! His mother and I were cheering him on. This is still one of my most vivid memories of him—when he was "normal."

By eighteen months Tariq was just beginning to speak and had a small but useful vocabulary. He had been meeting all of the developmental milestones, and I imagined that before long he would play Little League baseball. In my mind's eye, I beamed with pride and cheered as he fielded a ball or swiftly ran the bases. I would be there watching as my father had watched me. Down the road, I imagined having philosophical discussions with him as a young man. Our relationship would be close and warm; he would come to me comfortably whenever he wanted. I would give him space when he needed or wanted it. In these ways and others I planned on being the perfect dad.

At eighteen months, Tariq was treated for an ear infection and, after that, he was never the same. I began to wonder if my dreams for him would ever be realized. He became frustrated and withdrawn. He cried a lot and didn't sleep well at night. I worried, especially at night when I was awake with him. My daughter, Antoinette, had just been born, and at first their pediatrician thought Tariq's change could be an emotional response to no longer being an only child. His mother and I hoped that the doctor was right, but I was scared about what it would mean if he was wrong.

Soon Tariq stopped talking and stopped playing with the toys he had received for his birthday—like the little workbench with its nuts and bolts and tools. My parents had given it to him; it was just like one I had when I was a little boy. Instead, he began playing with a transparent rattle that had brightly colored beads inside it. He seemed fascinated by this toy and played with it for days and weeks on end while ignoring virtually everything else around him, including his baby sister.

When Antoinette was born, I was thrilled to have a daughter. I thought then that I had a perfect family—the "rich man's family" of a boy and a girl. Life seemed complete; I felt lucky, but that feeling didn't last for long. I became tense and anxious about Tariq. Both his mother and I wondered if either of us had done anything to cause his condition. Still I kept telling myself that everything would be okay.

The awakening was rude. That exciting time when every day brought a new accomplishment was gone. My sweet toddler was gone. Tariq became very agitated and upset if the rattle was taken away. His life, which had been such a great joy to me, became a worry that preoccupied my every moment. I was glad to see him when I got home from work, but the fun of playing with him was gone. Since he still liked being touched and cuddled, although now he always turned his face away from me, I clung desperately to the hope that Tariq would become "normal" again, that he would talk again.

When Tariq was two, I spent the summer at home with him while I was on vacation from my teaching position. The pediatrician had said that he might just need time. I worked hard to get Tariq's attention—to establish eye contact and a connection. I would put him on the swing in the backyard and stand in front as I pushed him. All the while I tried to catch his gaze for a fraction of a second. He would turn his eyes to the side on purpose; he was a master at avoiding contact.

It felt like a personal rejection. This part of Tariq's developmental disorder was especially frustrating because, although I was skilled at helping children with learning problems, all my efforts with my own son were fruitless. Eventually, but not until he was diagnosed with autism a few years later, I learned that he was easily overwhelmed by stimuli, and I had to back off.

As his third birthday approached, it became clear that Tariq could not attend regular preschool. His lack of speech alone indicated that he was developmentally far behind other children his age, but this was very hard to accept. His mother and I enrolled him in a preschool that took children with special needs, but he didn't fit even there. The psychologist there thought Tariq might be hearing impaired. On his advice we went to visit a school for young children with hearing impairments. As I write these words, I can feel the way my insides shook as I was struck by the fear that my child would be walking around with two hearing aids like the children I saw there.

I wondered what his life would be like. He would be different, I told myself, just different. Little did I know what was really in store for me and my child.

Now began the trips to numerous specialists and special schools.

There were many sleepless nights waiting for test results and no answers to the mystery of why Tariq had stopped speaking.

A specialist found fluid in Tariq's ears blocking his hearing, and he was treated for this condition with medication. My hopes rose—it seemed like such a simple solution to Tariq's problems. Although tests of his brain stem indicated that his ears worked, it was impossible to tell if his brain comprehended words. The fluid cleared up, but he continued to express himself only with grunts and babbling and crying—no words—and began to constantly twist and turn to get away from face-to-face contact. Still I dreamed at night that the babbling would turn into words. After all, that's what babbling leads to for the average child.

Tariq was in an early-intervention program for children with developmental delays by his third birthday, and he was the most difficult child in the school to manage. He required one-on-one attention at all times. He couldn't or wouldn't stay in his seat for more than a few seconds if left unattended. Whenever I wasn't teaching myself, I spent the day with him in school, helping the teachers.

Eventually my son was diagnosed as being afflicted by a "pervasive developmental delay," a broader term for autism. The condition can be found in twelve of every ten thousand children. The team of professionals that evaluated him at the hospital where he was born used the words *autistic-like* and *retarded* in their diagnosis. I went numb at first and then became livid with rage at them. While the anger long ago subsided, the tears are still never far. The professionals seemed to have no hope for my son. How could they give him such a diagnosis? How could I give up on Tariq? The words I was hearing sliced through me like a knife.

"Has anyone told you that your son is retarded?" With these words, the social worker broke the news to us. What a way to tell parents something of this nature!

As I remember it now, I withdrew inside myself as I learned about the disorder. It was painful to read that autism was a severely incapacitating and lifelong disability. It was hard to comprehend that my child's brain cannot process what he hears, sees, or feels. The information that he takes in is distorted or fragmented, making it incomplete and confusing. We were told that communication with others, or the world outside him, would always be extremely difficult.

I couldn't talk about it. I wanted to, but the words just wouldn't come out. They stuck in my throat, especially the word *autism*. Once in a while I would blurt out my worry that my son still wasn't talking even though he was over three, and at night I cried and cried. There was no comfort. Professionals, relatives, and friends rarely seemed to know what to say or how to say it.

Like many parents in similar situations, I spared no expense in the quest to find a cure for Tariq. Speech and movement therapies and even vitamins and a special diet were tried to help him. The burden of the debts from these treatments was for years a constant reminder of my hope for a cure. My dreams died a slow death as I ran out of treatments to try. As I became strong enough to face it, the reality that Tariq's condition was lifelong slowly came into focus.

Unfortunately I got no help from within my marriage and felt most alone at home. To put it simply and kindly, the strain of Tariq's disability added to the other stresses that led to a divorce. After years of trying to go through it together, it was easier to try it alone. My ex-wife and I tried several custodial arrangements in an effort to find what worked best for the children and ourselves. It was extremely difficult and the details are lengthy and involved. Suffice it to say that as a single parent, I faced a life that had changed permanently and profoundly—something I had neither planned on nor allowed myself to imagine. But now I was comprehending what had transpired.

Every minute of every waking hour was affected—the list of Tariq's special needs seemed endless, and the amount of care required was overwhelming. Since he rarely slept through the night, I was constantly exhausted. This lasted for over seven years, and the feeling stayed in my body even longer. I never knew what would happen next. Tariq was perpetual motion, and it was hard to tell what you would find as you followed or chased him from room to room. The entire house had to be childproofed lest there be danger to Tariq or to my possessions. Even the refrigerator had to be locked.

Because he had no sense of danger, there was always the possibility my son would run into traffic, burn his hand, or step over the edge of the pool into the deep water. The only part of my original dream that came true was that Tariq became a fast runner, but unfortunately this made for even fewer relaxing moments.

Once, at six years old he got out of my apartment in the middle of the night. I was terrified at the thought of how I might find him as I ran looking for him. My heart pounded so hard that I thought my chest would burst. Even though I found him playing happily in the playground a few blocks and a few busy streets away, my heart kept pounding for what seemed like hours. Tariq's death is the only thing that I can imagine that would be more difficult than his life.

I decided to enter psychotherapy, and this certainly helped me to keep going. It was one of the best things that I ever did for myself. I come from a family that doesn't often express feelings verbally or directly. This was something that I desperately needed to do now to survive. It was like finding water in the desert. My therapist helped me to express my feelings, but it was hard to make sense of them—to reconcile them to the reality I was experiencing. It was good to have found a way to express my emotions but I was being flooded and overwhelmed with them, and, despite my therapist, it felt crazy at times.

Why couldn't I calm down? The constant emphasis on doing more for Tariq that came from many professionals was not helping me with my guilt or with the "acceptance" that I was supposed to reach. It felt like there must be a defect in me that kept me from accepting my son as he was. Was I a bad person?

At this point, over ten years ago, a colleague and close friend showed me an article in the then-current issue of the *Journal of Counseling and Development* that talked about the grief experienced by the parents of children with disabilities. It was written by Milton Seligman, who is a professor at the University of Pittsburgh and, as I would later learn, is also the parent of an adult child with a disability. As I read sentence after sentence of Seligman's article, I came to a deeper awareness of myself. Many disconnected feelings and thoughts began to make sense. When I completed the article, I leaned back in my desk chair, took a few slow deep breaths, and thought, So that is what Tariq's life is all about to me; I am a bereaved parent.

From that day onward, my life began to change for the better. I had a new lens through which to analyze my experience. My new self-knowledge helped me in the process of learning to cope with the many problems associated with having a child with a disability. It still took time and help from others, but I understood my thoughts and feelings better. As I look back, I believe that the failure of my therapy in this regard was partially a failure of my therapist and partially a general lack of understanding in the field about the grief experienced by parents of children with disabilities.

I still struggled through some horribly dark moments, but I began to reclaim my life. Cindy, the friend who showed me Seligman's article, helped me by encouraging me to talk and by listening to everything I had to say without expressing any judgment or expectation. She eventually became my lover, and we later married. Life did indeed go on with new dreams.

I had entered a doctoral program in psychology before knowing for sure that my five-year-old son was disabled for life. Since I was doing everything possible for Tariq, I concluded that delaying my own development would serve no purpose. It was trying at times, but my professors and my boss at work were very supportive. There were things to look forward to once again—both personally and professionally.

When my daughter Antoinette learned to read, I was very, very thankful. Every time she learned a new word it let me know that her brain was normal. It was unbelievably exciting to live through this period with her—not to mention the great relief it was to know that she was all there and could learn in the standard ways. I could literally breathe easier and have done so ever since.

By this time I understood "normal" human development as the miracle it really is. My tears as I observed Antoinette daily breaking the code to read were born of intense joy. She has a special talent in art and writing that fills me with pride and gratitude, especially when she gives me a drawing or a painting or shows me something she has written. There is little that I take for granted anymore. Life is truly very fragile at times. You never know when something might break and what that will do to your heart.

For my doctoral dissertation, I decided to research the qualities of the families that had coped successfully with having a child with a disability. It was a way of focusing on the positive. Besides the obvious interest that I had in knowing as much as possible for myself, I hoped that what I learned might be of use to others. In fact, the research process led me to further integrate the thoughts, feelings, and experiences that I had begun analyzing both in therapy and on my own. I hoped to help bridge the gap of understanding that frequently exists between the families of children with special needs and those professionals whose job it is to assist them.

As I neared completion of my doctoral program, this dream came true when I began to speak to countless groups of parents and professionals in various communities about my life and my work. While these presentations were often draining, they also inspired me. I became effective at helping people to connect across the chasm that too often divides parents and professionals. I helped to develop a training package for the New Jersey Department of Education to foster parent-professional collaboration, and the final project is now being implemented throughout the state.

In 1991, the *Journal of Counseling and Development*, which had been so helpful to me, published my article, "Lost Dreams, New Hopes," about my personal experiences and their impact on my professional life. It is used as a handout in counseling and special education classes, and I still get letters and phone calls from people who have read it.

In 1992, another dream came true. My independent practice as a psychologist grew to the point where I was able to be completely self-employed and specialize in working with the parents of children with disabilities.

I have come a long way. My son's disability helped me to develop more ability than I thought I had. He gave me the opportunity to do something special. The knowledge and wisdom that I acquired through losing my dream of a normal child are helping me to be all that I can.

Tariq's disability was so severe that he needed round-the-clock care by the time he was eight and had to be placed in a residential program. Putting him into residential treatment was the hardest decision that I ever had to make.

As much as his disability has hurt and continues to hurt, Tariq has made me aware of the value of life. He is so innocent and generally happy, smiley, and cuddly. Tariq is such a gentle soul that he has always been a staff favorite wherever he has been in school. These thoughts always bring a calming stillness to my heart and a smile to my face.

As difficult as it has been, I have been able to adjust and live a relatively normal, happy, and rewarding life. I am experiencing more fulfillment than I ever knew was possible. I feel whole and loved and loving. I have learned so much from the other parents I have met who are working through the many aspects of their own grief and are then emerging hopeful, strong, sensitive, and proud.

Sometimes I'm not sure if I deserve such a full life. I feel like a plane crash survivor, with devastation all around me—particularly in the hearts of those parents in earlier stages of recovery than I. Every time I walk into an early-intervention program, I feel this. Every time a couple struggling with this kind of grief is referred to my practice, I revisit my own pain. As I listen to their story, I am inevitably reminded that I deserve to feel good sometimes—I have paid my dues.

The process of grieving, coping, and "going on with your life" is the focus of this book. I have included many accounts of life with children with various chronic conditions and disabilities besides autism. I believe that what I have to offer that's unique is my ability to integrate my personal experience, my clinical expertise as a psychologist who specializes in helping the families of children with disabilities, and my research and knowledge in the field.

Regardless of the nature of their child's disability, parents have many similar experiences as they learn to survive and cope. It is the challenge of a lifetime to do everything possible to help your child and to maintain hope and fight off despair while striving to live as normal a life as possible. Trying to be realistic but hopeful is sometimes quite a paradox.

I trust that my readers will be able to learn to help themselves by understanding their own experiences and those of others they will be reading about. They will be aided, as I am, by current psychological perspectives on the many issues facing the parents of children with disabilities and special needs.

The chapters that follow in this book trace the parents' journey. They tell of some of the mountains to be climbed, not one at a time necessarily or in any particular sequence, but a little of this one and a little of that one, until eventually you are healed enough to feel whole again. Chapter 2 describes that flood of emotion and frantic thoughts that occurs when you realize that there is something wrong with your child. Making sense of these emotions that signal the experience of loss is vitally important. Chapter 3 explores the somewhat predictable stages of working through this grief and attempts to understand what "acceptance" might mean when your child is alive but not who you expected.

One of the most trying challenges parents face is accepting and just being with a child every day who is so different from the norm. The behavior of children with limited ability, understanding, or language can be very perplexing. There is a great deal of embarrassment that parents experience when their child acts "weird" in front of others. The subject of bonding with the child and applying the principles of child guidance is dealt with in the fourth and fifth chapters. Most books on parenting do not apply these concepts to children with special needs.

The sixth chapter is devoted to the experience of fathers in this situation. Since most men don't speak much about emotional experiences, let alone grief, this chapter is meant to fill a need that I have not seen adequately addressed for fathers.

What happens to your marriage while this grief process is going on is explored in chapter 7, which deals with male-female differences as they apply in this situation. This is another topic rarely addressed adequately and where guidance is sorely needed.

Parents with disabled children worry about what happens to their "normal children" and how to "be there" for them. Sibling rivalry takes somewhat different forms because of the profound difference in the family structure that disability carries with it. Chapter 8 is devoted to this theme.

Chapter 9 provides suggestions for getting support through relatives, friends, groups, or informal networks with other parents in similar situations. There is such a healing power in opening up and confiding in each other. This chapter seeks to unlock that power.

From there we move to the final chapter, which concerns dealing effectively with the powerful professionals involved in our children's daily life. We want these professionals to rescue us and fix our child. We get angry when we can't get the services we want and need. At times we have to confront them. At other times we have to learn to work together.

All along this journey, whatever the sequence might be for each individual, we hopefully gain wisdom, develop a personal philosophy, and derive a meaning from our experiences that will sustain us.

It has been quite a trek. I look back now with a confidence born from my survival and recovery. I can look forward to the joys and challenges of my current marriage and family life. My work feels successful every time I can empower another parent by helping him understand his thoughts and feelings, find humor in his situation, and go on to cope with his problems. I hope this book does some of that for you. I feel good about how far I've come, but the cost has been great....My only wish is that I could have learned so much some other way, without going through it myself.

TWO

Feeling the Impact:
Lost Dreams and Growth

The dream of a perfect child can die a painful death. If you have a child with a disability, you certainly want compassionate words. When you find out your child is disabled, you just want it all to go away, and it won't. Dr. Elliott Lube is quoted in *The Bereaved Parent* as saying, "When your parent dies you have lost your past—when your child dies you have lost your future."

The Japanese writer Kenzaburo Oe has quite eloquently described this very intense and exceptionally personal loss. In 1964, when Oe was twenty-nine, his first child was born with brain damage. He named his baby boy Pooh and described their very close bond in a story called "Teach Us to Outgrow Our Madness." Oe and his fragile child became so close that Oe said that he believed he would die when Pooh died. Oe was convinced that he and his son shared sensations so completely that he directly felt the physical manifestations of his child's pain.

Oe perceived his child's force on his dreams as that of a nuclear explosion—a personal holocaust. Coming from a man who grew up in Japan in the aftermath of Hiroshima and Nagasaki, this is an especially powerful metaphor to describe the change in his personal world. Oe's novel *A Personal Matter*, written the year Pooh was born, was the first of a series whose central character is the young father of a brain-damaged child. Oe wrote of his connection to his child and of his quest to survive the personal devastation he felt. He won the Nobel Prize for literature in 1994.

The purpose of this chapter is to help the reader understand the natural and normal feeling processes that are triggered by worries over a child's development, troubling observations of the child, and the diagnosis of a disability or chronic illness.

Let's start with pregnancy, when expectant parents the world over worry that something could go wrong with their baby during the pregnancy or birth process. They are routinely told to calm down and that everything will be all right. When their infant's early development is slower than expected, or when a parent intuitively senses that something is wrong, medical professionals generally, and often wisely, urge parents to be patient because there is a wide range of "normal" development. Unfortunately, patience is not always rewarded.

Approximately 10 percent of all children born have or develop a disability or chronic illness in their early years. The impairments may be "mild," such as a learning disability that will only be diagnosed after the child starts school, or they may be more "severe" handicaps such as deafness, blindness, cerebral palsy, heart disease, mental illness, and juvenile diabetes. I have put quotation marks around *mild* and *severe* because when a parent learns that a child isn't normal, it usually knocks that parent over for a period of time, whatever the severity of the disability. There are different incidences or odds for each disability, but when it happens to you, it's always 100 percent. You are totally surrounded by your fate, as the father, played by Nick Nolte, in the movie *Lorenzo's Oil*, highlighted when he said that he felt like "a loser in the genetic lottery."

Every expectant parent has a lot of dreams—the kind you have when you're awake. Will the child be a boy or a girl? Who will she look like? What kind of personality will he have? What will she be when she grows up? What kind of things will you enjoy doing with your child? What new and exciting places will you go? How your life will be different! In all these ways and more, children are very important to parents. They can be a source of great joy—or of devastating sorrow.

Although people have children for different reasons, most couples look forward to having children as the fulfillment of their marriage. Since parents take great pride in and have great hopes for their children, when something is wrong the impact is profound. All the positive feelings are deflated, and the wonderful pride and hope that filled life so naturally are difficult to recover. The dreams for a normal, healthy child evaporate; the real child cannot live up to the original expectations. There is often a profound sense of failure for bringing a "defective" child into the world and often, too, a horrible guilt for feeling so disappointed in your own child.

As a child I was very shy and reserved, so I expected my son to be dynamic and articulate—to give voice to my life through his existence. Like so many parents, I wanted to recreate myself and come out better. I gave my son the middle name Donato, the Italian equivalent of Donald and my grandfather's first name, which means "gift." His first name, Tariq, is the name of a star and of a famous Arab general from the tenth century. In the Mideast the Rock of Gibraltar is sometimes called Tariq's rock, named for where that general crossed over from Morocco to Spain.

I had big dreams for my son....I guess I wanted him to do things that I hadn't—to be the man I hadn't yet become. These dreams set the scene for Tariq to enter my life, but it was to be otherwise. He has taught me to live myself and not through my children, just as his disability has opened me to the world of my inner life of dreams, hopes, disappointments, and joys. This process has included understanding the meaning of each feeling. At times it hurts so much to feel them that I want to block them out. The feelings, however, are messages from the inner self about what is going on, and they serve as needed guideposts on the inner journey.

As John Bradshaw says often in his lectures on public television, "You can't heal what you can't feel." This seems simple, but generations have been taught to ignore or mute painful feelings. For this reason, these particularly powerful and spontaneous feelings are socially unacceptable. The idea that feelings interfere with thinking discredits people who seem to be emotionally involved in whatever bothers them.

One Family's Journey Begins

The Warrens stand out in my memory from my doctoral research because they were so highly articulate about their feelings. Through their willingness to share their experiences, they had helped the families of other children with hearing impairments. They are a warm, friendly family of moderate means who live in a row house neighborhood in Baltimore. My first interview was with Linda, a tall, slender, red-haired woman who told her story with intensity and fervor. At the time, her son, Ben, who has a severe hearing impairment, was ten years old, and his sister, Anna, was twelve.

According to Linda, she and her husband, Bill, noticed that something was different about Ben when he was about nine months old and had not begun to vocalize the way their other child had done at that age. They clapped their hands when the baby was sleeping. He woke up, and they concluded for the moment that he was not deaf.

When Ben was a year old, they told the pediatrician that they didn't believe he was hearing properly. Although she was sure that something was wrong, Linda had a hard time convincing the doctor. The doctor stood behind the baby and clapped. Ben blinked, and the doctor said there was nothing wrong. Linda was still concerned because her baby had not begun to babble. At the time of the next checkup, the doctor clapped his hands again, and this time (luckily, according to Bill and Linda) Ben did not blink, so a referral was finally made to an ear specialist.

The ear specialist diagnosed fluid in Ben's ear when the boy was seventeen months old. The fluid was drained with tubes, and there was a slight improvement; Ben began to babble, but he did not talk. Linda became very alarmed. But when she told the doctor, he responded, "Why do you worry so much? You must be a worry wart."

Intuitively, like so many mothers, Linda knew something was wrong. Ben didn't act anything like his sister had. Bill had confidence and trust in Linda, and he had observed on his own that something wasn't right with their son. Bill and Linda kept pushing, so the doctor ordered a brain stem test at the hospital. Both parents waited anxiously for the results. Eventually Ben was diagnosed with a severe to profound hearing loss. Linda and Bill told me that they were both devastated. Even though they had long suspected that something was wrong, the diagnosis made them numb. They couldn't believe what they were being told. They recalled being worried, angry, and sad.

They went to another hospital to get a second opinion. This time they were told that their child had a mild to severe sloping hearing loss with some hearing in the upper range. Linda hoped that this meant her son could be normal. She could not really believe otherwise; Bill hoped she was right. Together they clung to their dreams for their little boy.

The Warrens' experience can be generalized to many other families. Frequently parents, especially mothers—who usually spend the most time with the child—get a sense that something is wrong with their child's development. Others, including doctors, try to calm the anxious parent. Doctors, too, can be subject to denial. It's hard to give bad news. The doctor doesn't want it to be true either. Denial on the part of a professional, however, frequently makes things worse. When a doctor is in denial regarding a child's disability, a parent's anxiety may increase in response; "if the doctor thinks my child is okay, I must be crazy."

At times when she was "really down" after the diagnosis, Linda turned to her husband. She realized that their son was different and that she could not change that. Allowing herself to cry helped. She also tried to be "good to herself" by not worrying about housework. At times she slept a lot to get through the day. She was not ready to reach out, and being alone helped her to grieve and heal.

Bill told me that his emotional reaction was not as intense as Linda's, although at one time he had cried unexpectedly while telling one of his best friends about Ben's disability. As he told me this, I reflected yet again how hard it is for most men to admit their tears.

Ben's disability was tough for this family, but they have survived and even flourished. They love one another deeply and enjoy life. As Bill put it, "Once you accept the fact that life is not a level playing field, you can learn to deal with things." Their acceptance gave me hope.

Getting in Touch With Your Inner Self

When Tariq was six, I thought that I was ready to help other parents understand their feelings about children with disabilities. I quickly discovered that I was only a novice. I would stand in front of a group, talk about some of my experiences, and then ask the people present how they felt about their own children's disabilities. An uneasy silence would ensue. Someone might ask a question, and I would answer. It was difficult to get people to open up about their feelings. At this point in my training, I was in supervision with a senior psychologist, Bert Kauffman, a retired professor in independent practice in Philadelphia. Bert methodically taught me how to help people develop a vocabulary for their emotions. He patiently pointed out how asking people if they were angry might not help them to discover if they actually were. His way of teaching would be to ask if I was the slightest bit annoyed or troubled about something. If so, he would ask me to explain it to him. From this experience, I learned quickly how to have this kind of dialogue with an individual. Combining Dr. Kauffman's instruction with what I was learning at Temple University about group process, I was able to apply these techniques to working with groups. I developed the Feeling Checklist as a way to help people explore their responses to their child's impairment.

The following exercise is presented here to help you explore your feelings. I have used it with numerous groups of parents and professionals to facilitate talking about feelings that commonly arise. If you are a parent, imagine a typical day with your exceptional child. If you have a brother or sister with a disability, likewise imagine a typical day. If you are a relative or friend, do the same. If you are a professional, imagine some of the children you have worked with and developed strong feelings for, or imagine that you yourself have a child with a disability.

Now, whatever your relationship may be with the child, look at the following checklist and circle those adjectives (they're all negative) that describe the way you feel during a typical day with the special child.

When you have finished, take a few moments to look over the list. Then discuss your responses with someone close to you.

The Feeling Checklist

shocked	anxious	unhappy	fuming	remorseful
numb	worried	sad	furious	regretful
dazed	disturbed	blue	disturbed	tainted
uneasy	restless	negative	upset	unworthy
indifferent	fretful	crushed	annoyed	embarrassed
sluggish	nervous	dejected	uptight	victimized
emotionless	afraid	disheartened	touchy	unholy
half-hearted	pained	gloomy	distraught	culpable
dull	tormented	hopeless	agitated	penitent
drugged	distressed	discouraged	troubled	guilty
apathetic	worked up	melancholy	grumpy	
afraid	ashamed	hollow	angry	
		guilty		
		depressed		

Typical Parent Group Responses

The language of feelings is crucial in helping parents to express themselves. I have met with one group in Philadelphia many times over the past eight years. All of its members are parents of children with visual impairments, and many of the children also have chronic medical conditions, learning disabilities, and mental retardation. As part of their education, some of the children receive mobility instruction with canes, and specialized computer technology, in addition to braille, is used to facilitate reading and writing. The parents, too, are groping in the darkness and the shadows, but of their inner lives. One purpose of the support group is to provide the parents with a way to navigate through their feelings, just as their children are learning to navigate through the physical world.

One Saturday afternoon, after the twenty or so parents sitting in a circle had completed the checklist, I asked if they noticed any patterns as they were looking it over. I suggested that we go around the circle and share whatever felt comfortable for each individual.

"I checked off almost everything; I've felt all these ways," blurted out a woman sitting across from me. Her response is a frequent one when parents participate in this activity.

Then another woman spoke up, "A lot of these have to do with being mad, but I've just been thinking that all these words are negative. Where are the positive ones? When do we get to that?"

Indeed these are very uncomfortable feelings, but all of them are normal and natural. Sometimes it's helpful just to say they're real. Let's take a look at how they make sense and how they might lead us to hope and other more pleasant feelings. Denial, anxiety, fear, guilt, shame, depression, and anger are feeling states that are evoked by grief. Although it may be difficult to recognize or admit to these feelings, acknowledgment of them is the gateway to recovery and the renewal of hope.

The man to her left spoke next. His voice cracked as he remarked, "I don't know what I'm supposed to say, but I'm very frustrated. I've got a lump in my throat. That's what I kept thinking about after I read the word *disheartened*. I don't think I've ever admitted this even to myself."

A small, thin woman with a worried look spoke next. "I keep wondering what I did wrong—if I did something wrong. I have a lot of these feelings, but that is what I keep thinking about." The lines on her face seemed to tell the story of her worry.

"I just wanted to make one big X and be done with it. This is so hard to think about. I'm with everyone else," remarked a woman with very thick glasses whom I had noticed earlier because she had to hold the paper barely an inch from her glasses to read it. She showed admirable courage in choosing to live her life fully by parenting children despite her own disability.

"It makes me feel better to hear you say that," responded the next man. "I always feel bad…like I'm feeling sorry for myself that my son is blind…and like I shouldn't do that."

How wonderfully comforting it can be to discover that we're not alone. As one person after another disclosed his or her feelings, the comfort level increased. People spoke more and more freely—as is usually the case when they feel understood.

"I get so furious every time my child has to go into the hospital," said one of the women in the circle. "My son has a brain shunt, and they're always telling me not to worry. How can you be calm when your child has to be hospitalized every six months? These doctors make me so mad when they say that."

Anger frequently bubbles to the surface in these kinds of meetings, as evidenced this time by the father who spoke next. A small man with a bushy head of dark hair, his face bursting with emotion, he blurted out, "My wife and I have been through so much. Our daughter was born without eyes—her optic nerves have just a little pea-sized undeveloped eye. It's not fair.…" His voice trailed off, and his eyes filled with tears.

A hush came over the group. Sometimes a calming feeling results when a message from those deep feelings is articulated. We waited for the next person to respond.

After a few moments, the next woman spoke. "I was never much of a worrier. I always told myself that I would be different from my mom. Now all I do is worry. What will it be like for my daughter when she grows up? She's only seven now, but can she ever be independent? Nobody can tell me. If she can't, who will take care of her when my husband and I are too old? That whole second column in the list was about being worried."

"You're right," said the next woman. "These words go together in groups. I'm not sure why." She had sensed, as others often do, that the words in the second column are synonyms for various feelings associated with the grief process.

"The first column is how I felt in the beginning right after my son was born. I couldn't believe it. He had water on the brain, and his skull was enlarged. I couldn't feel anything. It was like this was happening to someone else—like in a movie." She was describing the numbness that comes when we first sense, or are told, there is something wrong with our child.

"I never say anything, but I want to say something today," said the next man in the circle. "That column that starts with *unhappy*, that's me. I'm quiet because I'm crushed. People ask me how I feel, and that's it. I'll never play football with my son; I'll never do so many things. He's making progress. I can see it, but I'm so discouraged. I feel bad about that. Why can't I just be excited for him? Why can't I just accept this?"

His wife spoke next. "Well, I talk a lot—maybe I talk for both of us. I wish Bill would talk more, but I can't tell you how glad I am that he spoke today. That third column hits me. A lot of my friends had babies the same time. Every time they talk about their kids, I'm speechless. My son will never do the things they're talking about. I want to crawl under a rock."

This woman's description of shame precipitated an uneasy silence in the group. Many parents of children with special needs have felt this way at various times in their lives. When our natural excitement or interest in our child is deflated, we may want to hide, and that makes us feel shame. This can occur whenever our child's growth isn't as exciting as that of other people's "normal," or more typical, children.

This group activity helps people to recognize and make sense of their feelings about their child. I developed the lists of synonyms rather simply from a thesaurus. Just as there are many shades of every color on the spectrum, there are different intensities of these feelings. Each feeling resonates somewhat differently based on an individual's temperament and past experiences. It is not possible to pass through grief without experiencing each of these feelings in a manner particular to each individual.

Such intense and complex feelings occur at other times in life. The people in the group were able to readily identify these times:

when someone dies who is really close to us;
the end of an important relationship;
when we sustain an injury that limits us from activities we enjoyed;
when we lose a job we really liked or needed;
when we move from a community that meant a lot to us;

when we have failed to achieve a goal that we really worked for;
after a miscarriage;
when we are disappointed in a normal child who turns out to be
     different from what we planned;
during and after a separation or divorce;
when we lose a friend;
when a chronic illness takes hold in a friend, family member, or
     self.

The woman whose child was born without eyes spoke up: "I was thinking, who died? I never thought this way before, but I think we've lost all of our dreams for a normal child. Now I know why I've cried so much—it makes sense. I almost didn't come today because I didn't want to get upset. I can see what I've been going through. I'm not crazy. None of us are." It does seem "crazy," however, when your feelings don't make sense or when they seem out of synch with reality.

"I think I agree with Mary," responded the woman whose child was born with hydrocephalus (water on the brain). "It seems so simple now, but it's been so complicated and really difficult."

"Do you ever get over this stuff?" asked the man who had earlier mentioned his sadness. "How long will I feel this way?"

While grief is painful, it does subside over time. This process is spontaneous and unlearned—it has a natural course. Holding back the feelings can lengthen the amount of time it takes to process the loss.

At times, a parent may feel the need to talk to someone close. If you are unable to resolve your feelings in this way, or feel "stuck," it is wise to consult a professional psychologist, psychiatrist, counselor, social worker, or pastoral counselor who has training and experience in helping people with grief and loss.

With my group on that Saturday afternoon, I tried to impart an understanding that acknowledging all feelings, both pleasant and unpleasant, is essential to psychological health. All feelings motivate people to behave in ways that nature intended and help them meet many of life's challenges, including, of course, the challenges parents must meet to survive and to help their children.

Denial

An initial reaction to any loss is shock and disbelief. The parent of a child with a disability may respond, "Not me, not my child!" Other people may find it hard to understand this denial. There is pressure to "face reality." Despite this, I constantly told myself that my son Tariq would be OK, that he would talk again and catch up.

Denial serves an important role in everyone's personality structure. If anyone thought constantly of all the terrible things that could ever happen, how could he live? How could he manage to go out the door? If he were to prepare for all of the bad things that could happen, he couldn't have a life. What parents would want to have a child if they thought of nothing but what could possibly go wrong?

According to psychologist Ken Moses, in his video *Lost Dreams and Growth*, denial buys us time to discover the inner strength to handle a problem. He based this theory on his own experience as the child of Holocaust survivors and as the parent of a child with a disability. In addition, external support is necessary. Denial provides the time to find out which relatives can be relied on and which friends can understand. It also keeps people from falling apart while they're doing this.

Denial makes the amount of pain bearable. Parents may deny their feelings and maintain that they are not upset. They may deny the permanence of the handicap and believe that the child will grow out of it. They may admit the disability but deny the impact by reasoning that this problem won't change their lives. Denial is necessary until parents find the inner strength and the external support necessary to face painful reality.

Anxiety and Fear

When a parent is upset, others usually want her to calm down. She is unpleasant to be around so her uneasiness is treated as a problem. But anxiety by itself is not a problem. It is a feeling state that serves an important purpose.

It doesn't help when someone says, "Calm down—things are not as bad as you think." People can't calm down just because someone else wants them to or because they would like to. The psychological system is mobilizing energy for the tasks ahead. This arousal is the effect of anxiety, and it fills a vital need. The feeling can range from a relatively light sense of insecurity to a panic attack.

While extreme anxiety can be debilitating and needs treatment with psychotherapy and sometimes medication, a moderate amount is probably necessary for everyday functioning. When your child isn't developing normally, it is necessary to mobilize even more energy than normal to make the efforts necessary to cope. I was constantly on edge for years, concerned about Tariq's safety, and my anxiety helped me to anticipate problems he might have and to solve them *before* he faced certain dangers. This process often required enormous energy to face the tasks of problem-solving. Denial and anxiety together help to prepare for these tasks

While anxiety is a general feeling, fear is specific. Although it's common to be afraid of the changes that are coming when we experience a loss, it is wise to remember Franklin Delano Roosevelt's, "The only thing we have to fear is fear itself," and to concentrate on doing what you can to keep your child safe. The unfortunate reality is that when your child isn't normal, *there is something to be afraid of*: Coping with a child with a disability or chronic illness is tough. Fear is a healthy response that mobilizes energy. Parents who have a child with a disability are also often afraid to have another child. Even when the problem is not genetic, some parents cannot even discuss the possibility of trying again. When you have faced the odds without fear and lost, the possibility that something could go wrong becomes very real.

Years after Tariq's diagnosis and my divorce and remarriage, when Cindy and I were expecting Kara, I know I felt more nervous than the average parent. Having faced the tragedy of disability before, the worry was based in reality. Parents can have more than one child with disabilities. We'd been told our daughter was fine, but what if the genetic counselor was wrong? I remembered the discussions about birth defects in the childbirth classes. Everyone was silent. The instructor, who was a parent herself, quickly moved on to the next topic. I didn't blame the other parents-to-be. I wished that I could tell them about my pain and I knew my worries would not go away until I was sure this baby was healthy.

Cindy and I faced our fears together, and, fortunately, we had a healthy baby. Kara has been a source of great joy every day, especially as she learned to roll over, creep, crawl, walk, talk, and let us know what she wants and likes. Her development helps to reassure me that I am a vibrant person who can survive tragedy and maybe even come out better for it. I didn't worry so much when we were expecting our second daughter, Zoë, and, fortunately, her development has delighted us all along the way as well.

While I was writing this chapter, I heard a news report that a six-year-old boy with autism had gotten out of his family's apartment and been run over and killed by an early morning commuter train. I got an especially queasy feeling in my stomach when I heard that the accident had taken place near the train station that is only a block from our house.

I shook internally, remembering how I had lived with the fear that Tariq might get out of the house and wander onto those same tracks, and my heart filled with grief for the boy's family and with relief that my son has the all-day supervision he needs. A few weeks later I found out from members of the Autism Society that the bereaved family had recently moved to the United States from Korea in order to get the more advanced care that is available here for children with autism.

Guilt

It is not unusual for parents to blame themselves for something they did or did not do prior to birth that caused their child's impairment. The very process of diagnosis often exacerbates feelings of guilt. Every time we take our child for help somewhere, we hear a line of questions something like this:

When did you first notice something was wrong?
What was your pregnancy like?
What was your mental state during the pregnancy?
If you were working, when did you stop?
Are there any similar problems in your family?

These questions can be particularly painful for mothers who are led to wonder what they might have done wrong during pregnancy. Fathers may doubt that they took enough care of their spouses. No matter what their religious background, somewhere in the back of many parents' heads comes the question, is this a fair punishment for something I have done—or even thought?

Since it is commonly believed that good things happen to good people, it follows logically that bad things happen to bad people. Why do some people have impaired children and others have normal children? This is a gut-wrenching question when a child has been diagnosed with a disability. A parent feels terrible if she believes she has caused this tragedy. I recall how I blamed myself and wondered if the conflicts between me and Tariq's mother had caused or contributed to his condition.

When Bad Things Happen to Good People by Harold Kushner is the book I recommend most frequently to help grieving parents to deal with their feelings of guilt. I reread it myself every few years. It is a common belief that God is just. When people try to deal with guilt, they often come to the conclusion that they deserve what they got and somehow their misfortunes come as punishment for sins. As a rabbi and the parent of a chronically ill child who died, Kushner speaks to the unfair and uncontrollable distribution of suffering.

Whatever the reason, the world is not as orderly and understandable as we might like. Guilt helps precipitate a long, drawn-out thought process that we can use to determine the meaning of other feelings, thoughts, beliefs, and actions. As difficult as this process may be, it always makes people laugh when I remind them that people without a natural sense of guilt often find themselves in prison.

The resolution of guilt is an individual matter. Quite naturally, but painfully, parents wish that they could have done something to avoid the tragedy. They are able to move on with their lives after settling for themselves what their responsibilities actually are toward the child. Learning that autism is caused by defects in the neurological system, for example, helped me realize that marital conflict and divorce could not cause it, and that helped me to move on. It is a tremendous relief when you no longer believe that you did something to cause this terrible thing to happen.

Shame

Guilt and shame are often confused. While guilt refers to the uncomfortable feeling attached to violating an inner standard or taboo, shame, on the other hand, is much broader and involves a failure to live up to one's inner ideals. Shame makes us feel small, powerless, and inadequate. There is a way out of guilt because a person can make up for things done wrong. Shame leaves us wanting to hide, with no easy way out.

According to psychiatrist Donald Nathanson, the antidote to shame is pride. When your child isn't normal, there are countless occasions where you may feel a shame response, and far fewer opportunities to experience pride in your child's accomplishments. This fact has another negative impact: It is more difficult for you and your child to have a mutually satisfying relationship—the kind that reinforces the pride of the parent and child as well.

Shame affects the daily lives of parents and children when there is a disability in the family. Nathanson developed a construct called the Compass of Shame that delineates the four basic responses to shame: withdrawal, attacking the self, attacking others, and avoidance or denial of the feeling. All of these reactions were expressed clearly in the comments of the group members as well as by countless other parents I have met, talked to, and counseled. Still they kept searching for a way to feel good. Being able to find pride in themselves and in their child is the only way to relieve the pain. This can only happen as parents redefine who they are and what is possible for them and their children.

Depression

Depression has been called the common cold of the mind. It can be brought on by a loss or disappointment of some kind. No one is a stranger to the experience of feeling down or "blue." It is a natural reaction to stress or tension.

For a time after their child's condition becomes clear, parents may feel physically or mentally drained and be unable or unwilling to perform even routine tasks. There may be little interest in activities that previously brought pleasure. There may be aches, pains, fatigue, poor digestion, or too much or too little sleep. When these symptoms are severe or prolonged, the parent may be experiencing clinical depression—a disorder of mood that calls for professional help in the form of intensive psychotherapy and quite possibly medication.

To feel okay, a parent must feel valuable, competent, capable, and worthwhile. When a child isn't normal, a parent's sense of self can be violated—evoking feelings of incompetence, weakness, worthlessness, etc. I certainly encountered this when I couldn't help my son in the way that I wanted to by fixing the problem.

Most of us spontaneously want to cheer up people who are depressed. Professionals too frequently respond by saying "You're not worthless." But discouraging feelings of sadness does not alleviate them; does not cheer people up. It does, however, help to accept parents' sad feelings and acknowledge that losses are hard for all of us.

Like the other feelings that cluster together in the grief process, depression serves a vital role in helping redefine our sense of self. Struggling against sadness helps us to explore and come up with new ways of feeling competent, valuable, and worthwhile.

Anger

Anger, one of the most intense and least understood human emotions, is probably the scariest and most socially unacceptable feeling to own up to. It often arises with the thought, "Why me? Why did this have to happen to me?" Losing something precious hurts and seems unfair. Parents want someone or something to blame. It might be themselves, each other, the doctor, toxic waste, or, in the case of adoptive parents, the birth parents.

Angry parents in this situation are trying to make sense out of what has happened—If we are decent people, how could this happen to us? Parents need loved ones and friends to allow them to experience anger, to cry, and to scream. Indeed, what has happened is terrible and makes no sense. Trying to be patient by holding the anger in only prolongs the pain.

There are people who neglect and mistreat their children horribly and yet have perfectly healthy offspring. Sometimes parents of children with disabilities resent people who have healthy children, a common but uncomfortable reaction. If the universe is unfair, it sometimes seems reasonable to become embittered and chronically angry. But most parents don't want to go through life this way, so a new sense of what is fair is needed. Harold Kushner speaks to this age-old question about justice that appeared in the Bible. He reminds us that "Anguish and heartbreak may not be distributed evenly throughout the world, but they are distributed very widely. Everyone gets his share."

It's hard to accept that some things happen for no reason. Over one hundred thousand children are born with disabilities each year in the United States, distributed throughout all classes and ethnic groups. While it is true that poor nutrition and medical care and environmental pollution contribute to higher incidences of mental retardation, learning disabilities, and neurological damage in children, often no cause for these conditions can be found in an individual child. No expectant family is exempt from the possibility that their child might be a "statistic."

Resolving anger depends on coming up with a new definition of fairness in the universe. If you believe that the universe is fundamentally unfair, you will remain chronically angry and embittered— walking around with a chip on your shoulder. On the other hand, many parents have been able to use their anger to activate and energize themselves in the struggle to get the best possible services and education for their child's special needs. In this way parents can actually make the world behave more fairly toward their child.

Hope

The spontaneous feelings of denial, anxiety, fear, guilt, shame, depression, and anger eventually give rise to hope—as all of these feelings are shared and validated with supportive others. There is a way particular to each person to acknowledge the loss and focus on the future. Parents come eventually to think about their child with less pain, believing that no matter how difficult life may get, they can pull through. A sense of relief and normalcy is restored when hope is resurrected.

There is relief, too, in acknowledging and talking about the impact of resolving your negative feelings. Some adjectives that describe this emotional state are:

reassured	confident
upbeat	encouraged
positive	strong
optimistic	proud
heartened	steady
gladdened	peaceful
secure	

These positive feelings were missing from the checklist earlier in this chapter. As emotional wounds heal, these new feelings arise. How individuals experience them varies widely. While denial and anxiety are common initial reactions to learning of one's child's disability, the other feelings occur in no particular order and may reoccur throughout the life of the child. Each person brings a different set of thoughts and beliefs to his relationship with the child, and there are no rules for how to grieve.

Some people, most of whom don't have a child with a disability, say, "God gives special children to special people." I myself find no particular comfort in this statement, and, in fact, usually resent it. It's fine for whoever can truly believe it, since that person will feel no pain, but I can't believe that God or any higher power would do such a thing. I do believe that my experiences with my son have transformed me and made me somewhat special. I only wish there had been another, easier way to have accomplished this. The German philoso-pher Friedrich Nietzsche believed that life does indeed break us at times, but that when we heal, we are stronger where the break occurred.

Because grief, especially prolonged grief, is painful and not acceptable to talk about, most of us try to make it "go away." Unfortunately, this doesn't work. There is no joy without pain. The steep price for actually avoiding grief would be to live without compassion or love for others. As long as we are alive and continue to live and love and dream and strive for things we want, we will experience loss.

We grieve spontaneously after losses. It's as natural as losing a seed to form the sprout, or the transformation of the bud to a flower. Every loss sets the stage for future growth, however reluctantly we may face it. As Kahlil Gibran wrote, "Your pain is the breaking of the shell that encloses your understanding."

THREE

The Other Side of Sorrow:
Working Through the Grief

Grief can drive you places you never expected to go," according to Michael Dorris in *The Broken Cord*. In that book, Dorris tells his moving story as an adoptive parent of a boy who is eventually diagnosed with fetal alcohol syndrome (FAS) after years of slow development, learning problems, and seizures. As Dorris points out, "When you decide to have a child, you are hostage to an uncertain future."

So where does the grief take you, and when does the pain of the lost dream end? When will you feel better? Is it ever possible to actually "accept" what has happened? Sigmund Freud said that mourning a child is a kind of work that you have to do in order to move on, and that those who don't do the work will stay in a state of melancholy. Part of our basic human condition is that we spontaneously ponder our experiences and try to make sense out of our myriad and sometimes confusing feelings and thoughts.

Probably one of the best ways that I can explain the sequence of grief is to share some of my own visions. My dreams changed as I went through an inner transformation. At first, when I knew that something was wrong with Tariq but couldn't accept the severity of the problem, I would dream at night of my daily encounters working with Tariq doing things that the speech therapist showed me and things that I had read about. For instance, I would imitate his repetitive movements, I would flap my arms when he flapped his. When I would do this during the day, Tariq would usually notice me and stop what he was doing for a few moments. He would give me a little smile and then go back to what he was doing in his little world.

29

By night, in my frequently recurring dream, Tariq would look at me intently, as he would in my waking life, and then slowly form a word or two. I would feel the excitement in my chest as my heart beat faster. The sound of his voice forming words was a dream come true. I would rejoice, hug my son, and hold him next to my chest. In the morning I would wake up full of hope, believing that Tariq *would* talk, and I kept working with him.

By day the dream fueled my efforts and kept me going by renewing my hopes. I would tape Tariq's grunts and groans and babblings and whatever other noises came out of his mouth and listen to them, searching for progress or meaning. At times I thought I heard some. But no words came back after years of intense effort and the same dream over and over so many nights.

Over time I began to wake up exhausted and overwhelmed. It was hard to go on. My hopes were fading. While writing this chapter, I retrieved one of the tapes from a dusty box in our basement. Listening for just a few moments brought back the feeling as if it had all happened yesterday. I heard myself patiently trying to coax meaningful sounds out of my son. I couldn't listen very long. I realized that Tariq still makes the same vocalizations, the only difference now is that his voice has undergone an adolescent transformation to a deeper tone.

Speech can be delayed, but when a child is not speaking by five there is little chance that normal speech will develop. Still, I continued to hope and be very disappointed. All my life, whenever I worked hard at something I had gotten results—things had worked out. I could remember so many examples, such as developing from a physically awkward child to a competitive athlete in high school.

In the beginning of my relationship with Cindy, I had a daydream that our love could heal Tariq. In my fantasy, I would see us sitting in a grassy spot under the willow trees in the park near my apartment. Tariq would come running to us with a daisy in his hand, saying, "Look at the flower!" I would hug Cindy, and we would both hug Tariq in a romantic tableau of love healing the hurt and the disability.

It was so hard to admit to myself that this was not to be. Fortunately I got some help from my unconscious. Somewhere around Tariq's eighth birthday, I had a somewhat different dream. In this dream, my son spoke to me in sentences, and I was amazed, relieved, and overjoyed. I ran to share the news with Cindy, who was in the other room. As the dream continued, however, I woke up within the dream and knew that I was dreaming and that Tariq had not spoken.

When I actually woke up, I felt a deep relief, a sense that I could live with things the way they were. I didn't have to keep pushing myself. If a miracle came, I'd accept it, but Tariq's inability to speak was just a fact. Now I could be a whole person despite his silence. In my sleep, my mind had let me know that having a normal son was an unreachable dream.

That dream repeated over three or four years, and then I had a new dream. This time Tariq talked to me again. Looking at me intently with his big brown eyes, he told me that he loved me, felt my love for him, and knew I had done everything possible for him. He told me that he was happy in his own way and that he wanted me to be happy. Then he went back into his everyday state of autism—playing with his tongue, making unintelligible noises, and being unaware of my presence for long periods of time unless he wanted something. I felt sorrow and longing for what could have been if only he could have continued talking.

Waking up from this dream is harder to describe, but there was a definite sense that I had moved a little further on my journey. Tariq was a part of me—not all of me. I was a whole person—not just the wound from the loss. I had not bled to death, nor had I drowned in my grief as I had often feared. Instead, by inviting the feelings in, accepting the lost dream, living with it, and incorporating it, I had grown.

Stages of Grief: Working Through It

Elisabeth Kubler-Ross brought death and dying out of the closet in 1969 with *On Death and Dying*, her book based on her work with dying cancer patients. She did for death what Freud had done for sexuality. Because of her work it had become far easier to talk about loss, and in this respect alone her contribution is monumental.

Kubler-Ross conceptualized five stages that characterize reactions people experience to impending death: 1. Denial, 2. Anger, 3. Bargaining, 4. Depression, and 5. Acceptance. It is now commonplace to hear people casually talking about these stages and wondering where they might be in dealing with a particular loss.

These stages have been adapted by numerous writers to fit the parents and family members of children with disabilities. As discussed earlier, the birth of a disabled infant sometimes feels like the death of the expected normal, healthy child. When I present work-shops to groups of parents, I often ask them what stages they have been through. The group can usually identify stages very similar to those in the Kubler-Ross's theory, which validates the model. (Of course, not everyone goes through the same stages in the same order, and they may overlap or repeat.)

This subject brings to mind the myth of Procrustes, the innkeeper, who believed that people should fit exactly in their beds. All of the beds in his inn were the same length and when travelers stopped, Procrustes would stretch those who were too short and cut down those who were too big to fit the beds exactly. Procrustes was the mythical forerunner of inflexible thinking. People should not be stretched or cut down to fit the psychological theory. With this in mind, let's see how a parent might work through the heartaches without taking the Kubler-Ross stages too literally.

There is little disagreement among anyone I've read or talked to that some form of denial comes first. Denial creates a necessary buffer zone, because it takes time to learn to deal with a new reality. The thought, "Not me, it cannot be true," is a virtually universal response to loss. Although people may say "Face reality," the initial reaction of disbelief is perfectly normal and healthy.

Because it is hard to believe what has happened, parents may resist recommendations from professionals who bear the bad news. Some people try to push their child beyond his or her abilities or delay the enrollment of their child in a special program suited to his or her needs. Others may delay beginning prescribed medications while they "shop around" trying to get a more hopeful or less serious diagnosis. It is not uncommon, for example, for the parents of a child who needs a hearing aid to at first keep the child from using it because they cannot accept the seriousness of the problem and the implication that their child cannot hear adequately without the device.

Parents may fantasize about a miracle cure or refuse to believe that the disability is severe. Sometimes doctors *are* wrong, and upon first diagnosis it is nearly impossible to predict how far a given child can develop. And it's true that many parents through hard work, hope, and love have helped their children develop far beyond the expected potential. Each person must find his or her own blend of hope and reality.

In the award-winning film, *My Left Foot*, based on author Christy Brown's true story, we see Brown severely handicapped with cerebral palsy and unable to speak. Everyone but his mother, who always believed in him, thought he was severely retarded. Eventually Christy was able to begin expressing himself by writing on the floor with a piece of chalk held between the toes of his left foot. He had long understood his surroundings, but he had been locked inside his own body until then. Once Christy began to communicate in this unique way, his mother found a special program for him. He was able to learn to talk and became proficient enough with his left foot to express himself further through art and writing.

Many parents share the attitude of Christy's mother. She saw her child's potential despite the obvious and didn't let the negative assessments of others blind her. Despite her child's obvious deformity, she developed a strong bond with him, just as is recommended by such authorities as renowned pediatrician T. Berry Brazelton of Boston Children's Hospital. Such parents help many children with serious impairments to eventually astound the "experts." What resembles denial may instead be an unconditional love and hope that results not in a cure, perhaps, but in tremendous progress for the child.

A few years ago I was fortunate to meet Kathy Buckley, the first deaf comedian on the "hearing" circuit. She provided the evening's entertainment at a statewide conference for the families of children in early-intervention programs from across Pennsylvania. I was a presenter at the gathering, and my wife and I got the opportunity to eat at the same table with Kathy at the banquet. Kathy was articulate, impassioned, and funny.

During her presentation she related how she had spent three years in a school for the mentally retarded because no one knew she was hard of hearing. Could such a waste of human potential be funny? "They thought *I* was slow!" she quipped, bringing laughter and tears to the hundreds of parents in the audience, many of whom had experienced the gloomy predictions of experts.

People who don't understand why parents might deny aspects of their child's problem can seem condescending and impatient. It may appear to them that these parents are being irrational, but grief cannot be understood simply as a cognitive phenomenon. It is a complex and compound feeling process. While some parents get stuck in denial, most move on—when they are ready. As the Talmud so wisely states "The sun will not set before its time."

If we look at the loss of a hoped-for normal child in terms of psychological trauma, then an extended period of healing is necessary to bring the parent back to a state of psychological well-being. As in the case of posttraumatic stress, the sufferer tends to keep reliving the incident and has the tendency to expect the worst after such a sudden and terrible shock. The numbness is an emotional anesthetic. The sufferer may even feel that he's watching his own life from a distance or that it is someone else's story. This split between affect (feelings) and cognition (thoughts) keeps him from being over-whelmed, and it is helpful in gaining perspective and integrating emotions.

During my doctoral program, I met Phyllis Morgan. She was a teaching assistant and fellow student. Her husband had one of the first kidney transplants, and they had been coping with his condition for many years. She had trained many doctors and nurses in helping people to deal with loss. Morgan, as everyone called her, was spon-taneously warm and supportive. She related how numbness was often what allowed her to get up in the morning and function. The scary part, she pointed out, is knowing the numbness is going to end—that you are eventually going to feel its source.

Psychologist William Worden calls working through denial the first task of grief work and labels this stage "accepting the reality of the loss." Part of the acceptance of reality is to believe that the child will never be normal but at the same time that she is loving and lovable, and this can take a considerable amount of time.

When a disability is detected at birth, it is, of course, traumatic and devastating, but parents in this situation have told me that they experienced very little denial of the reality. "Invisible" disabilities, such as autism, learning disabilities, attention deficit disorder, and emotional disorders that are diagnosed well after birth, are often much more difficult to accept.

Crying Out in Pain

Significant loss always causes mental torment, but when a parent "loses" a living child, there is no obvious right or capacity to grieve. Other people often don't want to hear about it, and because the loss of the dream cannot be openly acknowledged and publicly mourned, the resultant grief is "disenfranchised." Sometimes people deny the pain even though they may accept the reality of the loss. They often feel pressured to be moving on. Of course, they want the anguish to end.

The words of the great Russian novelist Leo Tolstoy can be

comforting in this regard: "Only people who are capable of loving strongly can also suffer great sorrow; but this same necessity of loving serves to counteract their grief and heals them."

As denial has been worked through, parents begin to get angry that their child's condition will not improve significantly. This anger may be the first outward expression of pain. It often takes form in the questions "Why me? Why my child?" Intense rage and resentment may arise at the apparent unfairness. I remember resenting the cosmic injustice of my son's condition when so many healthy children were born to parents who abused or neglected them. I would lie awake with the same thought repeating over and over until my head would throb.

On the other hand, great energy and vitality can come from this anger and the resultant activity can be rewarding. It gave me the drive, for example, to work with my son every day. Passive acceptance of his condition would not have done this. Many parents want to work personally with their children because they know this kind of "homework" can make a difference. Wanting to prove the experts wrong spawned the ambition in me to make more money to pay for my son's therapies. Many parents have told me that they didn't know what they would do, who they would be, or how they would function without the anger.

The anger stage occurs when we look for where to point the finger of blame. Many people even experience a crisis of religious belief because the God they though to be just, now seems unjust. Some years ago *People* magazine interviewed Sylvester Stallone, who said that when his son was diagnosed with autism, he went out into his backyard, looked up at the sky, and cursed God. A mother who sought my professional counsel recently told me that she no longer believed in the hell she'd learned about in church since finding out that her only child had autism—according to her, she was living it here and now.

The feelings of anger may be spewed out and displaced in all directions, making it difficult to cope for all who are involved—including professionals. Sometimes this kind of anger leads to isolation. It often seems that no one can possibly understand how you feel. You may feel guilty for being angry, especially if the depth of your anger is frightening. If you sometimes hold your child accountable for putting you through such a horrible tragedy, you will probably also feel guilty for blaming such an innocent soul.

In my case, Tariq was five before I was able to admit to myself that I was angry at him. He was simply not who I wanted him to be. Even now I am uncomfortable acknowledging this. It feels like a defect in me, a flaw that I would rather hide if I could. Isn't a parent's love for a child supposed to be unconditional? I first realized my anger on one of those many nights when Tariq woke up and I heard him making noises and playing in his room. It took me a few minutes to wake myself fully in order to get up and try to rock him back to sleep. I was quick but not quick enough this time. As he had on other occasions at home and in school, he had a bowel movement and started playing with it and smearing it all over himself and the walls and furniture.

I was so furious at him for doing this to *me*—for making me go through this when most other five-year-olds, even with disabilities, knew better—I wanted to throw him out that window in his room; I really did. I didn't touch him, however, except to lead him to the bathtub and start cleaning him up with warm, soapy water and a washcloth.

I felt the rage within me boiling, ready to erupt, and I was terrified of what that might make me do if I couldn't control it. Remember the television show *The Incredible Hulk*? In each episode, David Banner would tell someone, "Don't make me angry! You won't like me when I'm angry!" If he did get angrier, the civilized Banner turned into an out-of-control monster. I took a few slow, deep breaths. As I washed Tariq, and put clean pajamas on him, I thought once again about those abusive parents with healthy kids. Now that I knew my own anger, I wasn't mad at *them* anymore. I hugged my child. I understood. This was an example of what William Faulkner, in his Nobel Prize acceptance speech, had called the human heart in conflict with itself. It's part of the agony and sweat of the human spirit—not that I didn't still long for that dream of pure untainted love for my child devoid of anger. I was able to realize from understanding my own passionate anger that I was capable of controlling it. I now had empathy for people who lose control—they need help to learn it. What a fine line divides us!

Let's Make a Deal

Fantasy may help to fight off the overwhelming feelings of sadness. Parents may imagine a miracle cure. Perhaps by working extra hard, the child's condition will improve. Having been unable to face the sad facts in the first stage and having been angry at people and God in the second stage, perhaps now some kind of "deal" can postpone the inevitable.

The professional literature often refers to this phase as "shopping" for a diagnosis, hoping that there is a way out. If the right program or the right teacher will make this problem go away, then life can go back to the way it was before. To the outside observer, whether professional or not, it may seem that the parent is grasping at straws.

Parents frequently complain to me that their pediatricians are particularly impatient with them when they want other opinions and other less established treatments. I advise them to calmly ask their child's physician for an extended consultation at a time when he or she isn't rushed. Many times the physician will respond quite differently when approached in this way and when the parents come prepared with questions and information. Given more time to discuss things, the physician may be more supportive of an alternative treatment and more understanding of the parents' wish to try another approach. If not, then the family might want to choose a new pediatrician.

Bargaining is the third way of buying some time. Usually the bargain is with God or our "higher power." Tariq graduated from the early-intervention program at four and half years of age and was due to start public school in the fall. He wore a little cap and gown with his classmates and squirmed though the ceremony in my arms. I just couldn't accept that he needed to go into a special-education class like the ones being recommended.

At the time, the choices were a self-contained classroom for multiply handicapped students or a specialized program for autistic children. I thought these places would make him worse since he would have no normal peers as role models. I couldn't imagine his condition would be permanent. I couldn't find a nursery school that would take him to give him that extra year that I hoped would help him to catch up.

I put an ad in the paper and found a small Montessori school that would accept him and give him extra help for an increased fee. I took on extra teaching and therapy cases to make the money. After trying extremely hard for over a year, it was clear that Tariq wasn't improving. The teachers couldn't manage him and give enough attention to the other children at the same time. The parents of the other children, who had at first been patient, were now concerned and complaining.

I took Tariq to the Center for Autistic Children, a specialized program that I had visited a year before. When I first went there it had looked cold and pessimistic—therapists working one on one with children who couldn't benefit from group activities. I had sworn to myself at the time that I would keep my son out of such a place at all costs. But now I had spent over a third of my annual salary on private school and therapies with no visible results, and I was going through a divorce. My parents, grandparents, and siblings had lent me money, hoping along with me to find a cure.

This time the center looked different: It appeared that one-to-one therapy was a realistic place to begin with my son. The social worker, the therapists, and the psychiatrist were warm, caring people who loved children like Tariq, knew how to work with them, and helped me feel comfortable with my decision to accept their help, which I had previously refused. What a difference a year made!

From All Walks of Life

Isolation is a major effect of this kind of grief for a lost dream, so it helps to know that people from all walks of life react in similar ways. Rich or poor or in between, black or white or Hispanic or Asian, you have to go through the same things. Parental grief is a normal reaction that aids in attaining inner peace and serenity. My research into how families coped successfully with disability was planned to help me grow while I completed the requirements for my doctorate.

One of the most articulate families I've ever met came from the inner city of Philadelphia. The Greens are African American, and their son, Walter, who was eight at the time, is physically disabled due to cerebral palsy. Their oldest child, Nick, was eighteen and had just gone away to college, majoring in special education. Sean, the youngest, had just turned two. Their story is included here because they can serve as role models for the collective experience of many families.

When I first went to their home, Charley Green was working at his job with the transit system, so I began talking to his wife, Shirley. She had a lot to say and hoped that it might help others to hear it. She began by recalling Walter's premature birth after only six months of pregnancy. Soon after his birth, the doctors told the Greens that their son would be a "vegetable." The doctor thought that Walter was probably deaf, probably blind, and would never talk. The parents were asked if the hospital could keep their baby and try experimental drugs since this infant was not expected to live.

Charley and Shirley were vehemently opposed to experimental

treatment. They were overwhelmed with worry and short on hope. Shirley recalled that every time the incubator was opened their son would fight hard. He would grasp the opening until the nurse removed his tiny hand. As Shirley remarked, "Do you think God would give him the ability to fight like that if he was going to die?" She said Charley's attitude was, "Good, bad, or indifferent, he's my son, and he comes home with us."

Walter spent the first several months of his life in an incubator, but as soon as possible his parents brought him home. Because they were so upset with the negative prognosis they had received in the hospital, they changed to a private pediatrician. The new doctor saw the baby as developmentally delayed because of the premature birth and predicted that Walter would "catch up." (How many parents have heard similar reassurances and kept their hopes up?)

Despite the more positive prognosis, Walter's first year was extremely hard for his family. He was hospitalized for pneumonia four times within those twelve months, and each time Charley and Shirley were worried that their son might die. At six months, there was still no specific diagnosis, so the Greens took their baby for a developmental evaluation. Walter was diagnosed with cerebral palsy.

Shirley told me she cried uncontrollably right on the spot when they were told, and for weeks afterward she cried profusely almost every time she was alone. She looked for someone to blame. She had worked as a secretary until shortly before Walter was born, and at first she blamed herself. She wondered what would have happened if she had not been working. The doubts lessened, but they would not go away.

When Charley got home, he gave me his perspective. He was a big man who spoke softly but with great intensity. He took out a few record albums from his jazz collection and put one on as we began to talk. The sounds of John Coltrane and Miles Davis formed the background for our dialogue.

Charley said, "I'm a believer, and I don't believe it's over until it's over. If I had followed the doctor's advice, I wouldn't even know my son now." He described his shock, "I see all his fingers, all his toes, and so on, and then I hear he's going to be a vegetable. It was too much. I was in hell...."

After Walter was diagnosed with cerebral palsy, Charley found himself drinking too much and picking fights with his wife. He was resentful and blamed himself. He wondered if he had done everything he could do—maybe he should have spent more time with Shirley, and maybe he should have gone with her to the prenatal appointments. He found himself lashing out at others. He wondered if his seed was bad.

Shirley had told me earlier that Walter had ultimately strengthened their marriage. He became the catalyst for her and Charley to really talk to each other. Up until his birth, their marriage had been "up and down," and they had separated whenever they weren't getting along. After Walter was born, the couple focused on their marriage and how to make it work. Shirley tried to understand her husband better and appreciate his sensitivities.

Walter helped Charley, too. He described himself as a man who doesn't show much emotion except when he is angry. "Shirley could see what was going on," he recounted, "and said that I was holding it in and that I had to let it out." As Charley and Shirley learned to express themselves to each other, they argued less. They solved problems together.

As life went on, and Walter grew and did well in school, their pride in his progress eased their shame about his physical disability. They stopped blaming and attacking each other. When describing his son's progress in keeping up to grade level academically, Charley beamed and told me, "That's my main man."

Shirley and Charley did not plan to have another child. Shirley's new pregnancy was not discovered right away since she was on a diet and was losing weight. When she found out she was pregnant, she worried that something would go wrong, but it was too late for an abortion. Amniocentesis showed possible complications. Shirley and Charley were sick with worry.

Fortunately, fate was kind. The new baby was delivered by cesarean section, and both parents were relieved when she had no birth defects. Betsy's first year went smoothly. When the baby took her first steps, Shirley finally stopped blaming herself for Walter's disability. "Betsy's first steps told the whole story," she told me. Shirley believed that Betsy was "like the string who pulled the whole package together." The Greens had gained a new sense of who they were as a family.

Redefining Who You Are

When reality can no longer be denied, when angry energy does not change the child's condition, and there are no more deals to be made, a sense of depression sets in. Sadness grips the heart as reality must be dealt with. The truth is extremely painful and often overwhelming. During this period, parents may question the meaning of life and their value as human beings. Because of the intense grief and shame, they may avoid others with normal children.

The depression that accompanies a loss varies from person to person just like the entire grief response. It can be deep and compelling, as described by William Styron in the personal account of his own battle with depression, *Darkness Visible*. It is a pain that can be unimaginable to those who have not suffered it, and as Styron recounts, it can "frighten the soul to its marrow." If your child's diagnosis is made a relatively long time after birth, your grief reaction may be more intense because your hope for a normal child lived longer. Your bond with your child is stronger, too. Whatever its intensity, sorrow is the natural response that has been waiting in the wings while we go through the other stages.

It's hard to feel like you're a good parent when your child isn't "normal." Energy and hope are in short supply. Many people report a feeling of hollowness, headaches, difficulty with sleep, eating problems, and other physical symptoms. Self-confidence may be shot. It helps to consider that there is a task involved. Worden defined this task as adjusting to an environment in which the loved one is missing, but in this case it is the typical child that is absent.

When someone dies, people often become more aware of all the roles played by the deceased loved one, and that can lead to the realization of how much or how little the loved one actually meant to them. Similarly, when the loss is the dream of a normal, healthy child, parents may not have been aware of all the facets of that dream. As opposed to the dreams about life with a normal child, experiencing life with a child with a disability demonstrates exactly what is missing.

The task of adjustment requires adapting to the demands of everyday life with the special-needs child. New coping skills must be developed. Parents may have to give an injection to a diabetic child or learn sign language, or develop other new skills.

A lot of fear can be involved in moving on. In our culture people tend to minimize this reality. Often we hear clichés like "Cheer up, things will work out." These are not comforting words while the loss of the dream is teaching otherwise. Things don't always work out, and, when they don't, it hurts horribly. For instance, when a relationship fails, it can be very hard to fall in love anew. When we are redefining ourselves, we fear being hurt again, rationalizing during this phase of grief that if we refuse to dream again and love again, then we can't be hurt again.

For parents who have lost a dream, the dilemma is how to adjust to the child we actually have. We need to formulate new dreams and goals based upon our child's real abilities. Doing this is part of healing and growth, and it takes time. How much? As long as you need.

Alexandra Bricklin, whose daughter Rebecca has pervasive developmental disorder, talks about how her tears operated during this period of grief. She expressed it in a poem:

Frozen Rage

As I grieve frozen rage,
I remember my child's birth.
Her newborn skin so tender
pushed against my harshness.
I felt frosty burning,
then warm tears.

Something is wrong.
I was born open
but mamma built me walls...

As I grieve frozen rage,
My icy heart drips.
Warm tears
melt anger away.

Giant Steps

The Green family has more to teach us about how to come out of the feeling of sadness. Shirley described to me the periodic bouts she experienced with overwhelming sadness. As Walter was developing in his early years, it was particularly painful for her to watch him trying to do things that he just could not manage. One example she recounted was learning to crawl without the use of his legs by just dragging himself around with his arms.

Her sense of guilt was intertwined with her pain because she was still blaming herself for Walter's condition. One way that Shirley coped was to allow herself some time each day just to be down in the dumps and not fight the feeling. She would give herself a time limit and then get back to whatever she had to do. By accepting how low she felt and just letting it wash over her, she was able to rebound feeling refreshed.

When Walter was two years old, he was placed in a special preschool. He was labeled mildly retarded with cerebral palsy. After three years there, he was reevaluated by a new school psychologist who determined that Walter had been misdiagnosed and was not retarded. Shirley and Charley jumped for joy. Things were nowhere near as bleak as originally predicted.

Not long before I met Charley and Shirley, Walter had been hospitalized for eight months. He had an operation to straighten his legs and intensive physical therapy to help him begin to use his legs with the help of braces. Shortly before leaving the hospital, Walter was able to walk with the aid of braces and a walker. When the time came for Walter's discharge, the nurses, physical therapists, and the orthopedic surgeon all shed tears of joy along with Shirley and Charley.

Shirley told me how she could feel the weight of sadness lifting from her heart. She began to envision more successes for her son. Charley had been greatly disappointed that he couldn't play sports with his son, but, nonetheless, he told me that when he saw Walter walk with those braces, after years of therapy and surgery, it was more exciting than the Super Bowl. Charley called this his proudest moment.

Although Walter still needs to use his wheelchair, most of the time he faces life with great vigor. He takes horseback riding lessons weekly and goes deep-sea fishing with his dad. A normal measure of hope has returned to this family. As Charley and I finished talking, we sat back and listened to the last side of the albums he had selected when we began. It was the soprano saxophone of John Coltrane in his exciting rendition of "My Favorite Things." It reflected Charley's loving acceptance of his child, and it was a fitting conclusion to our dialogue.

A certain warmth and closeness comes from sharing each other's stories. Renewed interest in others can signal growth and a movement out of self-pity. Charley and Shirley show how parents can redefine themselves when something is wrong with their child. Going through such an experience in a loving relationship can help to prove that life is still worth living after a serious loss.

Acceptance

Many people question how the acceptance stage can apply to parents of children with special needs or disabilities. The very term *acceptance* seems to imply that a completion has occurred. Instead, because the child lives, the grieving experienced by parents is in some ways more complex. Helen Featherstone, a parent, poses a striking comparison between the death of a child and life with a disabled child in her book *A Difference in the Family*:

> The most important difference between mourning a death and mourning a disability is that the child in question is not dead at all. Instead of an aching hole, the empty bed, the now useless baby clothes, parents face the insistent demands of a child who needs even more care than an ordinary infant would. They must shoulder the heavy responsibility of leading this child into life, and love him as though he embodied all their dreams. While death provides a moment's respite from ordinary demands, disability generates new tasks and necessities.

Although it may take a considerable amount of time, feelings of depression and anger eventually subside. Elisabeth Kubler-Ross stresses that this is not a "happy" stage. For a dying person, the pain is gone and the struggle is over. For the parents of children with disabilities and chronic illnesses, the pain has lessened but the hard work is beginning. On the plus side, we have become stronger and more able to deal with the everyday challenges of parenting a child with extraordinary needs.

Acceptance might be thought of as "going on with your life" and reworking the dreams for your child. It is a time to focus outward and make realistic plans for your child's care. Having worked through feelings of anger and guilt, it becomes possible to feel better and begin to trust yourself again. Then parents can trust others and ask for help when needed from family, friends, and professionals. You now have a realistic hope that the family will survive the crisis. There are rough times ahead, but the disability is real and can be worked into everyday life.

The task of acceptance involves withdrawing emotionally from the dream of the normal child and using the resultant energy to form new dreams and new relationships. It can be very difficult to withdraw this energy from old dreams. It may seem like withdrawing love from the child if parents stop hoping for a cure and move on to making the best of the situation.

In some respects, acceptance is the most difficult task of all. There may be a fear that new dreams will only be crushed if they arise. No one wants to be hurt again. Learning to love the actual child as opposed to the dreamed-for child involves making new goals and hoping to achieve them. If we regard the completion of this task in this way, it actually lessens the burden. The "down" periods are less severe and people bounce back sooner.

People respond to crisis from within the context of their individual lives and from within the collective lives of their families. While the model discussed here explains much about the experience of having a child with a disability, each person will experience each stage differently. The length of time each stage will last, the sequence of stages, and how they may overlap or repeat will vary. If grieving for previous losses was arrested or blocked, those old feelings will no doubt come up and complicate the current loss.

Recently I received a phone call from a woman in great distress. Carol had been referred to me by a close friend of hers who knew about my specialty in psychotherapy. Her seven-year-old son had asthma, and her four-year-old boy was extremely active. She seemed stressed to her limit. During our initial consultation, Carol blurted out all of her frustrations, including how horrible she felt to be admitting that she was having a hard time raising two very bright children.

She impressed me as an extremely articulate and intelligent woman as she vividly described her daily life as a full-time caregiver. Her face was drawn tight, and her speech seemed pressured. Her older son was easily upset and had a hard time sleeping because he worried so much. The younger son was so active that he would walk away whenever he had the opportunity and would sometimes turn up as a lost child at the supermarket or shopping mall. As tough as all this sounded, I got the feeling that there was something else going on for Carol.

I asked her if she had experienced any major losses recently. Sure enough, both of her parents had died in the past ten years. Her father had died suddenly from a major heart attack. Her mother, who had lived somewhat longer, had died from cancer while Carol was engaged to be married. Neither of her parents lived to see her get married. Carol had always imagined that her parents would be fine grandparents, that they would have helped and supported her in many ways. She especially missed her mother because she had imagined that her mother would have guided her through the pregnancies and the transition to parenthood.

As we talked, it became clear to Carol that her parents' deaths had compounded the loss of her dream for perfect children. She imagined that her parents might have been disappointed because of their grandchildren's emotional and behavioral problems. Only with these considerations in the open and in perspective could therapy proceed. Carol said it was a relief to "unload" her story.

Chronic Grief

On every occasion that I have spoken to parents about the stages of mourning, people have found the ideas extremely helpful. It never fails, however, that someone immediately responds, "When do you get over this? It happens to me over and over." In fact, this is true for most parents in this situation. We tend to revisit the grief as the child grows and matures, so there is no simple solution or resolution. It's just there.

Paul Monette describes this problem well in *Borrowed Time*, a memoir of his relationship with a friend who died from AIDS. He writes that his cup is neither half full nor half empty. It's just half. Although you may cry when you revisit the loss of your dream, over time it becomes a land beyond tears. Life is now about survival and meeting the challenge.

One of the small things that still remains difficult for me is passing a Little-League baseball game on a summer's night. When I hear the crack of the bat, I want to stop and watch and see my son there. I want to cheer him on, and then I'll get a tear in the corner of my eye or a lump in my throat. It *never* doesn't hurt.

I have been fortunate—I have survived and time and people have been kind to me. I have gotten over isolating myself from people with normal children. I can't describe how good it is to enjoy hearing and sharing the joys that a father experiences when he beams with pride about his child. It's a normal part of life that lets me know I'm whole.

So living with and raising an exceptional child is not something that you merely accept once and get it over with. The impact on daily life extends through the entire family—mother, father, child, and siblings. The experiences of the Smith family illustrate the chronic nature of grief and how families can cope with this unavoidable reality—this glass of hope that sometimes evaporates slowly over the years.

The Smiths, another family I met during my research, lived in a row house in a small town in New Jersey. Jim Smith worked as an electrician, and Mary had been a full-time homemaker until recently, when she began working as a secretary. Jim Smith Jr. seemed normal at birth, but gradually lost both sight and hearing, and now, at age twenty-two, had left home to attend a two-year residential vocational training program as a deaf-blind young adult. He is the middle child of three.

When Jimmy was about a year old and Mary was feeding him, she noticed a little flickering in his eye. She told her husband, but Jim did not see it. She lived alone with her worry. By the time Jimmy was two, his father eventually saw the flickering. The family doctor believed that it was nothing serious.

When Jimmy was three and a half, Mary took him to a pediatrician because his eyes were jumping all the time. The pediatrician referred the Smiths to a neurologist, who diagnosed a strabismus, the inability of one eye to focus without the other due to an imbalance of the eye muscles. At age four, an ophthalmologist examined Jimmy and found optic nerve damage that had probably begun at birth.

Jim and Mary told me how devastated they were by the diagnosis. At the time, Jimmy had to sit closer to the TV than his sister, Susan, who was about eighteen months older, but in every other way he still seemed normal. He could hear and walk, and he even rode a tricycle around their suburban neighborhood.

Jimmy was hospitalized for numerous tests. Doctors found no cause for his nerve damage and could offer no prognosis. Mary was afraid of what the future would hold for her son. Her first thought was to shelter Jimmy and keep him inside to protect him. Jim countered that they should let their son do whatever he could and treat him as normally as possible. Mary agreed, and Jimmy continued to ride his bike and play with other children.

Jimmy went out for sports and even though he could not see well enough to hit a baseball, the coaches were kind and let him run the bases. He was also in the Cub Scouts like most of the other children in the neighborhood. When the other Cub Scouts were climbing trees, his father would climb part way up with Jimmy, and he would then go as far as he could on his own.

At around age nine, Jimmy began to lose his hearing. At first his sisters and parents spoke loudly and then even shouted. As Jimmy's capacity for hearing diminished, he also began to lose his speech. Eventually he had to learn sign language, and his family learned sign language to communicate with him. Because of his limited vision they had to make signs in the palm of his hand. As before, doctors could find no reason why Jimmy was losing his hearing.

Adjustment was a constant process for the whole Smith family as Jimmy's condition worsened. As a teenager, Jimmy began to have problems with his balance. At the time I met him, Jimmy was learning to use a cane but was having a very hard time accepting the progressive loss of his mobility. Sometimes he even refused to use the cane because of his feelings about it.

Jimmy and I discussed this on the telebraille device that allowed us to communicate. I would type on a keyboard, and my message would be communicated to him in braille. He would type in braille, which would be transmitted into letters on a monitor. Before this technology, only those who knew braille could communicate with him. I felt fortunate and blessed to have met this young man.

Friends, neighbors, and relatives all wanted to communicate with Jimmy, so a sign language class was begun in the Smith home. Jimmy was the teacher, and every Friday night people gathered and had a good time learning. At the end of the year, Jimmy gave each of his students a report card—in braille. Both Jim and Mary look back on the sign language class, which lasted for four years, as some of the happiest times in their life with Jimmy. Jimmy has a good sense of humor, and most people enjoyed being around him, so the house was frequently full of friends and relatives.

One of the hardest times for Jimmy was adolescence. When he was little, he had friends in the neighborhood, but when they reached their teen years, they no longer wanted to be around Jimmy, who by then couldn't see at all and had lost most of his hearing. In effect, the family became Jimmy's social group, and they frequently went places together. At school Jimmy did have one good friend, who was deaf and had cerebral palsy. The friend could drive, and they went places together when Jimmy was on vacation.

The constant adjustment to Jimmy's lessening ability to function independently had been especially trying. This is the main dilemma for the families of those who have a degenerative condition. There is one loss after another; it's not just revisiting the loss of the original dream. Jim and Mary are constantly faced with getting used to a new and lower level of functioning. They struggle and revive some hope based on their son's ability—repeating this process again and again only to see components of that ability disappear. These folks are real survivors. They're always warm and friendly and caring. We cross paths at least once or twice a year, and they always ask how my son, Tariq, is doing. I know they don't expect him to be better. The way they ask just lets me know they care.

As Long as It Takes

The impact of the lost dream upon the family is lifelong. Whether looking at feelings, stages, or tasks, working this through is a long-term process. Many factors affect how each individual and family responds. The nature and severity of the disability are, of course, major factors in how the loss is experienced. The ability to cope and deal with adversity is another major component.

Taking individual differences into account, most families display similar characteristics as they adapt to everyday life after experiencing grief over their lost dream. Once they have faced and dealt with the reality themselves, parents become able to discuss their child's disability with other people. Once parents have worked through their anger and no longer see professionals as the enemy, they are able to collaborate with them in making needed plans. They stop blaming them for not curing their child. Family members find themselves more able to pursue their own personal interests. Their lives are bigger than just the child with special needs; they are able to be loving but not overprotective toward the child.

In 1993 Eric Clapton won a Grammy for "Tears in Heaven," a song about his three-year-old son who died in an accident. Clapton said in an interview that writing the song helped him to accept his loss. I listen to the song frequently because I find comfort in Clapton's artistic expression of his journey to find peace. Clapton sings that time can bring you down, bend your knee, and break your heart, but nonetheless he finds peace "beyond the door" because "there are no more tears in heaven."

In other words, we have to keep living. The point of the song for me is that on the spiritual level, in the moments when we can transcend momentary experiences, all is at peace. My son knows my name. He holds my hand. Life is still hard, but Tariq and I are at peace—just as we are in my dream.

FOUR

Day by Day:
Tuning In to Your Special Child

I was the type of parent who refused to give up the hope that my child would be normal again for a long time, despite a good deal of evidence to the contrary. It was not because of lack of effort that my son did not turn out to be another Christy Brown. By doing all that I could do, I was able to look at myself in the mirror, hold my head up, respect myself, and go on with life. People who don't try everything that they think they should may live an existence haunted by guilt and doubt.

While I was writing this chapter, I talked at length with Dr. Bert Ruttenberg, who had been Tariq's psychiatrist for several years. He believed and helped me to see that my efforts contributed to making Tariq more of a person and more likable to others. Tariq's personality engages people's interest and their wish to help. He certainly needs a lot of help, and it is to his lifelong advantage that people like giving it to him.

As Bert so wisely taught me, the more a child is loved, the more lovable that child is. A child who is rejected, on the other hand, will tend to be angry, and others will tend to shy away or reject that child. It is comforting to know that Tariq's lovable personality is my legacy to him even after I am gone, and it will help him get what he needs for the rest of his life. The acceptance of a child with special needs can challenge our ability to love as well as our notion of life between a parent and child. Giving everything and expecting nothing in return— no ballet recitals, no home runs, no A's on the report card—is the lesson that a child with a disability teaches and perhaps forces a family to learn. This unconditional love is a positive regard for who

50

the child is in essence, not what he or she will achieve or acquire in life.

Unfortunately, it is not an easy lesson nor one that is eagerly embraced at the outset. When a child has a disability, grief and disappointment can cloud over and complicate everyday life. There is a constant process of reconciling the dreamed-for child with the actual child and restoring pride in the family, the child, and the self as we hope and watch and help our special child to grow. The key to reviving pride and hope is to build a mutually satisfying parent-child relationship. This chapter will take a closer look at how this is possible amid the stress of everyday life that begins with pregnancy and its build up of hopes and worries.

Most women and men have some fear of giving birth to an abnormal child. The barrage of information about the impact of food, drugs, alcohol, tobacco, and pollution on the developing fetus serve to heighten the fears that universally haunt expectant parents. In *The Earliest Relationship*, T. Berry Brazelton and Bertrand Cramer explain that these fears are counteracted by visualizing the infant as perfect. Positive wishes for the baby and wishes to be perfect parents heighten through the pregnancy. It is a normal and natural defense that blocks out the worries that might otherwise predominate.

Men and women differ during this period. Because men's bodies do not change during pregnancy, they are, in general, able to put aside the worries for long periods of time. On the other hand, morning sickness, fatigue, emotional lability, and the growth of the fetus inside them are constant reminders to women that the pregnancy is real.

Some parents even imagine what they will do if they have a baby with mental retardation, cerebral palsy, or any of the abnormalities embodied in the families they came from. These scary dreams and fantasies explain why most expectant parents constantly want reassurance from their obstetrician that the fetus is normal. They never tire of hearing that over and over, and then, when the baby is finally born, they want reassurances from the baby's pediatrician that everything is developing normally. Even experienced parents may find themselves getting up in the middle of the night to check on the baby's breathing, particularly if the baby hasn't made any noise for a while.

One major psychological adjustment is the parents' need to feel better about themselves through bonding to the actual baby. In order to do this, they must first mourn the perfect imaginary infant that got them through the pregnancy. This creation of the imaginary infant is a normal part of the parenting process and is identified as image-making, the first stage described in *The Six Stages of Parenthood* by Ellen Galinsky, which focuses on how parents develop as their children grow and their personalities unfold. As mentioned previously, parents have mental pictures or dreams of how things are supposed to go when the child is born. Parents remember the child they once were and then form images of how they would like to have been treated by their parents.

Galinsky sees parents as having myriads of images that filter in and out of their thoughts, as opposed to one dream. She therefore sees parenthood as a journey of images failed and achieved. It is a sequence of stages that parents are led through in response to their children's growth. After *image-making*, which occurs during pregnancy, and has been discussed in this and the previous chapter, comes *nurturing*, which extends from birth through the first couple of years. Next comes the *authority stage*, as small children begin to show independence and assert their wills, and parents have to learn to set limits. Then the *interpretive stage* follows, when children reach the "age of reason," and parents explain the world and their values. The *interdependent stage* comes when teenagers challenge authority, and finally, *departure* occurs when parents let go and take stock of their successes and failures as their children move out into the world.

The initial stage of bonding with the actual child and letting go of the image of the perfect child can be far more difficult when the infant presents an actual defect or congenital disease. The gap between the real and the imaginary is much wider and harder to accept. The child is like a mirror to the parents of both their positive and negative traits. A visible abnormality, such as a cleft lip, unconsciously stirs up an inner sense of inadequacy in parents. "What's wrong with us?" is the question raised. It is no wonder that a child with a disability or chronic illness is a trauma that wounds the parents' self-esteem. Having known this pain first hand, it is something that I live in dread of happening again—indeed at times it has haunted me. At this point, I'll take a page out of my own life to illustrate these points.

Fountain Time

Some times are harder than others, as Michael Dorris points out in *The Broken Cord* when he describes Adam's birthdays—reminders of the pain and "the rage that he was not born whole." For me, the holidays, which every year quickly follow Tariq's birthday on November 29, make for an especially difficult period. Images of warm cozy family life fill our heads from Thanksgiving through Chanukah, Christmas, and the New Year. It's a time to be close, to give thanks, and to look forward. It's a time to celebrate the lives of children—a time when families get together and look back and assess where they are, notice changes, and remember losses.

Cindy and I entered the 1993 holiday season looking forward to the birth of our second daughter. Zoë was due to arrive in late November, and in order to combat our fears, we had amniocentesis performed as we had with our older daughter, Kara. Seeing the electron microscope pictures reminded me of my old biology textbooks, but these were exciting pictures of our baby's genes. It was a great relief to know that our baby had the right number of chromosomes, but it felt like we might be intruding into nature—looking too deep. How dare we! But we needed to be reassured. Now that we knew the baby would be a girl we began to imagine what her personality would be like and how she would fit with the rest of the family, with our toddler, Kara, in particular.

We kept busy and active trying not to be too nervous as the due date approached. On the Saturday after Thanksgiving, we took Kara and Antoinette to pick up Tariq and go shopping for Chanukah and Christmas gifts. As usual, Tariq was glad to see us when we picked him up, smiling broadly, grabbing me by the hand, and pulling me from the living room of his residential unit to our car. Even though he has no concept of the days of the week, he senses the increased activity and the excited mood around the holidays. He knows the general feeling but not the specifics attached to it. Somewhat fortunately, he is unaware of what he is missing, but I can't help but ponder what these holidays would be like with him if he were "normal."

As we approached the mall, I began to wonder what it would be like this time. Would it be upsetting being with Tariq? Would my eyes glass over? Would I get grumpy and irritable? How would I handle it? I began to focus on the anticipation of my two daughters, and that helped my mood to lighten.

As we parked and got out of the car, Kara got excited by the decorations and the sound of Christmas carols. At two and a half, it was all new to her, and she could talk about it. It was exhilarating to be a part of her excitement. Anotinette wanted to shop on her own for some presents. At twelve, she was old enough and really enjoyed that—it made her feel mature.

Tariq had a look of wonder on his face. He clung to my hand and pulled me toward the mall entrance. Kara held Cindy's hand. She put her head next to Cindy's stomach and said, "Come out baby! Come see the toys. I want you to play with me."

We all laughed. It was a warm memorable moment. Even Kara had a warm fantasy of the baby as a playmate. Tariq just kept walking happily, sharing the feeling of our family's humor but not the idea, which he couldn't comprehend.

When Tariq was born, I looked forward to shopping for toys for him as I envisioned having fun playing with him. Since he hasn't played "normally" with toys since he was eighteen months old, this part of my life with him has been an unfulfilled dream, and our little outing this day reminded me of that. Images of Christmases past danced through my mind. I recalled how for years everywhere I went I tried to pick toys that Tariq might like, hoping that he might get interested and have fun or learn something.

Gradually, over a period of years, I had learned to let go of that image of playing with my son with exciting new toys, like cars and trucks and games, on Christmas morning. Since it was not a realistic image for Tariq, I tried to create a new image—a more workable one. On this day, I couldn't help wondering what I would be buying him if he was "normal." At first my mind went blank. What are fourteen year olds into these days? I thought of one of my nephews who is a year younger and fairly typical to get a perspective. Baseball cards, sports equipment, CD's, computer games, and clothes came to mind.

Well, I could buy Tariq clothes, and I enjoy doing that. He's a good-looking kid; people always comment on that, so it feels good to pick styles and colors that enhance his appearance. Teenagers enjoy getting new clothes for gifts. Tariq wouldn't notice the same way. However, he would get the positive feelings of others seeing him in a colorful new sweater. Looking at it this way gave me pleasure in buying him some presents appropriate for his age. That helped me feel like a normal parent and got me out of the strong feelings that seem to cave in on me when I compare my son to a normal child his age.

We split our family up for a while because Tariq just liked walking, and it was difficult to actually shop with him. Antoinette on her own, Cindy and Kara, me and Tariq. We would meet again in an hour. We had learned various strategies like this to deal with the stress that could drive us apart if we didn't figure out how to manage it. I would miss the rest of the family, but I could have an enjoyable interaction with my son.

The mall was crowded with holiday shoppers whom Tariq didn't seem to notice. He did notice a vendor selling soft pretzels and pulled me over that way pointing to his mouth, signing that he wanted to eat. Then he pointed to the center of his chest indicating "please." It was wonderful that he communicated; just this brief connection about a basic need gave me a warm feeling. That exchange of affect is the basic vehicle of the relationship he and I have. Indeed, as I have learned, it is the basic vehicle for any human bond—affect is the bridge between people.

This approach of joining Tariq where he is at is something I learned during his years at the Center for Autistic Children—the simple but profound contribution of child psychiatrist Bert Ruttenberg, who founded that center nearly forty years ago. As opposed to wishing and pushing for a child to be normal, this tactic accepts the child where he or she is and encourages further development. Even more, it fosters an enjoyable relationship for both parent and child. Learning how to tune in like this has been a vital part of my own healing process.

I bought a few pretzels, and we sat down next to the fountain munching on them. It was pleasant "going with the flow" and just being there—a concept called floor time by child psychiatrist Stanley Greenspan. This is basically unstructured time when a parent follows the child's lead and the child's interests—the child is the director. With little children, you get down on the floor on your child's level. With older children, you can be sitting, walking, playing a board game or sporting activity.

The main idea behind floor time is to build up a warm, trusting relationship. A parent can't always just join a child where he's at, but the more the better. Greenspan recommends about thirty minutes per day. This joining with a child establishes a communication loop on the child's level in which feelings are passed back and forth. The warmth and trust that flows from this provides the foundation, or platform, from which to face all of life's challenges with a special child.

The cascading fountain was hypnotic, and Tariq enjoyed it, giving us some rare time to just sit together. I knew he was enjoying it. I was enjoying that he was enjoying it. He knew I was in tune with him and this filled me with a feeling of contentment, however momentary it might be. I knew he would be itching to walk again as soon as he finished his pretzel. I put my hand on his shoulder and squeezed tightly for a moment—he likes that kind of firm, deep touch. My thoughts drifted as I recalled other peaceful moments in my life sitting by the ocean and listening to the sound of the waves.

Just then Tariq got up, yanking my arm and interrupting my reverie and, in essence, demanding something from me. It was back to the present. He had had enough sitting and wanted to walk. That ended our stillness for a while. The good feeling I got from it fueled me, and being alone with him, I could just follow his impulses. If the whole family was together, I might have to hold him back, and he would protest—stamping his feet and uttering sounds of frustration. That kind of tension breaks my heart. It deflates my spirit and drains my energy. I hate that reaction and work hard to avoid it.

Whenever possible, I try to go at Tariq's pace and on the level of intimacy he can take. As long as I don't get exhausted, it makes our time together more pleasant. Over time, with any child, a parent can learn how to deal with the trouble spots that come up in the course of the day. This is the real art of parenting. This day it meant walking around the mall at a brisk pace. The walk itself was something I could enjoy with Tariq, although I would have preferred being outside if the weather was better. People must have been noticing—this wasn't quite normal—a tall, thin teenager smiling broadly, babbling like a very young child, holding his father by the hand, and leading him through the mall at a pace twice what everyone else was walking. Occasionally Tariq would twirl his free hand near his head and make a contented but unusual sound for someone his age, or stick out his tongue, seeming to enjoy whatever sensation he got from that.

I wondered what people thought was wrong with Tariq. Long ago I accepted that most people, relatives included, probably preferred not to think about it—a natural response to an unpleasant reality. If they did think about it, I thought that they must realize that it was hard being his dad. I imagined they knew how much I loved him. That was a pleasant projection. It had taken me years to understand and come to peace with Tariq as he actually is and to find and enjoy as many pleasant moments as possible.

This walk through the mall in harmony was one of the moments that told me I was a good father. Tariq felt good, and I felt good that he felt good. Like every parent in a similar situation, I need as much of that as I can get. It wasn't what I would have thought of as a Hallmark or Kodak moment before I had my son, but it is a valuable lesson about life and parenting even with "typical" children. Now let's take a closer look at how to develop that type of relationship with a child who has a disability and may be more difficult to nurture than a more typical child.

Julie and David, Her Busy Child

Julie had a very active four-year-old son and sought my counsel to help her relationship with him. "He's my only child," she told me with tears in her eyes and her voice trembling. "He was born when I was thirty-eight. I waited for him my whole life, and this is the way he is. You see it; everyone sees it—he isn't normal. That hurts to say. I'm not sure a good mother would say such a thing or would feel so very, very disappointed in her own child."

David was a bright-eyed, attractive child, but it was obvious that he was "different" from my first observation in my office. The new environment excited him. He fidgeted; he went from toy to toy never completing a play activity; and he didn't seem to listen to his mother. His mom told me that once he started crawling, he was never still for long. He got into everything around the house. In preschool, he wouldn't sit in the circle.

Julie always felt like people were looking at her when she took David places. His difference made her feel different, defective—at times even ashamed. How often I had wished that Tariq had turned out normal and how often I had felt the way Julie described herself feeling. Indeed, how often had I wished that Tariq's disability was as "mild" as David's.

"Their eyes seem to say that I'm the mom of a bad kid," she blurted out. Certainly her eyes told me how painful that thought was, as I observed a tear forming in the corner of one of them.

She told me how overwhelmed she felt just trying to keep up with David and keep him safe. He was very impulsive. If Julie wasn't totally vigilant, he would get out of the house and wander through the neighborhood. She cried as she related to me how he would never just sit and cuddle with her as other children his age did with their mothers. She never got that quiet time, and she longed for that. It was a part of her dream as a mother.

Recently at the play group she brings her son to, the daughter of one of her friends sat on Julie's lap for a breather. It felt so good to her.

As she soaked it in, Julie wanted those moments to last and last. Then she felt guilty for wishing for another child. She wondered why she couldn't just love David as he was at that moment, playing actively and happily with one toy after another. That was the real David. Clearly, there was something very special in this young boy's zest for life.

What a bind for a parent to be in! Yet understanding these complicated feelings is the door to the way out. It's the dilemma of every parent whose child isn't "normal"—how to help the child and yet simultaneously love and accept the child for who he is at the moment. It helps to remember that the child is not static, but rather a dynamic evolving organism with tremendous potential for growth. The potential, however, might be less or slower than a parent would wish for, and this is truly hard to accept.

From the first moments of a child's life, parents hunger for responses from their newborns. Infants begin their social interactions with soothing body contact, eye contact, and then later by smiling and making sounds. What expecting parents don't dream of a smiling baby who snuggles in their arms? So Julie's response of disappointment that she cannot have this is quite normal but extremely uncomfortable.

Babies come into the world "wired" in ways that elicit responses from parents and need this feedback to develop. The infant's responses fuel the endless work of parenthood by encouraging a strong attachment, reassuring parents that their love is helping. The parents' enthusiasm in turn encourages and nurtures the child's development through stage after stage. The child is also fueled from within. Anticipation generates energy in the infant, and a sense of mastery begins to develop very early on. This propels the infant toward the next achievement along with the responses in the environment.

When a newborn breaks into the tiniest of smiles, for example, the adoring parent enjoys this and will smile back and often talk to the baby. The baby may coo or gurgle and thrash around in response. This in turn causes the parent to continue the interaction. As child psychiatrist Daniel Stern has observed, the face of the mother and the face of the infant have a dialogue with each other. The baby is prewired to look at the parent's face because this is where the affective bridge first occurs. Thus, the baby is interactive from birth and an active partner in the relationship.

Stern's book, *The Interpersonal World of the Child*, has a painting by artist Mary Cassat on the cover. The baby is focused on the mother's face and reaching a hand up to it, demonstrating how the initial bond is built between the faces. The French sculptor, Auguste Rodin, conceptualized the face as the mirror of the soul, based on the premise that it is in the face that love is found. How common it is for a new parent to make silly faces in order to get a baby to smile and then to smile back in the quest for more of this most pleasant interaction.

As the baby gets older, the capacity increases for verbal inter-play—and it *is* play, genuine fun for parent and child. Then if a baby says, "ooh," for example, parents may say, "That's good!" or say "ooh" back in an encouraging way. Infants like to look at faces and can understand facial expressions and tone of voice, so the parents' natural response offers reinforcement for the infant, who is then fueled to do more and develop further.

It used to be thought that parents had the primary influence in the parent-child interaction. More recent research however, has shown how vital the child's response is to parents. In this early type of dialogue, each partner influences the other and sets up a response to the reaction of the other. Difficulties experienced by either partner can profoundly affect the relationship, as we could see with David and his mother.

When the baby's ability to respond to parental nurturing is impaired by some biological factor, the parents' expectations for the relationship are immediately violated. Their dreams are deflated, lessening their interest-excitement and causing their energy level to lessen. Quite naturally, this unpleasant feeling results in parents playing and talking less with an infant who doesn't respond, so the positive flow of affect is interrupted.

The infant, in turn, then receives less response from the parent and thus loses some of this source of motivating energy, making interactions less rewarding. This may lead quickly to a withdrawn and less responsive infant who slumps away from the parent instead of reaching toward the face. Studies by Brazelton and his colleagues have shown that the parent, in turn, then becomes withdrawn, or even frightened or agitated, and slumps away from the baby. Even a short gap in communication can leave parents feeling helpless and ineffectual.

Unfortunately, the infant who has trouble interacting and responding needs more—not less—help from his parents. He needs them to talk and play even more than they would if he were ideally responsive. Studies of infants with developmental disabilities have consistently shown that many of their behaviors, such as frequent and loud crying, difficulty in being comforted, and infrequent eye contact, discouraged their caretakers from responding. Thus the parental bond as well as the child's social and emotional development are put at risk for all sorts of problems. The infant may become withdrawn, and development may be slowed even more dramatically than the biological problem would seem to dictate.

Getting back to Julie, it was with good reason that she worried about her parenting. She had sensed that her interaction with her little boy was not helping him. Intuitively she knew that a change in her could help her son. From birth, David had a generally positive mood and was easy to comfort when upset. This quality had kept Julie going even when she was discouraged by his dislike for physical contact. Now he was beginning to become moody and disgruntled. Julie thought this was because she had to supervise and correct him so much of the time.

The tension between Julie and her son was living proof of a joint problem, and she experienced it as a maternal failure because she had expected everything to come naturally and blamed herself that it hadn't. She needed professional guidance to help her be more comfortable with her son and to encourage his development despite his overactive nature and all the practical challenges it created. Any child who has difficulty hearing, or seeing, or moving, or processing information will most likely have a similar effect on his parents. Now let's focus in a little closer at how to bond more closely when it isn't happening easily, and then we'll apply this information to Julie and David as well as to other situations.

Tuning In

Getting in tune with the actual child and letting go of the dream for the perfect child starts with the parents coming to an accurate understanding of who their child really is. Brazelton has made an important contribution to this task first stressing the positive in each child, demonstrating those positive traits and promoting bonding, and then helping parents understand their infant's limitations. The child with a disability or illness is first of all a child; the disability is secondary. Often parents' fears turn out to be worse than a realistic perception of the "damage."

Everyone is born into the world with a set of temperamental traits.

It is helpful to learn about these traits in order to be able to more objectively observe the child. It is a powerful intervention when the child's individual characteristics are identified by a skilled clinician, such as a pediatrician, psychologist, psychiatrist, or social worker. While this written explanation cannot approach substituting for that, it can be helpful. Each baby, with or without a disability, learns and grows at her own pace and with her own style. This section starts with a general overview and then applies this perspective in a way that can help a parent like Julie and her son, David.

Very early in the first weeks of life, parents begin discovering what pleases their baby and what causes distress. How often the baby needs to sleep, eat, and be changed becomes clear and routines are established. What stops the baby from crying, and how the baby prefers to be held are easily recognized. Observant parents who learn how to respond to the baby's cues answer their own questions and reduce their anxieties about the baby's health and well-being.

Getting to know the actual child occurs through holding, touching, and caring for the baby. The discrepancy between the imagined and the real child can then be resolved. It is a process of sorting through dream images and settling on what is realistic, thereby strengthening the relationship. This kind of bonding foreshadows the entire course of parenthood for children with both normal and special needs.

Some babies are almost always cheerful, while others are cranky. Some like to be held, while others prefer less physical contact. Some go along with whatever their caretakers' preference may be, and this is true regardless of how fast or slow a child's development may be. To further complicate matters, the child's traits may be very different from the parents'. This can create what has been called a temperamental mismatch and can set up a challenge for the parents who must learn to understand and respect innate rhythms or characteristics that may be very different than their own.

Child psychiatrist Stella Chess, a pioneer in this area, has identified nine temperamental traits. Looking at these attributes one by one in the child as well as the parent can dramatically improve the relationship, whether the child has a disability or not. It helps to know that in many areas nothing is wrong with either parent or child—they are often just different by temperament. This can be a powerful and healing revelation to parents. While it seems fairly simple, this material is unique and complex on an individual basis. It is the way in which skills and personalities unfold that makes each child's personality so unique.

Activity level may be the most obvious trait. Put simply, how much movement or bodily activity does a child prefer? Some children, like David, never seem to stop for long except when something new catches their interest. On the other end, some children prefer a low level of physical activity. When parent and child prefer a similar level of activity, it is easy for the relationship to be harmonious. A very active parent, for example, would probably regard an active child as normal. On the other hand, a parent with a low activity level may regard a child with an average level as overactive because the parent can't keep up without straining.

Biological rhythms as a temperamental trait can be regular or irregular and apply to sleeping, eating, and toileting. Some children never seem to nap, exhausting their parents, while others nap consistently, giving their parents much needed breaks. Those who eat regularly make meal times easier, and those who eliminate regularly are far easier to toilet train. While most would prefer children with regular rhythms, parents who have irregular patterns themselves tend to be more understanding of similar children. Children with irregular patterns may need extra care with emphasis on routine to help them become more regular and function more easily within groups such as in school.

Adaptability concerns how quickly a child can accept or get used to a change in routine. Some children react negatively to even small changes, such as using a different cup at snack time, while others readily go with the flow. Children who have trouble adapting are not helped by avoiding new situations. They need to be prepared and then gradually introduced to new things and thus helped to adapt. These children tend to be less distractible. The downside of being very adaptable is that it is more difficult to understand that child's needs and wants. Children and adults with this quality may have their needs consistently compromised.

The approach/withdrawal reaction has to do with how children approach new situations. Some children will initially withdraw from a new person, toy, or food. They need time to observe and approach slowly, often with support and encouragement. Other children are drawn in right away by the novelty of a new situation. They may need help to avoid potentially dangerous situations because they automatically approach without thinking or observing.

The physical sensitivity threshold is another trait that varies widely in children. Some are very easily upset by loud noises, bright lights, temperature changes, or differences in clothing. Others barely seem to notice all but the most extreme changes in their environment. The children who are easily upset may be regarded negatively, when actually they are just more sensitive. Being able to understand this can be a great help in the child's development.

Distractibility refers to how easily a child can be diverted from eating or playing by an unexpected noise or another person. Some children can concentrate easily despite their surroundings, while others are distracted by the slightest noise. Either extreme can present difficulties to parents. The very distractible child has trouble sitting still, while the child at the other end of the continuum resists switching attention easily to a new activity.

The persistence/attention span is a similar attribute. Some children continue an activity even when it is extremely difficult. Others give up right away. Those with greater persistence will be more likely to succeed in school, but they may also have problems switching attention when that is necessary. At its extreme, persistence after the job is done is known as perseveration, and it shuts the child out from making progressions to new or more complex activities.

Quality of mood is the final area in which children vary widely. Some children stay pleasant and cheerful most of the time and are considered to have a "positive" mood. Others are fussy and cry easily, presenting a "negative" mood. Parents of those with a more positive mood may have difficulty knowing what bothers their children. The parents of those who cry easily, on the other hand, may fear that their child is essentially unhappy and believe that they are not "good enough" parents.

From looking at these nine traits, Stella Chess and her colleague Alexander Thomas identified three major temperamental patterns. These patterns have been called *flexible* (or easy), *feisty* (or difficult), and *slow-to-warm-up*. There are advantages and disadvantages to each pattern, as well as strategies that are helpful with each temperament. Approximately 65 to 70 percent of children fit into one of these categories, according to the reseachers, with the remainder being a mixture of the patterns.

The *flexible* child has regular biological rhythms and is therefore easy to feed, toilet train, and take care of basic needs. Approximately 40 percent of all children fit into this category with these characteristics of a "perfect baby." Unfortunately, babies without these qualities are often considered "bad" because of a lack of understanding that these qualities are innate. Flexible children enjoy most new situations and adapt quickly. They seldom fuss and have a predominantly positive, cheerful mood. They have a low sensitivity to physical stimulation and a low intensity of emotional reaction. Flexible children have deep feelings as do all children, but they express themselves quietly. For this reason, they may get taken advantage of by other children, or they may get lost in the shuffle. They are easy to forget or take for granted when a busy parent has two or more children or when a teacher is trying to manage a large group.

The needs of flexible children are just as great as those of more vocal children. It helps to check in regularly, observe the child, and see if any particular help or attention is needed or wanted. Since they are not usually a problem, they rarely demand attention except in a crisis. It is vital to set aside special time so that flexible children receive the attention they need and deserve. Zoë, Cindy's and my younger child, tends to fit this profile. She is usually smiling and rarely upset, although she is shy and timid. When she does cry, it seems out of character and hard to figure. Since it doesn't take much to make her happy, we feel bad when we miss giving her what she needs. She provides, in her quiet agreeable manner, new challenges and rewards for us as parents.

About 15 percent of all children fit the *slow-to-warm-up* pattern. They are often regarded as shy or timid and need more time to warm up to new situations and people. Their biological rhythms may be regular or irregular. If pushed too hard, they tend to withdraw. They too express themselves quietly, sometimes nonverbally with their body posture or tone of voice. Kara, our older child, has such qualities, and she has taught me firsthand how to respond to children like her. In fact, she has made me more aware that I myself share some of these qualities. Despite their cautious nature, these children often become very attached to their parents and teachers. For example, once Kara has warmed up, she gets very upset and sobs when it is time to leave the home of someone she has become comfortable with. A trait that may be initially quite challenging can, over time, become quite an endearing quality.

Cautious children need to feel close to their base of security. The key for them is to go slowly, step by step. In this way, they can be drawn into new activities and situations. The parent can then back off and remain available when needed or wanted. Consistency in the environment and the daily routine also helps fearful children by decreasing the feeling of newness and adding to their sense of security.

The last temperamental type is the *feisty* child, who seldom holds back, unlike the cautious child. Feisty children tend to be very active, comprising about 10 percent of all children. They are intense and often fun to be with. They live with zest, while letting everyone know how they feel and what they want. On the other hand, feisty children can overwhelm their parents and caregivers because they are so intense, easily distracted, and often moody with irregular rhythms and intense reactions to various stimuli.

Feisty children need flexible parents who are sensitive to their feelings but able to set firm limits on unacceptable behavior. A parent who isn't flexible will be challenged to become so in order to have a satisfying relationship. The feisty child needs more time to experience his or her emotions before settling down. Only afterward can such a child be redirected to a new toy or activity when upset. Looking ahead in life, a child with these qualities may be more assertive than average and a real "go getter."

These intense children need peaceful, calm surroundings. By making the most of quiet moments, parents can strengthen their relationship as well as reinforce the child's more focused behavior. Feisty children also need many opportunities for active, vigorous play as well as more supervision to ensure their safety. The quiet moments can often be found to grow from those periods when the child has found something interesting to focus on. It helps when a parent is energetic and participates enthusiastically in these kinds of activities. This is a form of approval that such a child exalts in.

These were the strategies that I recommended to Julie for her son after observing him in my office and in the playground nearby. After conferring with David's teacher, it was clear that the same strategies would be appropriate in school. When I met Howard, David's father, it was immediately apparent that his son's activity level was not adversely affecting their relationship. Although calm and thoughtful in his demeanor, Howard had an easier time with his son because he enjoyed the vigorous physical play that is more characteristic of fathers' interactions with their children.

Howard did need, however, to look for and stretch out the quiet times to aid his son's developing ability to prolong his attention and concentration. Because he was unaware of the problem for so long, Howard and Julie experienced a good deal of dissonance whenever they discussed their perceptions of David. Under the guise of "boys will be boys," many children like David are not easily identified as needing help. Having an objective professional observer helped Julie and Howard to work together in their son's best interest.

Looking at the broad spectrum of these temperamental qualities in children is helpful in appreciating the uniqueness of each child. It gives insight into each child's behavior and needs. By tuning in and accepting these normal and natural traits, children get the message that who they are is good and worthwhile—they can feel loved and secure. Parents likewise can then get the feeling that they too are really decent folks because they can understand and love their child for who she or he is. It then becomes a building block in a relationship that feels good and is a source of pride to parent and child alike.

Floor Time

Julie got this harmonious feeling when she was able to match her rhythms and behaviors to her son's. I saw this happen while observing them at the playground near my office for one of their sessions of floor time in action. The guiding principle is that healthy emotional development is the foundation for social and intellectual growth. The first step to helping Julie was observing the child in action. I noticed David's agility in climbing and the sparkle in his eye as he took obvious pride in demonstrating his prowess.

This was the same behavior that often exhausted, stressed, and even angered Julie at home when it was more than she could handle. In the environment of the playground, however, climbing could be embraced almost unconditionally. I pointed this out to Julie. The only limits, or rules, during floor time are that you can't break things or hurt anyone. This is because there must be a structure in which the child feels safe and secure. Julie was then able to relax. It was a relief to have nothing else to have to correct David about, and he was able to play freely, which he did with great exuberance.

Next, I encouraged Julie to respond to David, which Greenspan calls "opening the circle of communication." The idea is to join the child in whatever he is doing while acknowledging the emotional tone, which in this case was excitement. Showing interest in what the child wants to do helps him to feel valued for who he is. In this case it was climbing, an application of gross motor skills.

"Wow! Look at my boy. You're really good at this," Julie remarked. In enjoying him and staying nearby in the playground, Julie entered David's world and "followed his lead," Greenspan's third step. This gave David the support to build his own drama and simultaneously, in this case, offered him an incentive to reach for Julie's slower-paced style. He paused for a moment and smiled back, clearly enjoying her enjoying him. Then he quickly moved on to his next challenge. His mother's support encouraged him.

"Look at this!" he exclaimed as he slid down a pole to the ground. He smiled as Julie arched her eyebrows in an approving glance and then moved on quickly again. By continuing to actively express approval, both verbally and nonverbally, Julie had encouraged David to "extend and expand his play," Greenspan's next step in floor time. Julie took pride in her son, and David took pride in himself. It seemed contagious—what a boost to the sagging self-esteem of both parent and child! Complimenting David on what he already felt good about added to his sense of competency. On the other side of the equation, finding the opportunity to respond to her son in this way helped Julie feel like a good mother.

After about twenty minutes of vigorous play, David came over to the park bench, from which Julie and I were both watching him, and sat on his mothers lap. The drama of our session in the playground had reached its conclusion. It was a fitting and welcome end to a vigorous performance. The child had "closed the circle of communication," the last of the five basic steps in floor time. Each child-centered activity had received approving expressions, gestures, and words, and now David was reaching out to his mother in a tender, well-deserved moment.

David demonstrated that he enjoyed Julie's enjoying this time. The drama of their relationship was unfolding. Julie began to feel more fulfilled as a mother. David's basic nature would not change, but their relationship could change. In the moments of mutual comfort and acceptance there was great warmth. This kind of reciprocal relationship sustains the development of the child and bolsters and heals the injured self-esteem of the parent as well as the child. Julie had entered

David's world as a partner and facilitator, something that had become rare in everyday life where she was forced to struggle to contain and control his extremely active behavior. The child was able to feel more comfortable in his mother's love. This renewed relationship would facilitate effective behavioral strategies during the rest of the day and guide David in further social growth.

The current video, *Around the Clock: Parenting the Delayed ADHD Child* with Joan Goodman and Susan Hoban, explores in detail the many challenges facing parents when their child has both ADHD (attention deficit hyperactivity disorder) and other developmental delays in areas such as language, coordination, and learning. Although the difficulties can seem insurmountable at times, when broken into smaller chunks, effective coping strategies can be developed. The video shows "behind-the-doors" scenes of what it is really like for two families in their own words.

The same basic floor time philosophy that we have been discussing can be a guide for engaging with babies or young children at the other end of the activity spectrum as well. Young children who are slow to respond or whose development is delayed also crave mutually pleasurable interactions. Holding or gently touching the child, talking or singing in a quiet, soothing voice, or rocking or swaying according to the child's preference can be quite pleasant and stimulating. Joining in the slower pace provides a motivation for the child to join the parent at a somewhat faster pace—the inverse of what happened between Julie and her son.

These activities can be built into the daily routine when feeding, dressing, bathing, and diapering or toileting. Siblings, relatives, and friends who are comfortable with the child can all learn to participate in this way—making for a more cohesive family life and facilitating an interlocking web of relationships that can be beneficial to all involved.

Donald was a man I met at a fathers' workshop I conducted. His child fit the slower-paced rhythm, and he had trouble bonding early on for this reason. He told me how much he enjoyed hunting and fishing and had, for as long as he could remember, imagined having a son to enjoy these outdoor activities with him. He wanted to teach his son these sports and enjoy the same kind of companionship that he had enjoyed growing up with his father. His son, Kevin, however, was born blind and with mild cerebral palsy. Donald was devastated. He thought all his hopes and dreams had gone out the window because his first image of Kevin was that of a totally helpless child.

It took a period of several years as Kevin developed for his father to come to grips with his son's disability. As Donald became more and more involved with his son's development by playing with him at his own pace, he learned what Kevin could and couldn't do and realized that there was nothing holding his son back from fishing. It would not be easy, but virtually everything that he had imagined about fishing with his son was possible. That realization helped Donald to remake his dream—hunting was still out, but fishing was in. Kevin would just need help baiting his hook and a lot of coaching.

Within months of that realization, on a warm spring day, Donald was sitting with Kevin on a bridge over a stream near their home with their fishing rods in hand and lines dangling in the water. It was a dream come true for Donald. The quiet challenge, the fun, and the relaxation that fishermen love were all there. What Donald had thought was out of the question at the time of his son's diagnosis was now firmly grasped in the bond between father and son.

Every child is constantly maturing, evolving, and dynamic. There is an unfolding of positive and negative behaviors that is not apparent at birth. In this process, knowing and accepting your child's actual developmental skills is a key for being able to relate in a mutually satisfying way. Expectations that are too high will be frustrating when they are not reached. On the other hand, expectations set too low provide for little excitement. There is a constant process of assessing the child's skills and joining where he or she actually is.

It is normal to wonder and not to know what is to come. The best antidote to the worry is to be able to find excitement and joy in the here and now. This positively energizes both parent and child to meet the main developmental challenges that lie ahead. As Gilbert Gaul, a Pulitzer Prize–winning journalist, observed in *Giant Steps*, "Life isn't made up of exclamations so much as a succession of small moments strung together like beads on a necklace. Where we go wrong is by expecting too much. Then disappointed and empty we have to find someone to blame." The resentment pales as we learn to live moment by moment and find those beads to string on our necklaces.

FIVE

Understanding and Guiding
Your Child's Behavior

"Simply imagine he's not your child. Everybody knows how to raise other people's children." Or so it seems. Whenever I address a group of parents about how to handle the behavior problems of children with disabilities, this statement never fails to evoke a round of hearty laughter. It's so much easier for all of us, even experts, to discuss other people's children. The balance between love and discipline is one of the toughest challenges of parenthood.

In the heat of the moment, it is difficult but vital to learn how to back off and look at your own life calmly and objectively. An important key to this approach is to seek support and insight from another adult—a spouse, a friend, or a professional with experience in the behavioral issues faced by parents of special children.

This chapter provides a framework to address behavior problems: first, get to know yourself and the deep inner feelings evoked by your child; second, understand the deeper meaning communicated by everyday problem behaviors; and third, learn to flexibly yet firmly apply behavioral strategies to implement change. Numerous other helpful books are available, and some will be cited here, but personal professional guidance is often necessary. If you are spending more time telling your child what not to do than enjoying your child, that may be the signal that it is time to seek help.

Getting in Touch With Yourself

The pressures of everyday life can push a parent to his wits' end. For many parents, not only is family life not like *Ozzie and Harriet*, it is also not like *Life Goes On* or *LA Law*, programs in which characters with disabilities have none but endearing traits. In real life, people who are disabled often have many annoying behaviors and habits that can try parents' patience. While a parent may have been sad holding and thinking about an infant or toddler with a disability, a preschooler's difficult behaviors may arouse anger that can be projected outward toward its source. This reaction, in turn, may produce guilt for not having been more understanding, resulting in a cycle that is not easy to break.

Not long ago, a father called me for an appointment. George, a well-dressed man of medium build in his early forties, seemed to have a lot going for him, but his outward appearance belied the inner turmoil he told me about. His finely tailored suit was complemented by a blue textured shirt and a rich looking tie of contrasting multicolors. George was a partner in a leading management consulting firm and was secure in his professional life. As he told me how he had looked forward to the birth of his son as the fulfillment of everything he wanted in life, his eyes glazed over.

He said that the frustration building up inside him was becoming unbearable. His body was reacting through colitis and a skin condition, and a concerned physician had recommended that he seek psychological help. George was obsessed with thoughts about his four-year-old, Billy, and he was becoming short-tempered with his wife. He was also grumpy with their two-year-old daughter for no reason that he could identify.

George's son had Down syndrome and many developmental delays. For example, Billy was not yet toilet trained and his speech was limited to a handful of words. George and his wife, Maureen, had heard me speak at a conference in Harrisburg; George had been part of a fathers' group that I had conducted there. He thought I could understand him, but thinking that he should be able to handle things by himself, he had been delaying getting help.

There was no one in George's everyday life he could turn to. Lately he said he was likely to start crying unexpectedly whenever he was alone in the car. He was very close to his wife; they had been together ten years and had always been able to talk about their problems. But now, when the subject of George's difficulties with Billy came up, they usually had to stop talking before it got tense and they became upset with each other. George told me that his wife felt that he was blaming her for giving birth to a child with Down syndrome and blaming the child for having the extra chromosome, his short forehead, and his slanting eyes. He didn't want his wife or either of his children to be the object of his grumpy moods and was worried that his crying so much meant that he was a weak man.

At least in my office, George's emotions were close to the surface, which is not very common among men. George triggered memories of my own excitement about Tariq's birth. As I looked into my patient's eyes, I sensed that my own eyes were televising my empathy of his predicament—rooted and intertwined with my own sorrow. His words flowed smoothly, as if he had prepared for the session.

"Sometimes I feel that my life is over, that I have no future. Maureen is afraid to try again for a normal son. Maybe this is all there is for us. When I'm thinking like that lately during the day in the office, I don't want to go home. It's hard for me to face Maureen and Billy when I'm feeling like that. It's so disappointing that Billy can't run up and hug me and sit on my lap and tell me what he has been doing all day. That's my image of what should be happening. Other people are so excited talking about their little children. I'm not even enthused about my daughter, Dawn, and that's not fair to her. I find myself running from them and feeling guilty that I'm not excited to get home after work."

I commented on how well George was expressing himself.

"Well, as a consultant, I'm a professional communicator, so I was ready to tell you why I'm here. I've read up on this stuff, gone to workshops and support groups, and gone through what I've recognized as stages of grief, but I'm stuck. Other people think I have it together—that I'm a good father. I hate when people say that I am because I know it's not true, but I wouldn't want anyone to know."

"Where are you stuck?" I asked.

"It's like I've got a chip on my shoulder. I'd love to be a bad dad of a typical son. At least he'd play sports and do other things that I could brag about. And most of all, he'd bring grandchildren with my last name to see me even if I was a jerk. Again, I know this isn't fair to my daughter. So I'm grumpy a lot. It feels like a contagious disease that is ruining my life and infecting my family."

In a situation like this, I try to get hold of some of the pressure points, or what child psychologist Saul Fisher calls the "pivotal areas" of everyday life. So I asked George to describe a typical day.

"What's so typical," he related, "is not sleeping through the night. Billy wakes up a lot around three or four in the morning; usually he wants to play. Maureen and I take turns getting up and getting him back to sleep. Lately it's harder and harder for me. I get so worked up, and I didn't used to. It's like that wakes him up even more and makes him stay awake longer. Then I start yelling at him. That wakes up Maureen, and then she gets mad at me. I can't blame her really. She doesn't get me up when it's her turn. I feel like a real jerk. Whether I get back to sleep or not my day starts out with me in a grumpy mood."

As we discussed the rest of a typical day, it was clear to me that George had a good feel for how to manage many situations that came up. He was sophisticated and knowledgeable as a parent. I couldn't help but imagine how well he might do with a "typical" son. By the end of the session, George commented that he was feeling a sense of relief, that he was beginning to unload something very heavy. I asked him to reflect on his interactions with Billy in the middle of the night, so that we could understand and modify how he dealt with this flashpoint.

When he came for his appointment the following week, George looked outwardly upset. He began telling me about his family history and why he had wanted a son so badly. His dad had spent a lot of time playing baseball with him and his older brother and taking them to Phillies games. He wanted to do the same with his son and pass on the tradition. He related how he had begun sobbing lately every time he passed a Little League baseball field with a game going on. He wondered if that was "normal" in his situation, and I assured him that it was.

"You know I feel guilty at times like that. It's not Billy's fault. It feels wrong of me to be upset about baseball. He's such a peaceful child. Everyone who works with him tells us how well he is doing with his ability. He likes playing a little rough with me at night, and I like that. I feel really good in those moments."

I intervened and asked what he was thinking and feeling the last time he was up in the middle of the night with his son.

"Well that was some tough homework you gave me to think about. I want to tell you the whole truth and get it off my chest. I wonder what you'll think of me after you hear this."

George's voice started to shake. His neatly pressed suit couldn't disguise his distress. His face got pale and his eyes widened. He leaned slightly toward me.

"When I got that angry way the other night, I wished that Billy would die and Maureen, too. Then I would be free of this burden—this horrible, ugly burden. Then I could go on with my own life....Right now I'm stuck with the two of them."

Then the tears started to roll slowly down his cheeks. George leaned back and slumped down in his wing chair. He reached for a tissue and took a few deep breaths before wiping away the tears.

After waiting a few more moments, I asked him what these tears meant today.

"I feel such a sense of relief that I told someone. I've been having these thoughts for awhile. How can you tell the woman you love that sometimes you wish she was dead? My tears feel like a release and not a sign of weakness. I'm not sure what you think of me, but your eyes still look at me kindly. I wonder if any of the other people in my support group have thoughts like these. Has anybody else ever told you something like this? Can you tell me that?"

Now that George was strong enough to admit to these scary thoughts, he might soon have the courage to ask others what they were really thinking inside. I pointed out that it is relieving and healing to hear from other people you know personally. As for what I've heard, I've heard similar things many, many times—often with tears. The anger is part of the sorrow, as I pointed out earlier. For many of us, the tears don't come so easily—not every man can cry like this—even though there are often tears on the inside. Admitting, accepting, and embracing your sorrow as normal but still uncomfortable is part of the healing process and the road to an inner peace.

Anger at the child causes the parent's image of him or herself to come tumbling down. Feelings of inadequacy often arise around behavioral issues, like sleeping. These feelings can be especially frequent and intense because of the high stress level experienced by the parents of children with disabilities. It is necessary for parents to admit to these uncomfortable feelings in order to reconstruct an image of themselves as "good" parents and then to think clearly and "objectively" about how to handle their practical situation.

Initially George wasn't ready to share his negative thoughts with his wife, but he wanted to eventually. He told me that he thought he could handle Billy waking up better now. I asked him to take careful mental notes of what transpired during those times. In the middle of the night, when his defenses were down, was when George had discovered the darker side of his personality, and times like these presented opportunity for growth. Having been there myself, in the middle of many nights with Tariq, I remembered all too clearly how horrible George could feel. I knew, too, that acknowledging such dark, frightening thoughts was the first step in breaking free of the shame of having them.

When I saw George the following week, there was a bounce in his step as he walked from the waiting room into my office. He looked at me intently and smiled. "I feel twenty pounds lighter", he began, "and less angry. I'm still short on sleep, and physically life is just as difficult, but I'm less angry about my situation. I don't feel my anger spilling out onto Maureen and Billy and Dawn. When it's my turn to be up with Billy, I've been a lot better getting him back to sleep. I am able to rock him and play lullabies and basically do what works without getting caught up in my anger, which had been making the situation even more difficult."

I commented that sometimes when we can change ourselves or the way we handle things as parents, it leads to a change in our child. Then I asked how things were going between him and Maureen.

"She thinks I'm handling things a lot better, so I told her what we talked about. She understood and hugged me after I got done telling her. The amazing thing, to me, was that she said that she had been feeling like I wanted to get rid of her and Billy. She said that some days she felt like life wasn't worth living, and that's not her. I've never known her to feel like that. Even more, now that I have been able to admit this stuff, I feel even closer to Maureen. I feel like before long I will be able to tell her anything again."

Then this couple will be able to comfort each other and work out the problems that come up. They might need professional guidance from time to time if they get stumped. This can be the case for any parent as a child grows and develops. George's need for intensive psychotherapy, however, would probably be short-term since his primary relationship, his marriage, could provide the emotional support he needed.

In this man's case, it was anger that he had to get in touch with in order to understand himself and begin thinking clearly about how to handle a problem behavior. In another situation, it could be embarrassment about a child's behavior in public, guilt over a previous strict punishment, or inadequacy in understanding a child's needs. Whatever the case, understanding and embracing your inner reaction and discussing it with others is the key to acceptance and figuring out solutions.

Understanding What Your Child's Behavior Means

Once a child becomes mobile and develops an increasing ability to communicate needs and wants, questions of authority assume heightened importance. Parents are faced with a set of questions that will be with them for many years, such as:

When do I say yes?

When do I say no?

How do I enforce the rules?

How do I know when I'm right?

What is safe for my child?

From birth, the child and parent have learned to understand each other through smiles, eye contact, crying, and cooing. As a child's mobility increases through rolling, creeping, crawling, cruising, walking, and climbing, parents will have more and more decisions to make about what to allow and how to enforce it. Near the end of the first year and onward into the second, what has been complex and subtle becomes more direct and verbal. Included in the parent-child repertoire of communication is the concept of "no," which can be conveyed verbally or physically.

It is very uncomfortable to be angry at one's own child. An angry parent can make a child feel unloved, humiliated, and abandoned, and we remember these feelings from our own childhoods. As Galinsky mentions in *The Six Stages of Parenthood*—and I have found confirmation in my work with groups of parents—an unmet expectation is usually at the core of parental anger. The upset is compounded by guilt in parents who are not aware of the source of their anger and who feel bad about lashing out. When George was up in the middle of the night with his son Billy, for example, he was confronted by his anger about the loss of his dream for the perfect child.

The challenges faced by the parents of children with special needs are sometimes overwhelming. It can be extremely difficult to remain objective. Not all children with disabilities have these problems, but they do have an increased risk of developing troubling behavior patterns. Some children draw attention to themselves within the family and the community through intense emotional expressions, biting, kicking, or other physically forceful behaviors. They often have more than average difficulty moving from one activity to another, and a lot of trouble separating from parents or significant others.

Their external displays also draw attention to their parents. When a child is having a tantrum in a supermarket, for example, other customers may wonder why the parent can't control that child. The parent is likely to be embarrassed and may think himself inadequate in the eyes of others. The frustration and anger generated during such moments can be very toxic to the family.

It is common, as in other experiences that evoke shame, to want to disappear or to want the child to disappear. It is hard to think clearly when embarrassed, particularly when well-meaning others offer unsolicited advice about what to do based on what they did with their own children or what they've heard or read.

The more normal a child looks, the more unsolicited advice parents seem to get, because there is no visible reason for the child's problem. Children who have attention deficits, autism, and other neurological problems draw unsolicited attention, which can make life even harder for the child and for her parents. When a child's abnormality is visible, on the other hand, it is more likely that the parents will be viewed with compassion.

Child psychiatrist Rudolf Dreikurs developed a way of understanding and responding to children's misbehavior. His approach works with all children, but is particularly valuable with young children and those with various disabilities that slow development or compromise the child's ability to communicate verbally. Dreikurs focuses on what the child is trying to communicate through the behavior that may be inappropriate. In this framework, all behavior—even what is frequently labeled "misbehavior"—falls into four categories: seeking attention, power, displaying inadequacy, or revenge.

First, all children need *attention*; meeting this need for babies and young children is a major part of parenting. Infants often cry in noticeably different ways when they are hungry or uncomfortable or need to be changed. Parents learn to recognize what their baby needs at the moment from the type of crying they hear. Likewise, it helps to think about what a young child might be asking for through her behavior. There are many possibilities; for example, the child may be:

- hungry
- sleepy
- scared
- overstimulated
- understimulated or bored
- frustrated with not understanding

- avoiding something
- allergic
- feeling sick

Young children who have limited verbal and nonverbal vocabularies must give their parents messages through their behavior. This is called "communicative intent," and behavioral messages naturally stimulate parents to wonder what is on their child's mind. When these messages are misunderstood, especially when the child is using socially unacceptable behavior to express himself, both parent and child can become intensely frustrated. Parents often understandably focus on what is considered unacceptable and try to stop it. Then both parent and child can become intensely frustrated.

Tension for both parent and child heightens when the parent tries to stop the behavior without understanding its intended message, and heightens still more if the child keeps doing the same thing. The unacceptable behavior may be the only way the child can express her need or want. Trying to grasp the intent provides a starting point for parents to receive the child's message and then guide her toward expressing it in a more socially appropriate way.

When you can understand why your child is behaving the way she is, you can have empathy for her point of view. Empathizing doesn't mean agreeing or giving in, but *understanding*. And empathizing makes it a lot easier to work on changing a behavior that is a problem. For example, three-year-old Joanne starts pushing her five-year-old sister when she is tired of playing with the blocks. Realizing that her child is bored enables her mother, Christine, to empathize with her child's limited language rather than criticize her for being physically forceful. Joanne can then be asked to point to what she wants to do.

Sometimes children want more than attention; they need a sense of power and a feeling of control over their environment. At times virtually every child wants to take over from the parent and be in charge. Doing so is an important step in gaining independence. Temper tantrums are an example of power plays between parents and children. When they occur, parents typically feel provoked and angry; some tend to fight their children, some tend to give in. Fighting may encourage the child to intensify his protest or he may submit defiantly. When parents give in to tantrums they are teaching children that having tantrums is a way to get what you want. Both of these responses can intensify the child's desire to win and be in power.

On the other hand, withdrawing from conflict can help a child learn how to use power constructively. It can be difficult to observe objectively and notice the patterns, but by observing a child's tantrums, parents can often learn to avoid the situations that provoke them. Not long ago, a woman consulted me for help in dealing with her son's tantrums. She cried as she told me about her son. Josh was three years old and had been enrolled in a special-education preschool program for the past few months. He had very little speech compared to other children his age, but Josh was making good progress in his program. He had tantrums that could last a half hour or more. These tantrums did not occur when his father was home, which made the mother feel even more inadequate.

His mother was extremely frustrated and felt ineffectual as a parent. Her upset feelings often ruined most of the afternoon for the mother as well as for the child. When I asked when the outbursts occurred, she told me every day, specifically when her son got home from school and she was fixing his lunch. As is frequently the case for a frustrated, overwhelmed parent, she had never considered that there might be a pattern.

I wondered aloud if Josh was hungry and did not understand the wait for lunch. That made sense to his mom. I suggested that she could have his lunch prepared in advance, so that he could eat as soon as he got home.

Josh's mother soon called to tell me that the tantrums after school had stopped, and their afternoons together had become enjoyable. It seemed too good to be true. Instead of fighting over waiting for lunch to be ready, more play, floor time, and positive communication was occurring as the boy's language developed. Of course, not every problem like this one can be solved so simply, but this example does illustrate one way to reduce tantrums by avoiding them and promoting mutually enjoyable interactions between parent and child.

Sometimes children get extremely discouraged and act out in order to *display inadequacy*. Of course, this occurs more frequently when children have learning difficulties. The child may want the parent to back off from expecting a new milestone, such as going from words to sentences, and the behavior can be an expression of helplessness. Despair and hopelessness may then be evoked in the parent, leading to passivity and a lack of response in the relationship. This is another negative communicative loop that reinforces the idea that nothing can be done and ensures that improvement will not occur.

An example of this behavior would be a child who is learning to eat with a fork and who cries and kicks the table whenever he drops food. Parents often don't want their child to feel so frustrated so they back off expecting the child to use utensils. The way to encourage adequacy, however, and thereby reduce frustration over the long term is to focus on the child's assets and encourage all attempts and little successes no matter how small in using the fork. When the child drops something, respond by encouraging him to keep trying.

Breaking the challenge into small pieces, such as any successful use of the fork, enables the child to have a feeling of success. And learning to appreciate small increments of progress helps parents to avoid hopelessness and helps children to persist in their efforts. Of course, this principle applies to all children, but special children need a lot more understanding in this regard because it takes them longer to learn and master tasks for which their disability may delay or inhibit learning.

I can still picture vividly how excited Tariq was when he learned to drink through a straw. He was nine at the time. What was a small event for other children was a big step for him. I was excited and happy for him. His big smile showed that he was really proud of himself.

Last, when children feel hurt, they may want *revenge*, displaying a tendency to retaliate in order to "get even." This kind of behavior often occurs during the preschool age range of three to five. For example, a child who does not want to put his toys away before bedtime may kick or bite the parent who is asking him to do it. This is a form of communicating or connecting by hurting. This type of behavior is also frequently perceived as a lack of respect on the part of the child. The unprepared parent will frequently feel wounded, and sometimes enraged by her child's behavior and may even be impelled to retaliate physically or verbally to get even. Such a response is likely only to intensify the child's attempts to strike back and result in steadily escalating emotional and physical tension.

Behavior that has revenge as a goal may be the most difficult type to view objectively; teamwork with a spouse or another supportive adult is often necessary to control it. It can be extremely difficult for parents to overcome negative feelings in this case, but avoiding retaliation is the key to a helpful response. Using time-outs, described later in this chapter, while accepting and verbally acknowledging that the child feels hurt and angry can neutralize the hurt, often visibly relax the child, and help him or her to feel loved, which ultimately makes revenge unnecessary.

Understanding that children are always trying to tell us something and that all misbehavior has one of these four purposes often serves to defuse the build up of tension between parent and child. I have often observed parents relax visibly when they start thinking this way about their child. Doing so makes it possible to look at how to change behaviors that are problems while acting as a guide and a positive role model.

Strategies for Change

Special children are undergoing constant change, just like their more typical peers. Styles of discipline that work today or tomorrow may not work next week or next month. Parents do better when they have a broad repertoire of positive strategies to deal with challenging behaviors. The goal of positive discipline is self-disciplined children who are responsible and cooperative at their own developmental level. An added value of using positive strategies to guide children's behavior is that it helps parents to feel positive about themselves and their children. The techniques outlined here are all aimed at guiding children toward learning what is expected of them in various situations, and at avoiding ineffective punishments including:

- Threats, which parents often don't carry out and therefore undermine parental authority
- Yelling, which often doesn't work and may teach children not to listen unless parents raise their voices
- Insults, name-calling, and negative comparisons to other children, which teach shame to the child
- Withdrawal of privileges that have no clear relationship to the problem behavior and creates resentment
- Spanking, which is most often a sign of frustration in adults and may teach children to become physically aggressive themselves or passive, timid, and afraid

Renowned child psychiatrist Haim Ginott believed that spanking teaches a child that when you're angry, you hit. While spanking may decrease an undesirable behavior for a time, it does not teach an acceptable behavior. Spanking may also relieve a parent's anger, but most parents feel guilty afterward. Many children are able to use that guilt to acquire all sorts of privileges after a spanking. As Ginott said,

"I've never known of a child who was spanked into becoming a more loving human being."

Stressing the Positive

An ounce of prevention is worth a pound of cure. Positive reinforcement of desirable behavior is the best prevention for negative behavior. It is all too easy to spend a lot of time focusing on a child's problem behaviors, especially since any behavior that makes the child appear "abnormal" is particularly unpleasant for parents. Reducing or eliminating that behavior may make the child appear and actually be more "normal," which is one reason we often focus on the problems— and so may overlook many of the child's strong points.

However, when a child consistently gets a lot of attention for a certain negative behavior, he or she learns that as a way of relating or belonging. Parents, on the other hand, often grow discouraged and feel guilty when they must constantly correct their children. While setting limits is, of course, necessary, doing so can be balanced by noticing and praising positive behavior. This kind of effort results in a child getting more *yes* responses and fewer *no* responses and has been called "catching the child being good," which feels better to parent and child alike.

Ellen Galinsky reported on an informal experiment in a day care center with the parents of "normal" children in which it was found that parents tend to overestimate the amount of time that their child is difficult to handle and to underestimate the time that she is cooperative. The "four to one rule," something I learned from child psychologist Lawrence Shapiro, can be helpful in sustaining a positive attitude. According to this guideline, you have to notice and comment on four positive things before commenting on one negative or undesirable behavior.

Responding to the positive also builds a positive self-image and confidence in the child. It is especially beneficial to notice and comment on positive behavior as soon as possible after correcting a child for an undesirable behavior. Doing so reassures the child that he is still loved and valued even though he has just been corrected.

Setting Limits

Children need both loving, positive attention and limits. A deficit in either area will inhibit growth. This is particularly true when the challenges are steep; children with special needs make more progress when reasonable expectations are made and held to by parents. Conversely, unrealistic expectations may be a blow to an already delicate sense of self-esteem. For parents, the inner struggle over setting limits and establishing who is in control is a struggle that continues until the child leaves home—with or without a disability.

At the core of many conflicts between parent and child is the expectation that the child should be acting differently. Successful limit-setting is based on realistic evaluations of the child's skills. Understanding a child's capabilities helps to avoid setting unrealistic limits, and it is important to understand the effect of the child's disability on whatever limit is being considered. The child may not be able to do what is being expected or may not be developmentally ready. Reasonable expectations can be formulated with help from other parents, friends, teachers, therapists, and doctors who know your child, as well as from books.

Stanley Greenspan recommends increasing the amount of floor time whenever increasing the child's limits. The resultant empathy and warmth will help the child to realize that you are trying to teach him or her through that pleasant connection as well as through limit-setting. The parent, in turn, feels less guilty for restricting the child. Greenspan also recommends teaching one key issue at a time and using broad enforceable rules that are repeated frequently, calmly, and firmly.

When we begin to set and enforce rules for our children, there is virtually no way to avoid revisiting our own childhood. Most parents consciously aim not to repeat what hurt them as children. In this respect, we may be recreating our own childhood in the hope of trying to be the parent we wished for. People who grew up with inflexible, authoritarian parents may strive to be flexible and empathetic and therefore find it hard to set and enforce limits. On the other end of the continuum, those who grew up with permissive parents may have longed for more structure and rules with the security that can come from firm direction. In either case, our techniques for dispensing authority will have to be reshaped over and over if we are to become successful parents who help our children to achieve their full potential.

The language that we use in limit-setting can be instrumental in helping the parent to remain firm and the child to cooperate. Positive rather than negative suggestions work best. For example, "Close the door gently," instead of "Don't slam the door;" or "Take little bites," as opposed to "Don't take big bites." It is also preferable to make pleasant requests, such as, "Take a few more minutes, and then we will go inside," instead of "Stop playing." Specific requests get better responses than general ones; for example, "Put the blocks here," rather than "Pick up the toys." These techniques help to create an atmosphere that minimizes guilt and prevents the slow build up of anger that can be so harmful to parent-child relationships.

Distracting and Redirecting the Child

Toddlers eagerly explore the world around them and often get into things that may be dangerous or inappropriate. Older children who are impulsive, overactive, or who are unaware of danger due to cognitive difficulties create similar concerns for parents. This difficulty is compounded because this behavior in a child whose same-age peers are more developed reminds parents of their lost dream. Parents can become physically stressed from the demands of extra supervision. Very frequently, however, this can become a pleasant, playful interaction by distracting and redirecting the child to a safe, acceptable alternative.

Distraction works well because it is a respectful approach to curiosity and short attention spans. An easy example would be a six-month-old infant who begins pulling on a parent's ear and won't let go, causing discomfort to the adult. Simply giving the child something interesting to play with can quickly alter the situation. The child is thus distracted from the ear and redirected to something else that is enjoyable.

With a child as active as my son, Tariq, this technique was extremely helpful. I think he was attracted to the gleam of a sharp kitchen knife because he would often get one and begin waving it around playfully. If I just pulled it away from him, a negative cycle would ensue as he got upset, cried, and stamped his feet. This could go on for an hour or more, with him trying more and more desperately to get the knife back.

An hour of that kind of conflict can really give you "a bad head." Calling Tariq's name gently and offering to trade him something else he liked, such as a koosh ball or a rubber snake would usually work. It was like magic to watch him come over and agree to the exchange. He would become absorbed in that and forget about the knife. Then he could be easily steered to another part of the house, restructuring the environment to avoid a reoccurrence of the problem. Instead of feeling like I was ruining his fun or that he was getting the best of me, I felt like a competent loving parent who knew and understood his child.

Ignoring Inappropriate Behavior When Appropriate

While it may be far easier said then done, remember that behavior that is not recognized is not reinforced by attention. As already discussed, children frequently misbehave in order to get attention. It is far easier to encourage appropriate behavior when attention for misbehavior is avoided as much as possible. According to mountains of behavioral research with laboratory animals, children, and adults, behavior that is not reinforced tends to subside or be extinguished.

This skill can be used to handle minor problems that are not destructive or dangerous, such as whining, sulking, mild crying, temper tantrums, attempts to interrupt, insults, etc. Of course, these problems often feel major because they challenge the authority and self-concept of loving, good natured parents. However, it should be noted that consistent, planned ignoring of a child's whining, for example, will usually result in decreased whining. At first there may be an increase in the rate, duration, and intensity of the undesirable behavior because the child is trying to get the parent to respond in the old familiar way. It helps to be prepared for this temporary increase that often precedes the gradual decrease.

Rick and Judy came to me overwhelmed with their son's whining and crying whenever it was time to go out and he was having a good time. Keith, who had limited speech at four years of age, would lie on the floor and refuse to cooperate. When I asked if the same problem occurred at school, Rick and Judy told me that their son's teacher handled him very well. I suggested that they ask the teacher what she did. They subsequently learned that Keith's teacher just expected him to cooperate and get ready to go out or move on to the next planned activity. He protested at times, but never as intensely as at home.

It was hard for Rick and Judy to ignore their child's whining and crying. They felt guilty and sad when he didn't want to stop what he was doing, yet giving in to this behavior was reinforcing it and giving Keith an unhealthy amount of power in the family. I suggested that they observe their son at school and see if he was unhappy when expected and required to cooperate. Both parents noted that when their son's whining was ignored, he quickly complied with his teacher's request and returned to a positive mood. By exploring their feelings and seeing this strategy in action, Rick and Judy were able to implement a plan that changed their son's behavior.

Structuring the Environment

Young children need to explore in order to learn. The downside is the constant concern about what harm or damage can be caused by an inquisitive toddler getting into something. In order to help them to have as much of this vital experience as possible, it is up to parents to structure the environment so that children can grow and be safe. This strategy often goes by other names such as childproofing or babyproofing. By limiting the need to say no, a more positive atmosphere is created in the home. Parents have less need to invoke their authority, and children can play happily.

As soon as babies can move around on their own, it is time to childproof the environment. It is important to have plenty of things that the child can handle freely, safely, and without distressing the parents. In the kitchen, for example, the lower cabinets can be fitted with childproof latches commonly available. One cabinet can be left open and full of safe, nonbreakable items like plastic containers and bowls so that the toddler or child can have fun while hanging out waiting for dinner.

Children with special needs require this kind of structure longer than their peers, and sometimes indefinitely. This can be painful to accept for parents as they watch other children moving on and requiring less childproofing, which in turn makes parents feel more free in their homes. This is another image violated, when you realize that you have to make childproofing an ongoing part of life.

Setting predictable schedules and routines is another part of structuring a child's environment. Dressing may come before breakfast, for example, and baths before bedtime. Children feel secure and their behavior is more consistent when they know what to expect. Tantrums that occur when a child does not want to switch activities can be minimized when the child understands that bath time comes before bed, for instance, and therefore it is time to stop playing and put the toys away.

Giving Choices

Giving children choices helps them learn to be responsible for their own behavior. This strategy also helps children to learn how to cooperate with adults as well as with siblings and with other peers. Simple choices allow a child to have an element of independence and control. When children can control aspects of their lives appropriate for their level of development, they are more likely to cooperate when they are not allowed to do something. Parents, on the other hand, have control over what choices are given and can thereby enforce the limits they want to set.

A skillful parent will learn how to structure choices that are appealing to the child and simultaneously acceptable to the parent. For example, if a child wants to take several toys in the car for a short trip to the mall, the parent may say, "Pick two of them; that will be enough." Similarly, to make dressing in the morning go more smoothly, a child can be given two choices of outfits the night before. Even children with very limited language may have strong preferences. Another time that this strategy might be useful is at snack time, when a child might be given healthy, desirable choices.

Natural and Logical Consequences

Giving consequences that are natural and logical are a way to correct a child's undesirable behavior. *Natural consequences* come from the laws of nature. For example, a child who refuses to eat a meal will get hungry, and this will usually occur before the next scheduled meal if the child is not allowed to eat until then. *Logical consequences* result from going against the rules of social cooperation. In the instance where Rachel won't share her toys with Melissa, Melissa might not want to play anymore or might refuse to share her toys with Rachel at a later date.

Natural consequences do not require any intervention by adults. The child who refuses to eat will automatically get hungry and ask for food. Learning will occur when the child is told to wait. When danger is involved, parents must intervene decisively. We wouldn't let a three year old run into the street to learn about how badly a car could injure him. Parents in this kind of situation need to set up a natural consequence. It could go like this:

"The street is not for playing—you could get hurt by a car. You can choose to play in the yard or inside. If you go near the street, that means you've decided to come in. What do you want to do?

Then, if the child goes toward the street, the limits have been violated, and she has to come inside for a while. Choices can be given again later. A child who doesn't understand danger, obviously, cannot be given this choice. Sometimes parents want to believe that the child understands even when professionals have doubts, and this can be extremely dangerous. If there is any doubt or controversy over how much the child understands, then it is advisable to err on the side of safety.

Many situations don't have natural consequences, so logical consequences have to be set up by the adults in charge. Logical consequences fit the need of a particular situation and guide the child toward socially appropriate behavior. They are given in a firm, friendly way. Sometimes it's hard to figure out how to do this in the heat of the moment. Let's take the example of a three-year-old who is riding his tricycle too close to the street. Commonly, a parent might tell him that if he doesn't stay on the driveway and away from the street that he will have to go to bed early. Going to bed early and riding a tricycle have no connection. A logical consequence, on the other hand, would be that if the child does not stay in the driveway, the tricycle will be put away until another time.

Giving Breathers (Time-out)

Giving a child time to calm down is an extremely effective strategy for helping a child regain control of himself. It is best when used as a last resort when other methods of discipline do not work. Time-out is appropriate for disruptive behaviors such as tantrums that can't be ignored, constant interference such as interrupting, or aggressive behavior such as hitting or biting. Time-out can be offered as a choice or can be a logical consequence. A child can be offered the choice of calming down or taking some time out.

In my experience, I have noticed that this technique is the most frequently used and misused strategy for problem behaviors by adults who are overwhelmed and frustrated. Often it takes the place of yelling, screaming, or spanking, but this is not the purpose. Children will not learn how to behave differently if they are merely excluded in an angry exchange with a parent or care-giver. As much as possible, time-outs should be used calmly, firmly, and with empathy. Not only can the child learn that he has to control his behavior if he wants to be around others, but parents can simultaneously get a chance to cool off and control their negative emotions toward the child.

The breather should generally last until the child has calmed down. A rule of thumb is that the length of a time-out should be one minute for each year of age. The idea here is not to use this technique to reject and isolate the child but rather to teach self-control. Eventually the child may decide on when she is ready to come out. The parent may say, "You can come out when you are calm and ready to play." This approach will help the child develop internal controls. For parents who are unsure of how much their child understands, it would be wise to consult with the child's classroom teacher or another professional. The location for the time-out needs to be away from people. Simply put, the child needs a quiet space. When the time-out is over, don't discuss it—just go on with the activities of the day. Talking about the time-out calls attention to the behavior you are trying to stop.

WHILE guiding the behavior of a child with a disability is full of difficulties, there are also many windows of opportunity to explore and understand every facet of our child's development. Simultaneously, as parents we can look into ourselves, our expectations, and our sorrows as our children struggle to grow and meet their needs. In these everyday routine behavioral events, there are countless learning opportunities for children.

The everyday hassling, limit-setting, negotiating, and problem-solving are all attempts at finding the right kind of connection between parent and child. All of the ideas and techniques described in this chapter are ways of helping to tune into your child and guide his or her development despite the limitations imposed by disability.

Children go through stages; parents go through stages; and we are in stages together. While parents need to be in charge, and children need to follow, the reality is that we shape each other every step of the way. Basically, regardless of our limitations, children and parents all want the same thing—firm, loving parents who know how to handle problems.

SIX

A Circle of Fathers:
Big Boys Don't Cry

He had been talking freely about himself and his child and the demands of everyday life, and then he stopped and looked up at the ceiling. The ten other men in the room, seated in a circle with me as the leader, all waited patiently and curiously for Ted to continue. We had gathered to discuss the challenges for fathers of children with disabilities. Before long the waiting became uneasy, so I asked Ted if there was anything else he wanted to share.

Still looking at the ceiling, he answered hesitantly, "There's so much I want to say, but if I say anymore, I'll cry...and I don't think I'll be able to stop."

It then became obvious that Ted was looking up in order to keep the tears in his eyes from overflowing. As he slowly lowered his head and faced the other men, a tear rolled slowly down his left cheek. What had just occurred was an awkward but tender expression of male emotion. The man who was sitting on Ted's right reached over and put his arm around his comrade. This incident was the catalyst for the other men to open up, and many did so with tears in their eyes and deep feeling in their voices.

Ted had unconsciously been speaking for more than himself in his comments. His openness had released the other men from the taboo against expressing the depth of their feelings. Is it because we have held it in so long that men believe that if we cry the tears won't stop?

Reflections on Male Emotions

I awakened to the sounds of jazz from our clock radio on a Saturday morning—the day before Mother's Day. It was a work day for me; I was scheduled to lead a men's group at a weekend gathering of parents of children with multiple disabilities. I had led several sessions for this group of parents in past years, but never a men's group, so today would be different, a challenge of a special sort because the emotions of men are so routinely cloaked. (We men are often a mystery to ourselves and each other as well as to the women and children in our lives.)

As I showered and shaved, the apprehensions I had contemplated the day before returned. What would this be like? Would the group see me as a real man, a man among men, or as a "wimpy shrink type"? I laughed to myself, realizing thoughts like these had begun when I was five or six years old. All boys want desperately to fit in and are terrified of being called a sissy. Well, here was that fear again—that was what these particular apprehensions boiled down to—proof of how powerful those early and universal experiences and their memories really are. Even real men worry, I reminded myself—this wasn't an episode of *Father Knows Best.*

Would the competition among us as men keep us from accomplishing anything? Would male aggression hurt any of us? Despite these lingering questions, I felt ready for the challenge. This particular blend of confidence and uneasiness reminded me of the angst or the slight edge that I needed to do my best work.

I wished that I could be there with my family in our yard. The forecast was for a warm and sunny day. Kara would be pointing at the flowers and smelling them. I wondered if the sunflower seeds that I had planted with Antoinette had sprouted yet. I realized that these thoughts were another form of ambivalence about this particular day's work. I wanted to go, and yet I wanted to stay. Although I have often felt this way, the feelings today were intensified because I'd be doing no ordinary day's work. Men's groups require a special effort; getting men to open up isn't easy.

I reminded myself that I would be home for dinner and there would be plenty of daylight left to enjoy the flowers of spring in the company of my family. Finishing my orange juice, I put my notes in my briefcase and headed for the car. The morning air was fragrant from the many varieties of flowers and shrubs that were in bloom in our suburban neighborhood. I stopped for a cup of coffee to sip in the car along the eighty-mile ride west on the Pennsylvania Turnpike.

Before I started the car again, I took a few minutes to review my notes for the day's workshop and some of my recent journal entries. I reflected on some of the concepts expounded upon in *Finding Our*

Fathers by psychologist Sam Osherson. In particular, how fathers have such an enduring impact on the lives of their children and play such a key role in their sense of identity. How men deal with women, other men, and children can often be linked to unresolved matters that existed with their fathers. In the world of work, men are also influenced strongly by their fathers. Many men, as well as women, struggle alone, sometimes throughout their lives, with their fathers in order to arrive at some clue for a sense of completion in one of the central relationships of life.

"The Tracks of My Tears"

I got back into the car and continued my trip. Yellow and white wildflowers were in bloom along the side of the road. My car radio was tuned to a jazz station. I thought about the first time I had seen my father cry. It was also the first time I was flooded by my own emotions; when my brother Don died.

Although it is still difficult to recall it, I feel that the only way I can explain my journey through a lost dream from a male point of view is to include my brother's death and what I learned about my father, my grandfather, and myself from that experience.

I had just turned twenty-nine and had recently married for the first time; my brother was almost twenty-three. I was the oldest of my parents' eight children. Don was the fourth and was still living with my parents at the time. It was a cold, windy December night in 1977. I was careful to avoid the patches of ice on the road as I drove home from a party.

I went to sleep expecting to hear from Don early in the morning since he and I had spoken the previous afternoon and had planned to meet and go jogging. He had told me that he was not planning to go out that night. So when I woke up to the phone ringing early that Sunday morning, I expected it to be him. Instead it was my mother telling me the news—that my brother had been in a head-on crash with a pickup truck. Someone had skidded on the ice. The other driver was in critical condition. Don was gone.

"He was going to call me this morning," I kept repeating to her. He wasn't supposed to have gone out. She asked me to come as soon as I could. My head stopped spinning just long enough for me to tell her that I would be there right away.

As I dressed hurriedly, I kept thinking that it just could not be.

That phone call was supposed to be him. He was supposed to wake me up....I would see him when I got there. The frigid December air filled my lungs as I started my 1971 Volkswagen bug. The ride, which routinely took twenty minutes, went quickly. I needed more time with my thoughts, but there was none. The house where I had once lived loomed before me.

When I pulled into my parents' driveway, my father came out to meet me. He had been waiting by the window, something he had never done before. He ran across the frost-covered grass to me and hugged me, weeping profusely. I could feel his chest heaving next to mine and his whole body shaking.

This was the first time he had hugged me since I was a little boy, when he used to call me over to him when he got home from work. It was the first time I had ever seen him cry. I'd seen him mad and sad, and more often grumpy, but never in tears, and I didn't know how to take it. It was my first hint of confirmation that Don's death was real— I would never see my brother alive again. In that outpouring of male emotion there was the gravest of seriousness. I had, of course, grown up with the adage that big boys don't cry, but now I was released from that. If my daddy could cry, then so could I.

My memories of my mother that morning are not as clear, probably because I had seen her cry before and knew what her sobs sounded like. It didn't take a death to release her tears, and her normal mood usually returned in a relatively short time. This time, though, she was devastated. She would become physically sick with her grief for many months.

A little later my grandfather called, "Hello, Robert..." His voice broke down, and he just sobbed uncontrollably. The other man in my life who never cried was in tears as well. I wanted to console him, but I didn't know how. Later that day, when I saw him, he managed to hold it in, yet in his eyes I could detect a pain that I had never seen before in this kind man, the patriarch of my mother's family.

I was kept busy that morning calling relatives and friends of the family and asking them to pass the word along. I was upset; my voice shook, but I didn't cry. I felt that I had to be strong and help my parents get through that day. As the oldest, this was my station in life, and I wanted to do a good job.

In the afternoon I went home, got in the shower, and turned on the warm water...and then the tears came. My whole body shook as my tears mingled with the warm water and washed over me. I had not willed them to start, and I could not will them to stop. After what seemed like a long time, my body slowly stopped shaking. My mind, my heart, my whole being was inundated with grief. All of my muscles had been heavy, but now they were relaxed.

The days that followed blur in my memory, but my images of Don's funeral are crystal clear. I can still see the sadness and the tears and hear the sobs and consolations of my grandparents, my aunts and uncles, my cousins and friends, and Don's many friends. The church was filled with people in shock—there is something unusually compelling about the sudden death of a healthy young person with his life in front of him. Add to that Don's naturally pleasant disposition and engaging smile and the dimensions of the loss become more defined.

People kept asking me how my parents were doing. Nobody asked me how I was doing. I imagine my brothers and sisters had similar experiences. Actually, it was a question that I didn't know to ask myself—I didn't know how I was doing. My surviving brothers and I were the pallbearers, and my sisters were with my parents and grandparents. They were crying, and we brothers were "sucking it up" and acting brave.

The casket was heavy with our family's grief. When we put it down at the grave site, my sobs burst out despite my will to hold them in and to silence myself. I can still feel my insides shuddering when I call this scene to mind. My brother Rich put his arm around me in a firm yet gentle way, and gradually I regained my composure. I can still feel his arm there when Rich greets me at a family gathering.

As I reminisce now, that outpouring of feelings by my father, my grandfather, and my brothers was the beginning of the growth of my emotional life as a man—as a more full and complete person. I wish there had been an easier way, but this was the path my life took. Then Tariq, by his very existence, would challenge me to grow further.

This quest inspired by my son led me to explore the unfinished relationship with my own father. For all of us, our fathers are the most powerful and influential men in our lives.

On the way to the father's workshop, I was nervous about how anger and shame and love for our fathers would play out in the group. Would our competitive fires lead us to fight and inflict new wounds or reopen old ones as so often happens among men.

I had met many of these men before, and we held each other in mutual respect—especially since we all bore the common wound of having a child who wasn't "normal." I thought that most of us could connect without taking out our swords. We were knights in the same army—at least that's the way I looked at it, and that helped me to prepare myself. I hoped the walls would come down and no one would be hurt because the common needs were so important.

Sam Osherson presents this dilemma as a normal and natural, albeit unpleasant, tension between unrelated males as well as between father and son. We have both a desire to connect with our fathers and with each other and considerable opposing impulses to shun intimacy. This may help to explain why men tend to be more comfortable expressing their feelings indirectly through telling stories about their struggles rather than by stating straight out how they feel.

I remembered how excited I got when my father came home from work when I was a little boy; how little and insignificant I felt when he was mad at me, yet how warm and wonderful it was when he would put me on his knee and say "How's Daddy's little boy?" I remembered the many conflicts with my father over politics and lifestyle when I was in college and in my younger adult years. Over time we had reconciled many of our differences and learned to respect those that remained. Many men recount similar experiences with their fathers yet still find something missing. Maybe this is the "father hunger" described in such well-read books about men as Robert Bly's *Iron John* and Sam Keen's *Fire in the Belly*.

We men are supposed to be the "strong, silent" gender, and most if not all of our experiences with intense passions are alone, unspoken, unshared. What a relief it is, I have found from my own experiences, to tell your story and to feel empathy from other men. So often we just want to be heard and appreciated as friends. Now I hoped to skillfully guide the men in the group today to have an encounter with each other that would be as powerful for them as my experiences in men's groups had been for me.

That power for me is manifest in my ability to relate more quickly and deeply with men wherever I encounter them, whether in my personal life or in my professional circles. Perhaps this is a result of listening a little differently, revealing a little more, or perhaps it's asking one more question that makes my interactions richer and fuller. Instead of avoiding what makes me uncomfortable in my everyday personal relationships now, I have become more able to wrestle with my difficulties as husband, as son, as brother, as father, as friend.

Recently I had been counseling the parents of an adult child with mental retardation. When I met the young man's father, a successful businessman, I asked him what it meant to him to have a child who was named after him who was very limited. "You know; you've been through it," he responded. How often men make comments like this as a way of joining with another man while still avoiding sharing what is really going on for them. Opening up is not considered "manly."

This time I responded, "I know what it's been like for me. Can you tell me a little about what it's been like for you?" Well, that's all it took—that one more question—for him to open up about his disappointments and his worries about the future. What bothered him the most was that his son could never be fully independent, and that his other son and his daughter would feel burdened by looking after their sibling when their parents were no longer alive. These worries about the future are common for fathers in these situations and are reported regularly in the literature. Once he told me these things, I could help this father think for himself about the problem about which he was consulting with me.

I was easily lost in my thoughts as I continued my journey. I have been that way since I was a little child. I got off the turnpike and followed the directions to the hotel where the families were staying and the meetings would be held. I had planned to arrive early so that I could join the people already there for breakfast. This would help me get comfortable with people and give me the "feel" of the group. I try to do this whenever I can before leading a workshop or a group. Still, I felt a nervous anticipation and my routine shyness, even though today was special in that I could renew friendships and acquaintances that had been developing over several years.

Joining in With the Families

The sight of children with wheelchairs or walkers or canes enabled me to quickly locate where the families were having breakfast. Like my own son, these children were growing older and bigger, and their limitations were more and more obvious over the years. Some of the children had cerebral palsy and therefore little use of their arms or legs; some had faces disfigured by this condition. Some couldn't see or hear. Some were mentally normal, while others would be considered mentally retarded. All of them had parents and siblings who just looked like regular people.

The children ranged in age from toddlers to young adults. I felt my own sorrow creeping into my chest. What is it about seeing someone who seems to have a worse problem than you that makes you feel a little better? "There but for the grace of God go I," or "Don't complain, there's always somebody worse off." At least my son wasn't physically disabled or disfigured—how weird to take comfort from that! But that is how it feels—odd but human. It was okay to think this or even say this here because these parents have the same experience when they encounter people with more severe problems than themselves. How odd, but how human—this was part of the spoken and unspoken bond that made us comfortable with each other.

The smells in the air led me to a sumptuous breakfast buffet: cereal, fruit, muffins, scrambled eggs, bacon, sausage, and juices. I filled my platter and found a space at a table with two families I knew. I am fundamentally shy, so I was relieved not to have to meet anyone new just yet. We greeted each other, and I just tried to blend in with the conversation. It felt more like home here—I was a fellow traveler, not just a professional "expert." My table mates were comfortable enough with me to call me Bob, yet at the same time my expertise was respected.

George and Isaac were talking about advocacy issues for children with disabilities. Their wives, Sally and Mary, were helping their children to eat. We all exchanged hellos. They asked me about how my family had been since we had all come together to the last gathering. Isaac is an African American who has been active in civil rights. From this perspective he seemed very able to identify with his teenage daughter's need for equal access and quality services and was very committed to the struggle for her long-term needs. George owns a hardware store in his hometown and is also involved in an advocacy group.

All around the room, men were well represented. This is very rare in my experience—these groups are usually predominantly women and led by women. The fathers of children with disabilities are invisible more times than not, and uncovering that mystery was part of my mission this day. The fathers of children with more severe disabilities tend, in my observations, to be more actively involved.

The "New Man"

Men frequently react in extreme ways, and fathers of children with disabilities fit this pattern. They are either very involved, or withdrawn and virtually absent, with the larger number seemingly uninvolved. From this observation, many professionals assume that fathers do not wish to be involved. Is this really the case, or do men grieve their loss differently and hence react and involve themselves in different ways?

Until the 1970s, the role of the father in child development was largely ignored in the professional literature. While regarded as providers and protectors, fathers were not expected to be involved in day-to-day parenting activities, with the notable exception of discipline. Who, for example, doesn't remember hearing "Wait until your father gets home?" In emphasizing the undeniable importance of mothers, social scientists lost sight of the father and the larger family context in which children grow and develop. The word *parent* became synonymous with *mother.* This same trend applied to fathers of children with disabilities. Consequently, the literature about these fathers is extremely limited.

By the time fathers were "rediscovered," many men were frustrated with their traditional roles. They had found that the "duty" to be a successful breadwinner sometimes choked the natural instinct to nurture, and that they could, in fact, be tender and nurturing with their children and provide discipline too. And, as more and more women worked outside the home, fathers of necessity became more involved in the day-to-day care of their children.

Cross-cultural studies reported by anthropologist Wade Mackey show that when men spend time with children alone, they behave much like women in their physical interactions, particularly in nurturing. This is true regardless of the gender of the child.

Developmental psychologist Michael Lamb of the National Institute of Child Health and Development, a leading scholar on fathers, reviewed studies that showed some significant differences between mothers' and fathers' behaviors with their newborn infants. Mothers spend more time attending to the infants' basic needs while fathers tend to play more. Fathers are also observed to be more vigorous and rougher in their play than mothers. Both fathers and mothers adapt their play to the child's developmental level, which implies that fathers as well as mothers are sensitive to child development.

Lamb also found a consensus in the professional literature that mothers and fathers initially respond differently to a child with a disability. Fathers seem less emotional and focus more on long-term problems such as the financial burden. Mothers respond more openly with their emotions and are more concerned with the burdens of the daily care of the child. Fathers who are less involved in daily interaction with their children tend to have a more prolonged period of denial about the disability and its implications. The growing literature about men tells us that men express their feelings differently and use denial more to avoid the direct expression of feelings. I wondered how that would be manifested in the group I was about to meet with.

It has been presumed in the professional literature that fathers have higher expectations for their sons and therefore are more disappointed when those sons cannot live up to their dreams. It is a strong blow to the male ego when the father has no heir apparent to his throne. The mother, likewise, has been unable to give the king an heir, and both have been deprived of "a chip off the old block."

There is some strong scientific data that sheds light on these generalizations. S. Philip Morgan, a sociologist at the University of Pennsylvania, conducted a study of fifteen thousand families and concluded that a family constellation with a boy is the likeliest to keep the parents together. Having a son tends to draw the father into a more active parenting role, and having more than one son tends to cement the involvement. In the May 1993 issue of *Child* magazine, Dr. Morgan reported a startling statistic. He estimated that each son reduces the risk of divorce by 9 percent.

Warming Up: Getting the Group Started

I needed a few minutes alone, so I excused myself from the table to check out the room where the group was scheduled to meet. Most of the families were just finishing up their breakfast and taking their children to the child care that had been provided by the conference organizers. The meeting room was next door to the dining room, and just outside it was a large window onto the golf course and the rolling countryside of Lancaster County. Inside was a circle of twenty-five chairs as I had requested.

The men began to gradually filter into the room one by one. They stood in small groups near the door exchanging hellos, introducing each other, and talking about what a beautiful day it was. "We'll spend part of our time outside," I promised, having decided on the spot that this was the way to join with everyone, in keeping with my own style of leading a group. It was getting crowded near the door as more and more men came into the room, but no one made a move to sit down. I sensed an awkwardness that had come up at other meetings like this when men and women had to separate. The women had their own meeting down the hall. There was no companion to shield the entry; the men were on their own, but looking to me, I sensed, to help them get comfortable with each other.

Finally they had to come in because there was no more room by the door. To get things started, I sat down and then invited everyone else to take a seat. I sensed a collective sigh of relief—things would get started; the leader would take over. The men in the group ranged in age from their twenties to their fifties or perhaps sixties. The group was mostly white with a few African Americans, one Hispanic, and one Arab.

George introduced me as someone many people there had met before, as the father of a child with special needs, and as a psychologist who spoke at many parent and professional conferences. I described some of the problems facing men who are fathers of children with disabilities, noting that men were often poorly represented at meetings for parents of children with disabilities. Where were they? Usually they were at home watching the children so that the women could attend, but the women still felt overburdened and stressed out. The men, at home, thought they were helping out. What a bind for both men and women to be in.

As I looked around the circle of fathers I saw many knowing glances and nods of agreement. I wondered out loud what would be different this particular day about meeting without the women.

I commented that men tended to drift away from their friends after marriage. The trend is to socialize with other couples (as described by Stuart Miller in *Men and Friendship*). Women, on the other hand, show a strong tendency to maintain their circles of friends. Now, having a child with a severe disability, which tends to isolate us even more, makes it even more difficult to maintain and build connections with other men. What do you do when you can't brag about your child's accomplishments the way other men do? What do you even say when you're asked how your child is doing? How do you handle that choked-up feeling you get when you're searching for the right words? Maybe we could connect with each other today, I added, in a way that we hadn't done before.

As a way of warming up, I suggested that we go around the room and introduce ourselves, sharing something about ourselves as fathers as well as about our expectations for what we hoped to get out of the group. There was a brief silence before a gray-haired man to my right began. Ben's child was in her twenties, and he had been coming to these events for years. This was the first time that he knew of that the men had met together as a group. He always got a lot out of these meetings, and he was looking forward to hearing what others had to say.

The man to his left, appearing to be about the same age, introduced himself. Jim's son was twenty-nine, and he and his wife had been dealing with disability for quite a while. They were very involved at home together, but his wife wanted him to be more involved in the meetings and conferences she attended. He wanted to support her better.

Next came Harry, a salesman who traveled extensively for his work. His special-needs child was six, and whenever he was home his wife seemed overwhelmed by the sheer amount of care required. He wanted to help her more and felt bad that he spent many nights away from home, but he, too, seemed overwhelmed and perhaps unsupported, although he was silent about those issues.

Steve, an African American, talked about how isolated he felt living in a rural area. He said that several times after these weekend gatherings, he had resolved to call Isaac, another African American at the meeting, and stay in touch. But he had never actually connected outside of the meetings. How often had many of us felt that way and not followed through, I wondered. Procrastination, particularly about cultivating relationships with others, is apparently part of the male mode of being.

Some of the men there were stepfathers. Jack was a house painter whose fiancée had a three-year-old son who had little sight and no hearing. He spoke simply and very intently, telling about how he was one of six children and how he wanted to be able to give his children more attention than his father had been able to give him. He was trying to learn all he could before getting married. He didn't know the best way to help his fiancée, but she had wanted him to be with her this weekend.

Getting Into the Real Stuff: Connecting Through Anger and Sorrow

Weren't all of these men displaying typically male responses to loss, talking about helping their partners and denying their own feelings? What are men expected to do in the face of loss? As Carol Staudacher, an expert in bereavement, points out in *Men and Grief*, keeping the lid on emotions, taking charge of practical details, supporting others, and taking on the loss as a challenge, or even a test of traditional masculinity, are all part of the script. Men are *not* expected to lose control over their emotions, to openly cry, to worry, or to express overwhelming sadness.

In an essay in *Uncommon Fathers*, Canadian political science professor Lloyd Robertson worries that his frustration and anger will overpower his love for his daughter, Katie, who was born with severe brain damage. He found himself more cheerful when he was actively involved with his wife in helping to meet Katie's needs and wants. Standing by and watching his child's struggle and his wife's pain was more heartbreaking for him than pitching in and helping with the work. This sort of involvement can break the irresistible pull of grief. Robertson finds a parallel in the enduring tale of "Beauty and the Beast," where the spell is broken when the hero loves another human being as much as he loves himself. In caring for one's special child, a father can learn about unconditional love.

Well here it was; right in this room. It was time for me as the group leader to intervene. Staying strong to support the wife was as far as we had gotten going halfway around the circle. Even though this was just a warmup, it was too rich an opportunity to miss, so I asked the group to begin to address what this situation meant to them as men as they continued to introduce themselves.

"I'm real mad about being here," said Chuck, a young man wearing a T-shirt from a long-distance race. "My daughter is just eighteen months old, and I want her to be normal; I resent that I have to be here this weekend, and I resent that my wife has to spend Mother's Day here." There was obvious emotion in his voice, and I could feel the atmosphere getting uncomfortable. What does it mean when men get angry? What is the appropriate response? I felt a little defensive that Chuck didn't want to be a part of this group, but I understood. I didn't want to be there either, and I wouldn't have been if my son was normal.

"It'll pass," said Ben. "I remember being angry, but you get over it.

It takes time. You'll get through it. My faith really helped me."

"You get a different perspective, and then you mellow out," added another middle-aged man.

"You just don't get it. I don't want it to pass. I don't want to be here. I'm just trying to hold on to some shred of normalcy in my life," said Chuck emphatically.

Jack rushed to Chuck's support. "You old guys just see things different." His remark provoked laughter, but the tension in the room seemed to grow.

"What do you mean 'old': We're just mature," remarked Mike, a man who hadn't spoken before. More laughter followed, this time seeming to unite the group, and Mike went on to tell about himself and his situation.

The next participant said, "Maybe Chuck is speaking for all of us when he talks about his anger. We've all felt that in some way." I had been feeling the group tension and through my knowledge and trust in group process knew that something would happen that could draw us back together. Perhaps this group was expecting me to do that job, and in some ways I certainly expected it of myself. Having a child who was thirteen at the time placed me in the middle of the group in terms of experience.

I needed to help the younger and the "more mature" to be useful to each other. How could I help them deal with their particularly male anger, which often implies rage and destruction. Men tend to use anger to mask other emotions that are much more difficult to express and admit to. How about the idea that your "defective" child was a personal failure? My worst nightmare would be to wake up and find that my son was two years old again and I had to go through all this another time. Surviving that again might be more than I could handle. As the leader, my job was to give voice and guidance to the deep passions that had surfaced in the group.

Tony introduced himself as another who had married into the situation of raising a child with a disability. His daughter's biological father had abandoned and rejected her and her mother. Tony got so attached that he adopted the child when he married. Tears were forming in his eyes. He talked about how bad he felt for his daughter and his wife and how hard it was for everybody. Then Tony began to sob, slowly at first, but then more intensely. The man to Tony's left put his arm around him. The rest of us waited, feeling our own wounds, I thought.

Suddenly Tony's nose began to bleed, the blood flowing freely. Did everyone stop breathing for a moment? Two more men rushed to help by taking Tony over by the door where he could stretch out on two chairs and lean his head back to stop the bleeding. The tears had stopped by now.

"Does he need a doctor?" someone asked. Tony said that he would be okay—that he wanted the group to go on; he didn't want to miss anything. I asked if he had nosebleeds often, and he responded that he had them whenever he got really upset. That let me know that it was okay to continue, but I remained on alert to get help if necessary. I returned to my seat and told the group Tony's wishes. From their reaction, I could tell it was okay for big boys to cry here. It was safe to continue the process that the group had temporarily suspended.

"Maybe Tony has expressed something for all of us with his tears and his blood, just like Chuck did with anger," I commented before asking the next man to introduce himself.

Harry, a gray-haired man with an adult child spoke next. "I knew what I was going to say before Tony spoke, but now all I want to say is that I'm at a loss for words. I just respect his feelings, and I'm one of the 'mature' guys," he said with a chuckle.

Fred was next: "My two-year-old son, our only child, sees and hears very little. It's been really hard. I'm used to a lot of excitement and action. I was in the airborne rangers, and my hobby is hang gliding. I did all the things I thought a real man would do, but nothing prepared me for this. Last week I went to a fathers' event at my daughter's school. There were five of us there. We were each off in a corner playing with our kid. Nobody really talked to each other like we are here. It's different here. I need more of this kind of head medicine."

Finally, it was George's turn; he would be the last to introduce himself. "I had two children already, a son and a daughter, when my youngest was born with some problems. He's three now. I have my own business, and I've been pretty successful, but nothing prepared me for this. I live in a rural area and to get my son what he needed I had to really fight and push for it. That little guy has really changed my life. I'm home a whole lot more now with my wife and my other children. I never really spent that much time at home before, although it was something I wanted to do. I really enjoy being home more. Sure, I wish my son didn't have these problems, but I'm a better person now, and I wouldn't want that any other way."

The introductions that I had planned fifteen or twenty minutes for had taken over an hour and a half. Tony's bleeding had stopped and he rejoined the circle. I had to modify my plan for the morning somewhat. Who says men have nothing to say? This group, as many others I've led, had certainly proved otherwise.

I wanted to keep my promise that we would spend some of this beautiful morning outside. I summarized what we had said and where we were headed. We would use the time outside to reminisce about our own fathers—some of the warm moments and some of the painful ones. There were several questions about my directions. In order to clarify, I shared some of my own experiences, including the first time I had seen my dad cry when my brother died. The point was to go into your heart—for the anger, the shame, the grief, and the love—and then to share it with a small group of men. The next portion of the group would present an opportunity to continue the more open expression of thoughts and feelings that had just begun.

I had the group count off, and then formed seven groups of three. Forty-five minutes were allotted to walk, talk, get acquainted, and do the assignment. Again there was some awkwardness and hesitancy getting started, but the warm sunshine helped us all to get moving. The men filtered out of the room in small groups onto the patio overlooking the golf course.

One group stayed on the patio, taking in the sunshine and the view. Another found a park bench near the first tee. Some walked down the "nature trail" that began behind the first tee and led away from the golf course. One group found a picnic table. Another group sat on a grass bank nearby. Wherever they were, they were talking intently.

From my observations, it was easy talking about themselves now, after the tears and the blood, but still hard talking about their fathers. When it was time to go back inside, the participants lingered—perhaps wishing to stay in their smaller more intimate groups. As we walked back in groups, small circles of fathers continued to talk with each other. It was wonderful to see men being this real and genuine. Something special had happened, and the group had bonded.

Winding Down and Looking Forward

No one wanted this experience to end, but when the group had reassembled in our meeting room, there were only forty-five minutes left until lunch. Hearing from each of the groups about what they had discussed and figuring out what we wanted to do in the future remained to be done. There didn't seem to be enough time—as is often the case when a group is going really well.

The task I had given to the small groups was more difficult for some than others. Some had fathers who were dead; others were not in touch with their fathers; and alcoholism had ruined some father-son relationships. Shame, anger, sadness, and loss were expressed by every man reporting from his small group. These were the small emotions that they had described occurring with their children. Some expressed relief to have talked about these things that they had kept bottled up for so long. One man said he found these more informal contacts with other men invaluable. Something similar had happened once before, by accident, in a hotel bar one evening during a previous weekend gathering of this parents' group. Wouldn't it be great if the group could communicate this way intentionally from here on?

Gradually, the participants got into it. Jim mentioned that his dad rarely expressed emotion of any kind. He related to my experience when he said he saw his father cry for the first time when his grandfather died. Jack, the painter, and Barry, a laborer, said their fathers showed only anger. Jack talked about how his father always seemed so critical of him. The tender moments were harder to verbalize. Jack talked about how his dad would always take him to a special display of Christmas lights every year and about the baseball glove he still used that his dad had given him for his birthday one year. Barry remembered being ashamed of his father's drinking and, sadly, couldn't recall a single moment that he cherished.

The tender moments were often described as fishing trips, playing catch in the backyard, learning to ride a bike while Dad cheered you on, sitting on Dad's lap on the tractor as he plowed the field—always one-to-one interactions between father and son. No one said that there were many tender moments. I was reminded of an interview with President Bill Clinton, who told the reporter that he made time each day when Chelsea got home from school. Clinton was determined not to grow old with the regret that he had not spent enough time with his child.

Disability had taught all of us how precious time is with our families. Work was now seen in a different perspective by many of us, while others were grappling with how to spend more time at home.

One man said that he couldn't talk like this to his wife because she expected him "to be strong." (In the course of the morning, several men had remarked that their wives wanted them to talk more.) I questioned how his wife would actually respond. Whether it was true or not, that his wife wouldn't be able to handle his passions, he certainly believed she couldn't. I suggested that expressing oursleves with the women in our lives might come more easily now that we had begun with each other. Perhaps if we had more continuing support from each other, our wives might then have more support from us. It could even be more like teamwork instead of each partner struggling alone, hoping for a breather from the other.

Each person must find his own way through the grief. For me, I couldn't imagine where I would be without having had Cindy to listen to me and to wipe away my tears so many nights. Clarissa Pinkola Estes, a Jungian analyst and storyteller, suggests that by "following the pain" a man can reach and discover his inner self. Certainly in relation to grief, sharing it with significant other people in your life is crucial. Sometimes sharing pain is the only way to lessen it.

Discussion turned to how to stay connected and how to get more of what had happened in the group. We talked of meeting again in six months and joining other groups in local areas. George invited everyone and their families to an annual summer barbecue at his house. The idea emerged to form local networks from the people present. Another idea was to have the more experienced men act as mentors to the younger men. I doubted that anyone in this group had read *Iron John*, but the idea of initiation, which is central to Bly and many others in the men's movement, was certainly alive here—more "mature" men helping younger men learn the ropes.

It was time for lunch, and since the door to the room had remained open after the break, women and children could be seen walking by on their way to the dining room. They were looking in and wondering, we heard later, what we were still talking about. Even though the meeting was over, no one left his seat. Indeed, it was hard to leave, so I stood up, formally ending the meeting. Others stood and gathered in small circles, and then, after several minutes, the fathers gradually left the room and headed to the dining room to rejoin their families.

The dining room was buzzing with conversation. The women wanted to know what had gone on in the men's group. They were amazed that we had run overtime. One woman told me that she and others were surprised that all the men had shown up. Looking around, seeing families enthusiastically talking about the morning, I was proud of the work the group had done. Being associated with these men made me feel good to be a man. While that day's work was done, there was still a lot left to accomplish in the struggle for intimacy and connection.

Continuing the Journey

With no time constraints, I took a more local route home through the farmlands. The next day was Mother's Day, so I stopped at a roadside stand to buy a flowering plant in a basket for my mother. She would enjoy the pink blooms on the impatiens. I remembered how she would read to me when I was a child and how she would nurse me when I was sick. She struggled to be a "good mother" for all of us. The women at the weekend gathering could not nurse their child back to "normalcy." My mother could not bring my brother back from his accident—sometimes love is not enough.

For the men I had encountered that morning perhaps the greatest frustration was that they could not fix anything and make it better for their wives or their children. In this respect, too, love is not enough. The pain makes you go places you never planned to go. Obviously the twenty or so men gathered for the morning group did not represent all fathers of children with disabilities. There are countless individual differences everywhere. The themes expressed by the group are, however, typical of those expressed by the many hundreds of fathers I have met as a group leader, researcher, and psychotherapist. I decided to write this chapter through the experience of this particular group in order to bring the ideas to life. I can't help but wonder what the future holds for the group of men that met that day.

The group demonstrated a very real and immediate need to connect. There were clumsy but very real attempts at intimacy. One example of this was the attempt to reassure the young father who was expressing an intense anger about the fact that his child was not "normal." It took time and some conflict to acknowledge that anger and let it be heard. Sam Osherson has demonstrated in his work how anger is part of the male style of connecting. Looking at this powerful emotion from this perspective enables us to embrace it instead of retreating from it. Perhaps we fathers of children with disabilities need the mobilizing effect of anger to pump us up, so that eventually we can face the shame and profound, long-lasting sadness that accompanies our problem.

Even though the fathers initially saw themselves primarily as support people for their wives and children, they were able to acknowledge their own needs once they were together with each other. I know of no other way to break through this wall of their own making that keeps fathers from working through and completing their own grief. One man "broke down" and really cried once there was permission to feel in the group, and there were tears in many others' eyes at various times.

The talk about their fathers and themselves as sons led to a longing for mentorship within the group. One man compared it to the sponsor concept in Alcoholics Anonymous. Invoking their experience as sons was important in bringing this out.

For professional people who are not sure what fathers in this situation need, it is good to get them together as a group and ask them. The ideas collected in *Getting Men Involved: Strategies for Early Childhood Programs* by James Levine can be a helpful guide. The fathers can tell you everything you want and need to know, but you have to question and listen skillfully because the male imperative to be strong in the face of tragedy can be tricky to overcome. In a males-only meeting, it is more likely that fathers can take off their armor and get to the real stuff inside.

It's obvious that men have a different tone of voice than women. What's not so obvious, but equally true, is that men have a different tone of grieving. Men's intimacy is different from women's, but not defective. Connecting with other fathers can have a powerful impact. This was demonstrated by our group of fathers who got acquainted with each other and became linked by common experience—the wound of disability in their offspring. We began as emotional strangers and departed as brothers.

SEVEN

Keeping the Boat Afloat:
The Couple's Journey

Family life can be a test of love and resilience, so taking good notes and understanding each other's needs and wants is vital to the success and survival of any marriage. After children arrive, there is a balancing act between caring for their needs and putting time and effort into the maintenance and growth of the marriage. This rite of passage in the development of family life is challenged still further by disability or chronic illness.

On the Sunday after my meeting with the fathers in Lancaster, Cindy and I packed a picnic lunch and took Antoinette and Kara along. After about an hour's ride, we arrived at Tariq's residential unit at the Devereux Foundation in West Chester, Pennsylvania. I got out of the car and went inside by myself to get Tariq. I had missed him, but was apprehensive about seeing him because he is never easy to manage, even for a few hours. I took a deep breath and released it slowly, preparing myself inside to remain calm and focused. Tariq was glad to see me and showed it by jumping up out of his chair, smiling, and immediately pulling me by the hand toward the door, eager to go outside. For an instant he looked so normal that I half expected him to say something to me, and then I remembered, for probably the millionth time, that this kid would never talk to me. For all the time that has elapsed, for all my knowledge and experience, here was yet another momentary coming to terms with the loss.

When I put Tariq in the backseat of the car, Kara was glad to see him. She kept saying, "Hi! Hi!" and waiting for a response that never came. Tariq looked away, out the window, while I engaged the child lock on the door beside him, so that he couldn't open it from the inside by himself. Although he is a teenager, Tariq's behavior is still more like that of a toddler, and danger always lurks nearby. Kara would not be two years old until August, but she was already aware in her own way that Tariq was part of our family and that he was different from other teens his age. She was amused by his mannerisms, which were much like her own. This was a two-edged sword. On one hand, Kara's awareness is a confirmation of her vitality to me and tremendously reassuring. At the same time, it is but another reminder, like the child lock, of Tariq's deficiency, which opens a pocket of sadness inside me.

I reflected on how Antoinette had tried so hard when she was little to talk to her brother and to play with him. Eventually she gave up trying to relate to him as a normal sibling because he seemed to ignore her. By the time she was five, she understood in her own way that he could not play and relate with her because of his disability. I recalled how saddened I was at the time because Antoinette's realization reinforced my own conclusion, which I didn't want to believe. I felt another twinge of sorrow now because I knew that Kara would learn the same thing. On the way to the park, Kara had imitated Tariq by putting her fingers in her mouth as he was doing. Fortunately, I thought, she wasn't smearing the saliva on the inside of the car window as Tariq often did.

We drove for about fifteen minutes past shopping centers and then into the countryside to Marsh Creek State Park, where late spring flowers and trees were in full bloom. The air was perfumed with the scent of honeysuckle. Sailboats and catamarans skimmed the surface of the water and circled the lake with their bright, multicolored sails reflecting onto the water. Canoers and rowboaters were careful to avoid the path of the more graceful but less agile sailboats. It was a perfect day, and I was eager to get out on the water and enjoy it with my family.

We decided to have lunch first, and so after parking the car, we walked up the hill to the picnic area. Tariq held my hand like a little boy, but the top of his head reached over my shoulder, now making it appear strange that he insisted on walking this way. We searched until we found a picnic table in the woods high above the bank of the creek overlooking the water. It was a peaceful view. We had brought food that Tariq liked, so we could enjoy a meal together without hassling over things that he wouldn't eat. We ate tuna sandwiches on whole-grain bread, corn chips, and fresh fruit, and enjoyed cold sodas with our meal. A pleasant breeze made for some enjoyable moments as we looked out at the sailboats.

Tariq finished first, probably because the meal for him did not involve talking and interacting with the rest of the family. He got up and started to walk away from the table. "Down! Down!" said Kara, her little voice punctuating Tariq's steps. Tariq turned, smiled, and returned temporarily to the table. Cindy commented on how that interchange was just like Kara's interactions with Harry, our family cat. Antoinette and I chuckled. Cindy's remark was both sad and funny, but as a family we held on to the humor of the situation because that is part of how we cope, and part of the way most families in this situation learn to cope. We knew we would have to leave the table soon, since Tariq had made his wishes known and would not be content to sit with us for long.

Since I am a faster eater, I finished and got up and took a walk with Tariq so that everyone else could finish eating with a minimum of pressure. Over the years we had developed ways like this to manage these situations. Kara's presence shed a different light on things; her fascination with Tariq helped us all, I thought. Her realization that she was already more advanced then he was gave me another dose of grief, while her affection for him warmed my insides; for whenever anyone found value in Tariq's existence I was comforted by a sense of value in my own self as his father.

After cleaning up, we walked down the hill back to the lake and the dock where boats are rented. We all fit around the picnic table for a family meal, but we could not all fit in one boat. Cindy got a rowboat for herself and Kara; I got a canoe for Tariq, Antoinette, and me, and we all put on our life jackets. Tariq resisted by twisting and squirming and making vocalizations that signaled his discomfort, but he eventually complied. Kara was proud of her life jacket and kept pointing to it, calling it her "boat coat."

Antoinette sat in the front of the canoe, eagerly anticipating helping to propel the boat. I sat in the rear and put Tariq down on the floor of the canoe between my knees. If he were "normal" he would have a paddle too, and I would be teaching him about steering, but he wasn't, so I would have my hands full just trying to keep him in the boat. I hadn't taken him out since last summer when he was several inches shorter and ten or fifteen pounds lighter. Now he was five feet tall and over a hundred pounds, so I felt some apprehension about the excursion. I had to keep the boat moving; the movement, as in the car, was soothing and peaceful to Tariq. If we stopped and just drifted, I knew from experience that he would try to stand up and get out. He put his hands in the water on each side of the boat and seemed to enjoy the sensation, humming to himself as we moved along.

A vision of the boat tipping over flashed through my mind. I wasn't sure how deep the water was, but with life jackets we were safe. There was no way, however, that I would be able to get Tariq back in the canoe after righting it. If he were a typical teen, it would be a father and son adventure to be recalled years later with a chuckle. Alas, it was not to be so, for we would need help, so I was staying within sight of other boats just in case. What would people think, I wondered. Tariq and I with a capsized boat would be a disabled duo, and what about Antoinette? She is an adequate swimmer and would manage, but she would be left out in a way because most of my energy would have to go toward dealing with Tariq. I was sure that people would help, but I didn't want their help because I wanted not to need it. And what about my wallet and some of the things in there that might be ruined? Talk about taking notes—I should have left it in the car.

As I recount this here, I can feel the tension in my chest and wonder how I came across to Cindy that day. I am grateful that I always feel understood by her even when my mind drifts off or I get grumpy or irritable or short tempered. Not that I make it easy either, for at those times I don't have it in me to give back to her because I want to get away inside myself. Not wanting to be alone, she pulls on me trying to bring me out of it. (My grumpiness may be an expression of my resistance to being in the situation with these thoughts about my son.) Eventually I surrender from my withdrawal and am glad to be back with Cindy and not alone with my darkest thoughts and feelings.

Out on the water, I steered the canoe toward Cindy and Kara, who was excited and pointing in our direction. We got close enough for Cindy and me to take pictures of each other and the children. Kara was having a great time, and she wanted to get out and take a walk on the water. Antoinette, Cindy, and I all chuckled, marveling in the sheer joy and immediacy of Kara's experience. Cindy wouldn't be able to keep her out on the lake much longer. It was getting hard to stay close together and stay out of the way of the sailboats, so we decided to split up for a while. I steered out across the lake, keeping Tariq balanced between my legs, while talking to Antoinette and trying to teach her a little about canoeing. We reached a tranquil little cove on the other side of the lake. The sailboats avoided that area since it was difficult to catch a breeze there, and people were fishing from their boats and from the rocks on the edge. Sometimes Tariq's babbling kept me from hearing myself think, and today it led me to flashback on all those sleepless nights when he was little. At other moments, I was impatient with Antoinette, and she seemed resentful that my attention was always divided and that she was always secondary to the task of keeping the boat balanced and Tariq in it. Who could blame her?

After a while it was time to return, so we headed out of the cove and pointed the canoe toward the flag that marked the dock. It was just a speck on the horizon that got bigger almost imperceptibly as we paddled along. Antoinette really liked this part, and she was feeling more at ease now. She was proud that she had been able to help paddle the boat so far out onto the lake. Tariq dangled his hands contentedly in the water and hummed to himself as we paddled and talked. I explained to Antoinette how we would chart a course through the circling sailboats that were tacking to and fro.

Thank God, I thought, for this moment when everything in the boat was in balance. As we got closer, I could see a woman in a red dress. That was Cindy, I thought; then I could see Kara in her arms; they were waving to us as we approached. I felt excitement in my chest for my beloved and for my baby. It was good to be back—to be reunited in a few minutes. As we approached the shore, I told Antoinette to take her paddle out of the water and to watch how I guided the canoe gently toward the spot on the shore where one of the attendants was awaiting us. The current carried us while I steered and squeezed my knees a little tighter around Tariq. As the bow touched the shore with a light thud, I took another deep breath and reached for Tariq before he could jump out and run away. Having anticipated his movement, all went smoothly.

The canoe hadn't tipped over (not that it wouldn't another time), and all in all it had been a peaceful day on the lake. I reveled in the moment. It was a day made possible, I thought, by the relationship Cindy and I had cultivated and developed over eight years. It hadn't been easy for Cindy to take on the role of stepmother in this situation. With Kara we no longer fit all in one boat as we once had. But we had learned how to steer, how to keep things balanced, and how to chart our course among the other boats. Through trial and error and frustrating experiences, we had developed the skills that began with keeping everyone safely in the boat.

We were all pleasantly tired from the exercise as we rode back to

Tariq's school and dropped him off. He seemed glad to be back and didn't particularly notice me when I left him with his counselor. This bittersweet moment did make the separation easier because on those occasions when he notices my departure, he cries and clings to me like a preschool child, which makes it hard to leave him. As we drove away, we talked about our pleasant outing, assuming it was so for Tariq also, but there was a lingering question that his enduring silence left imprinted on our experience.

A Biological Backfire

A successful marital relationship is based largely upon a basic faith in the relationship, or union, held by both parties. This kind of faith is often what makes it possible to work out problems or get through the tough spots. When a child is born "imperfect" or when a disability or chronic illness is discovered, the resulting evocation of powerful emotions puts the relationship on trial. As Josh Greenfield put it in *A Child Called Noah*, the "defect" can be a demoralizing symbol of a deep and profound biological failure to produce a healthy child. Even when two people share the same sorrow, their individual pain and unhappiness may drive them apart. How can we understand each other in the wake of such devastating pain?

The intense inadequacy, the self-doubt, and the loss of control that are such an integral part of the experience produce powerful reactions. Psychiatrist Donald Nathanson's concept of the Compass of Shame, described in his book *Shame and Pride*, is manifested as people frequently withdraw, avoid, attack their spouse, or attack themselves. The only way out requires working through the painful feelings with one's partner and arriving at some form of joint acceptance. As marriage expert Harville Hendrix puts it, marriage is therapy. And, as therapy, it often involves redefining one's values and relationship with the other.

In *Ordinary Families, Special Children*, Milton Seligman and Rosalyn Benjamin Darling conclude from their review of the literature that there is sparse and contradictory information regarding marital problems and divorce in families of children with disabilities. For a relationship that is fragile or unstable, disability can be "the straw that breaks the camel's back." On the other hand, couples with strong cohesive marriages may become closer and more loving, and those in relationships that haven't yet been tried by adversity may develop increased closeness and strength.

A recent (1993) television movie, *Born Too Soon*, based on a true story, showed how one couple survived by learning to understand each other. I include a summary here since the issues that they faced are, at least in my personal and professional experience, typical for most couples in similar situations. In the film, Liz and Fox are a professional couple, both journalists. When pregnant Liz's water breaks months early, she is terrified and blames herself for working too hard. Fox joins her at the hospital, pledging that they will go through the experience together. Their baby, Emily, is born weighing less than two pounds and her life begins in the neonatal intensive care unit.

At first, Fox is right there with Liz struggling to keep hope alive, but before long a rift develops when a doctor advises them not to get "too attached" because that will make losing Emily even harder. But Liz continues the natural process of bonding to her baby and becomes absorbed in her minute-to-minute care. Fox, on the other hand, begins to withdraw, by resisting having his picture taken with Liz and the baby in the hospital and returning to work.

After Liz is discharged, she spends all of her time at the hospital with her baby. As the emotional split between her and Fox widens, she finds support from some of the other mothers whose babies are in the hospital. When Liz tries to confide in Fox because she is always emotionally drained, Fox advises her to think of something else, even to do some work—a typical male response. His attitude leaves Liz alone and desperately overwhelmed with her feelings.

The couple argues over her involvement and his withdrawal. He gets mad at her for not taking care of the house, and she is furious at him for listening to the doctor about not getting too attached. Because she can't feed Emily or hold her, all Liz can do for her daughter is to be by her side in the hospital every day. Liz is in anguish because she feels that Fox wants to take away that tiny vestige of motherhood by asking her to deal with this crisis his way.

Fox, like many men, uses his anger to connect and tell of his pain. He admits to Liz only in the heat of an argument that he wanted a healthy baby and that he can't just sit there and watch their baby die. Liz is understandably too angry to accept this explanation for his abandonment of her and Emily. Through the arguing with his wife, Fox is eventually able to admit his real feelings. He has a change of heart and begins to take care of things around the house and to visit

Emily more often. Only then can the couple begin to understand and help each other through their grief.

When Emily needs another surgery, Fox and Liz wait through it together, but the baby does not survive. Fox and Liz are able to have a healthy baby a few years later. They had learned to understand each other, and fortunately for them, their biology had cooperated.

Do You Read Me?
Todd and Beth's Dilemma

Even a child's mild learning differences or disabilities can confuse and divide a couple. In general, more severe disabilities are diagnosed earlier, at birth in the hospital or a little later when something is obviously wrong and professional help is sought early, and couples get the news together. A child with a mild disability, such as an attention deficit disorder or a learning disability, provides a different sort of challenge. One parent may notice problems and tends to worry, while the other parent tends to be a container for the hope that everything will work out. The overall balance may work in the sense that the family keeps functioning, but it is very uncomfortable for both partners, each locked into his or her role.

A couple recently consulted me for help with their problems dealing with their son's reading difficulties. The woman, Beth, came in first by herself—as is often the case in my practice. Her son, Phillip, was now seven and over two years behind in reading. He was regressing emotionally, whining and clinging to his mother. Beth had recognized that there was a problem long before it was pinpointed in the reading process, but she wasn't sure what it was and doubted herself. She had talked to her husband, Todd, about it quite a bit, and he always said that things would work out even though he himself was also concerned when Phillip stopped enjoying school and began crying, wanting to stay home in the mornings. Beth felt increasingly desperate and worried about her son.

At his teacher's suggestion, Phillip had been evaluated by a reading specialist. Specific reading weaknesses were found, including difficulties in short vowel sounds and in connecting sounds with symbols. Remedial activities were suggested and some improvement had occurred, but Phillip hated going to the reading tutor. He had recently refused to go into the tutor's house when his father took him for his lesson. He had thrown himself on the ground and had a tantrum. Todd had picked Phillip up and carried him in, but little was accomplished since he was so upset. When the lesson was over and they went home, Todd punished Phillip because he didn't know what else to do.

At the time of the initial consultation, Beth felt that there was a stalemate. How could they force Phillip to read, an activity that he found extremely difficult? I listened to this mother's anguish. She and Todd were in their late thirties, and Phillip was their older child; they also had a daughter who was still in nursery school. Phillip was very bright and got excellent grades in everything but reading and writing (which depends so directly on reading). In tears, Beth told me of her worries that her son would be unhappy, would not succeed, and would never feel good about himself again.

Because Phillip had become very emotional, his teacher wondered if there was a problem at home that was affecting his school performance. Beth felt that she was being blamed by this suggestion. Todd had trouble understanding how upset Beth was, but he knew that his son's learning difficulties weren't her fault. They had both agreed on disciplining Phillip for his behavior at the tutor's. Nonetheless, they were very uncomfortable with what to do. Beth said that they both felt terrible about punishing their child when they knew learning to read was so difficult for him. All of the relationships in the family were strained. They hadn't had any fun together in months.

Beth said that she and her husband were willing to try whatever I suggested. The tension in this family had to decrease, so I recommended a moratorium on tutoring for the rest of the summer. Beth and Todd could take Phillip to the library, if he wanted to go, and then Phillip could pick a book on a topic that interested him. If he wanted to, he could just look at the pictures. In addition, I suggested that they just have some "family fun" over the weekend by doing something that they always enjoyed together. I insisted on meeting them all together the following week.

Phillip was extremely shy when I met him; on the way to my office from the waiting room he buried his head in his mother's side as a younger child would do. He sat on Todd's lap and snuggled up with his dad. While giving him time to "warm up," I talked with Todd and Beth, getting to know them a little better as a couple. What Beth had told me about her husband seemed accurate. He had been concerned for some time, and his son's unhappiness had now motivated him to accept help. He felt bad that he couldn't help Beth enough with this problem.

Gradually I worked their son into the conversation:

"How do you think Phillip is feeling about his difficulties in reading?" I asked them.

"He can tell you that himself," replied Beth.

"I feel stupid, and I hate myself, and I hate when they make me read," explained Phillip. He said all his friends were reading at a higher level, and he had to stay at the same level. I could see a glazed, worried look in Beth's and Todd's eyes. I gave Phillip some crayons and paper and asked him to draw a picture of his family doing something together. I showed him to a seat at my desk while I continued to talk with his mom and dad.

"Your son expresses himself so clearly," I said. Hearing a child express such painful feeling can be extremely difficult, and this is a common dilemma for couples like Beth and Todd who have articulate children struggling with a learning difficulty.

"Beth has a great bond with him, and I rely on her to let me know what is really going on," commented Todd, "but lately everybody's been upset, and it hasn't been working. I'm not sure why."

I asked Todd to tell me about his frustrations and asked Beth to just listen for a while. Todd was reluctant at first, but as he warmed up he spoke slowly and clearly, with obvious emotion, of his feelings of failure that he couldn't help his son with his reading and his growing isolation from Beth. The lines of worry softened in Beth's face as he explained himself.

"What would it be like if Todd talked this way at home?" I wondered out loud.

"I wouldn't know how to act!" remarked Beth emphatically. "I'm usually out in a boat with my emotions, and Todd is always there on the shore to reel me in. I don't know what we would do if he was out there with me."

"Maybe you could learn to row together," I remarked. "And temporarily I'll be there to reel the two of you in, if you need me, until you can do it yourselves." They were skeptical. They had been together ten years and were not sure they could change, but they agreed to try. I asked Phillip to bring his drawing over. He displayed a colorful and carefully conceived drawing of his family at the playground. They were all on the swings, and he was in the middle. I suggested that Todd and Beth give everyone their wish and have some fun together as a family over the weekend. I asked Todd and Beth to come to the next session without Phillip.

When I met them the following week, Todd and Beth were much more at ease. They had gone camping for the weekend, a favorite family activity that they hadn't done while they were "stressed out" over the reading problems. I asked them about their dreams and fantasies for their son's future. Beth spoke about giving Phillip every opportunity and being a good mother and making sure her son was genuinely happy. That seemed to be going out the window now. What would become of the son of a professional couple who couldn't read adequately for his age? Todd had imagined their son becoming a successful professional. Now he wondered if Phillip would even be able to go to college. Beth and Todd had not previously discussed any of this together.

I told them that a big part of dealing with a child's special needs is learning to separate the problem into manageable pieces rather than carrying around a heavy weight of worry and fear. I suggested a battery of tests by a colleague of mine who was a school psychologist and could make recommendations for Phillip's practical educational needs. At first they were reluctant to agree, for fear their son would be labeled negatively, but they eventually acceded because they didn't want to go on living as they had been.

While the diagnostic process was going on, I continued to meet weekly with Beth and Todd, coaching them on how to express themselves and listen to each other, a form of rowing the boat together. I coached them on going back to having fun with Phillip and following his natural sense of wonder about the world. One week Beth told me about Phillip's curiosity about bees. I suggested following up with anything related, including books with lots of pictures so that he could learn something without the pressure to decode the words.

In my sessions with Phillip, I observed how difficult it was for him to decode words and how he shut down entirely when he got frustrated. As Phillip felt less tension within himself and within his family, he was able to apply himself more. His teachers began to notice progress at school.

Fortunately, Phillip's test results were very reassuring. Intellectually he showed a pattern of average-to-superior abilities overall. While he needed special attention in reading, there were no indicators of emotional disturbance as the cause. Beth was overjoyed that she was not to blame, and she and Todd were proud of their son's essential brightness. The prognosis was that Phillip could make substantial progress with remedial help, provided he could continue to express his feelings and ask for help when he needed it. The roof had not caved in on this couple's dreams for their child even though there were uncertainties about how far and how fast he could progress. They could live with that once they had learned to share the burden.

Couples Groups

Groups have the power to teach in a special way. I learned one of these special lessons while I was working for the New Jersey State Department of Education as a regional trainer for an agency that serves children with both physical and mental disabilities. For many years my image of this rural area had been that it was a tranquil place where life was simple and close to perfect. That anyone's life there could be disrupted by a disability in the family didn't fit my fantasies. It was the week before Mother's Day, and I had been asked to give an after-dinner talk to a group of mothers. The twenty-five or so women I met that day expressed fantasies very different from mine about their relationships and their lives.

After dinner, while awaiting dessert and coffee, I talked about some of my experiences with my son and led a discussion about the journey from grief to coping with the day-to-day life of raising a child with a disability. To an outsider, such a topic for an after-dinner talk might seem grim, but for this group it was a lively and animated discussion full of humor and hope. What emerged as the main need was the women's desire to be better understood by the men with whom they shared their lives. Many were extremely frustrated because they felt alone with the emotional burden of their special children. They thought that their husbands were tired of hearing from them and might respond better to me as another man. They joked about feeling that they were nagging when they kept trying to get their point across. The social worker, who was present, was asked to set up a fathers-only meeting that I would address during the week preceding Father's Day.

On the evening before the men's meeting, I arrived early and mingled with the first few men, getting a feel for what they were expecting. All of them had been told that they really needed to hear what I had to say—that it would be new and different and that they hadn't heard it before. Was I a messenger for the women, I wondered? This felt strange—like I was being set up for something that I didn't quite understand.

When the meeting began, after dinner in a restaurant, I talked briefly about my own experiences and then led a discussion about the grief that parents in this situation go through. Before the discussion got too far, one man asked, "So what's new about this? Is this what you talked to our wives about?" I responded that it was.

"Well, this isn't new to us," another father replied. There were nods and agreement around the room. I was taken off guard, but now I knew the nature of the set up. I would handle this right now.

"Why do the women think this is new to you?" I asked.

There was silence, so I waited.

"Well maybe we don't talk about it," responded another man.

"Can women understand what men don't say?" I asked.

"You've got a point there," a father named Tony replied, "but there's nothing I can do about the situation, so I gave up talking about it a long time ago."

Now the participants began to discuss their frustrations as men and as fathers and the strain that their children's disability placed on their marriages. Several men openly admitted that their wives were dissatisfied with how they were handling their problems and admitted that they worried privately about whether their marriages would survive. The romance was long gone for many of them, and none could bring it back. Most of them had never really talked like this before to other men. They commented on how they were more open without any women present. At the end it was suggested that a meeting be held in the fall with the men and women together.

Now I had the confidence of both groups, and the stage was set. The women felt frustrated, alone, overburdened, and misunderstood. The men, on the other hand, felt nagged, frustrated, powerless, and also misunderstood. Here was a challenge! On the feeling level for me, it was like being a kid again—torn between my parents and wanting them to get along better. Then I was powerless, but now I was a mature and seasoned professional with the confidence that I could make a difference.

Bringing the Men and Women Together

According to a Native American proverb, you can only begin to understand a person after you walk a mile in his moccasins. For this reason, during the fall couples' meeting I decided to use role-reversal exercises to help the men and women understand each other. Role reversal would diffuse the tension between the spouses and the groups by allowing each person to experience the problems of the opposite sex.

On the way to the meeting, I recalled the healing power that I always felt while sitting on the beach watching and listening to the waves. I visualized the many times I had been there with Tariq, hoping that the waves would heal him somehow. He did seem more peaceful there, I had thought, and I felt more at ease with him. He was with me in spirit as I pictured him playing in the waves and laughed when he ventured out too far and got knocked down.

I imagined that I might be dodging some bullets tonight because I knew the pain of couples not understanding each other. I knew the death of romance in a relationship, and I knew the long-lasting pain that accompanies divorce. All of these deep emotions were present in this group, so I had to be objective to be effective. Arriving early, I met briefly with the social worker who knew the parents. She was there to facilitate a discussion for the women while I would do the same for the men. Each group would be asked to select a recorder and a spokesperson.

Close to fifty people were in the room, most of whom had come with their spouses. There were some stepparents in remarried family situations and some single parents. I could feel the tension and anticipation. My introduction consisted of reporting on the separate meetings of men and women that had occurred in the spring, and then I asked everyone to form a big circle to play an adaptation of the commercially available game *Gender Bender*, which utilizes role reversal.

First the women were asked to answer a series of questions on paper as if they were men. The men answered as themselves, and we compared the results. Here are some examples:

1. You are in the bathroom that has run out of paper towels. How do you dry your hands?
    a. on your pants
    b. shake them dry
    c. on the curtain

2. Which characteristic shows a woman has a lot of passion?
    a. red hair

   b. a fiery temper
   c. a wiggle when she walks

3. Do you think the women's liberation movement is
   a. completely justified
   b. partly justified
   c. an attack on men

There was laughter and relief of tension while the group wrote down their answers, which were collected and tabulated quickly. The number-one answer for the first question by the women answering as men was drying your hands on your pants. The men had the same answer. Number two was evenly divided between *b* and *c*; the men answered similarly. Number three was tougher because it was more serious. The women as a group correctly predicted that the men would say that they women's movement was partially justified; three even said that the men felt it was an attack on them. The women were surprised that three men felt the women's movement was completely justified. There was more laughter and relief around the room. Men and women were discussing heavy topics without hurting each other.

Now it was time for the men to answer some questions as if they were women. The women answered as themselves this time. The questions included these examples:

1. You found a *Playboy* under your son's bed; you
   a. leave it
   b. talk to him about it
   c. tell your husband to handle it

2. A man who doesn't talk much has
   a. inner strength
   b. good listening skills
   c. nothing to say

3. The thing men understand least about women
   a. fears
   b. strengths
   c. needs

For the first question, a third of the men said they would talk to their sons if they were women, and two thirds said that they would tell the husband to handle it. The women were evenly divided between those answers. Clearly the modern women present were indicating that they are different from our mothers' generation, and the men certainly had at least a clue as to the women's thinking on the subject.

For the second question, the men's answers were almost evenly divided among inner strength, good listening skills, and nothing to say. The idea of the strong silent type still had a lot of influence. On the other hand, the majority of the women's answers indicated that the man who didn't talk much had nothing to say. Only a few thought that such a man was a good listener.

The thing that men understand least about women was evenly divided between fears and needs, according to the men. The women answered that their needs are the least understood. By the end of the game, the group was warmed up and actively involved. It was clear that men and women spend a good deal of time trying to figure out each other. The last question was crucial, because understanding each other's needs is central to expressing real compassion for each other. It was time to continue the role reversal—but now about the very real situation of having a child with a disability in the family. Men and women were instructed to form two separate groups. The women were asked to discuss why it was hard to be a man with a special needs child and what women needed from men. The men were told to discuss why it was hard to be a woman with a special needs child and, what men needed from women. Each group was to pick a spokesperson and a recorder. One gender had to leave and go to another room. The women asked the men to leave. The stage was set for the real dialogue of the evening.

Stumbling Forward—Male Style

Sitting around in a circle spilling your guts isn't exactly a typical male activity, so it was no surprise that this meeting started out awkwardly and went differently from the predominantly female meetings that are typical of parent groups. When I went down the hall to the room assigned for the men's meeting, one man was already there and another followed me in. After a few minutes, no one else had arrived, so I ventured back out into the hall.

The rest of the men were standing around the coffee pot, fixing their coffee and munching on cookies. There was an awkwardness here—little conversation and many eyes directly and indirectly checking me out. It reminded me of how I felt as a child on my first day in a new school out on the playground, not knowing anyone yet and wanting to feel a part of things. I could lead by asking everyone to come down the hall to the assigned room, but instead I led by joining in, standing around, and getting a cup of coffee myself. "The women can see us standing around here from where they're sitting. They probably think we're not doing anything," remarked one of the men.

"So what are we going to do?" I asked.

"We need to get started," said Willie, the oldest man in the group. He was in his sixties and was a grandfather. He explained that he and his wife had come tonight to support their daughter, who was the single parent of a child with cerebral palsy. They had also raised a child of their own with a physical disability. Instantly he had the group's respect and admiration. Sensing this, I asked Willie if he was willing to speak for us.

"I've never done anything like this before, but I'll try. I've been a truck driver all my life. One of my daughters has a doctorate; she's the director of a state school for children with disabilities." Willie started asking each man what he thought about why it was hard to be a woman with a child with special needs. As the men stood around and sipped on coffee, the ideas flowed about what they thought the women would say they needed:

1. Women have it harder because they need more practical help in the everyday things. It's just too much to handle. A nanny would be ideal, but a teenager to help out for a few hours a day with child care or household chores would be great.

2. Women need more understanding and compassion from their husbands as shown by communicating more and listening to how they feel.

3. Women want to talk about other things too—not just the child with the disability.

4. Women need more physical help when the man is home; they're worn out from the everyday grind.

5. Women want men to play with the special child more and get to know more about him or her.

6. Women need men to take the children out and give them some free time for themselves.

7. Women want men to assume more responsibility around the house.
8. Men should pay more attention to how the woman is feeling and what she might need or want each day.

Now it was time to talk about what the men wanted from the women in their lives. This was much harder to get started. I asked how women could be expected to understand what men don't say. Again, in his own simple style, Willie started asking each man what he wanted. Once again we were able to develop a list:

1. We want the women to understand that we are trying to help in the way we know how and that we're frustrated when we can't make things better.
2. We need more time as a couple again, to be together without the children.
3. We want women to be more rational and less emotional, so that we can discuss problems and find solutions.
4. Let us as men take more responsibility with the special needs child. Sometimes it seems that the women can't let go of doing all the work and being overwhelmed all the time. Let's get more organized and distribute the work.
5. We need more strength and stability in our marriage. It would help if you told us what we were doing right so that we could feel more secure in the relationship.

The women had been done for some time when the men's group finished and had been sitting around in their circle chatting informally. Maybe the men took longer because they weren't used to conversations about relationships. It's easy to talk about work and sports, but this stuff gets hard. The women were eager to know what the men had been talking about, especially since it appeared that the group had just been standing around drinking coffee.

The men reported first. When Willie was about halfway through reading the list of why it is hard to be a woman and what women need, he was interrupted: "This is too good to be true. The doctor (pointing to me) must have been coaching you guys," remarked one of the women. The whole group howled with laughter.

Willie spoke with the wisdom of a grandfather, "He just got us started; we came up with this stuff ourselves." The women were satisfied for the moment, and Willie continued reading.

"This is incredible," remarked Mary, a red-haired woman of thirty-some years who had an eight-year-old child with a mental and physical disability. "You guys sure have done a good job keeping this a secret; I'm really glad we're finding it out tonight."

Now it was the women's turn to report on why it was hard to be a man. Mary was the spokesperson. She explained that since the women's group did not really expect the men to come up with much, they had developed a much shorter list. Nonetheless, the women did hit the mark as they reported:

1. Men have an extremely hard time with all of the intense emotions involved with the child with special needs. They want women to be more rational and more supportive of their style of caring.
2. Men feel unappreciated for their efforts for how hard they work to pay the increased medical bills, etc.
3. Women are so intense that men feel they're getting nagged all the time.

When Mary was finished, I intervened, "So how did we do at understanding each other?"

There was laughter and smiles. I pointed out that the differences in the male and female styles of relating that were expressed in the groups were similar in most couples, not just in those having a child with a disability. As Robert Bly pointed out in his dialogue with Deborah Tannen in *Where Are Men and Women Today?*, there is a lot of forgiveness that simply comes from naming the differences between men and women, and it doesn't mean that either one is wrong.

I recommended the book, *You Just Don't Understand*, by linguist Deborah Tannen, because it explains in detail the different conversational styles of men and women in easy to understand language. As Tannen points out, men and women have quite different definitions of the comfort of home. The man generally has been using language all day in his struggle to succeed at work. At day's end, at home with the woman he loves, he has nothing to prove at last and wants to be free not to talk. On the other hand, in a general way, the woman, if she works outside the home, has been careful not to be too expressive all day in order to avoid being called aggressive or neurotic. If she works at home caring for children full time, she may not have had an adult to talk to. At her day's end, when she is finally with the man she feels close to, she wants to be free to talk.

In the dialogue that evolved out of the role reversal, the men and women presented what they each wanted for themselves. Again the women were amazed at how specific the men's group had been. "I hope we can be like this one on one!" said Sally, a woman in her late twenties with a child in early intervention.

By the time the women's group reported on their wants, the men listened openly. The tension in the room was all gone at that moment. Mary reported that the women wanted:

1. The men to be involved in the child's education. They were tired of going to the meetings alone. They wanted the men to try whenever possible to take a few hours off from work to be with them at these times.
2. Some time alone without the children to relax.
3. To be able to talk about their feelings without the men getting defensive.
4. Time together as a couple.
5. Men to develop a better understanding of their child's special needs and not leave it all to the women.

By the time Mary finished, it was almost 9:30. The meeting had lasted thirty minutes longer than planned; babysitters must have been wondering when parents would return. After a brief summary of the evening's events, the couples were urged to continue the discussion by themselves, with friends, and in their ongoing support group. Some more involved problems could be untangled best by consulting a professional skilled in counseling couples and sensitive to the issues around having a child with a disability. I asked everyone to find their partner and end the evening by whispering something special in each other's ear. People began to file out arm in arm, hand in hand.

There was a long way to go, I thought, but there was no doubt that these couples had left understanding more about each other than they had prior to the evening's experience. In that respect, my work was fruitful. On the ride home, I pondered how I was just like the other men there. How many things did I expect Cindy to understand without talking about? How many times did I expect her not to be upset because it was too frustrating for me to listen about things that I couldn't fix? Each time I facilitate a group for couples I learn and understand more about what it takes to understand each other better. I bring something new to each group, and each group finds its own unique way of teaching itself.

While the stories in this chapter cover many of the difficulties encountered by parents with special needs children, it is wise to remember that every relationship is unique and special and needs to be understood in that way. The vitality of healthy children reinforces parents' efforts and keeps us all going. The joys of watching a child's development can be very exciting, but with a special-needs child these joys may be few and far between.

It is particularly necessary for these parents to have enjoyable time together as well as to develop the ability to enjoy playing with their special child through floor time. Whenever I speak to groups of couples, I ask early on when they had their last date. It is rare in my experience that couples go out together with any regularity due to the often overwhelming demands they face. Yet those demands make it all the more necessary to find time together for the sake of the marriage, which obviously will benefit the children.

The difficulties can be overcome. One couple that consulted me, for example, told me how afraid they were to leave their chronically ill child even with a trained respite worker. They realized that they were having a hard time letting go and trusting. They thought that no one else could comfort their child when ill or get emergency medical help if needed. The solution that they eventually found was to carry a beeper, and now they can go out with regularity and peace of mind.

Imperfect Relationships

Just as parenting even a typical child requires giving up the dream of the perfect child, a rewarding and enduring marriage calls upon us to abandon our longing for the perfect union where all of our needs are met and our partner is also totally satisfied. Relationships can be incredibly complex and seldom are quite what we expect. My own daily experiences remind me of my trials and frailties, and as parent and special education professor Helen Featherstone observes in *A Difference in the Family*, insight alone cannot solve every problem that comes up. It is, however, an important tool to maintain the love between a couple when the very fabric and meaning of life is challenged by disability in the family. For some people, a child's disability may reveal problems in a marriage that no amount of understanding and insight can repair or pave over, and divorce may ensue. For others, a child's special needs can be a red herring that distracts a couple from fundamental issues about their relationship. Problematic relationships can become considerably worse. Since, according to the U.S. Census Bureau, 47 percent of first marriages fail, and 57 percent of all marriages end in divorce, none of us can afford to be smug.

Hope for relationships can, however, spring from the crisis that couples experience when their child is imperfect. "Normal" crises like childbirth, moving, loss of a job, financial problems, trials in parenting, etc., all can strain a relationship in parallel ways. Many have observed that ordinary trouble differs only in degree from the strain caused by disability. In my view, however, having a child with a disability is a quantum leap away from everyday problems, but it is nevertheless an experience that prepares us to learn from life.

The stereotypes of female and male suggest a splitting of love and work. According to psychologist Carol Gilligan's *A Different Voice*, expressive capacities are delegated to women through communication in relationships, while instrumental or problem-solving tasks are regarded as logical and masculine. This neat but outmoded model collapses under the weight of a shared sorrow that neither love nor logic alone can heal. The state is then set for a far deeper connection and relationship, perhaps even more intimate than would have been possible with an easier life. The many voices that have been incorporated in this chapter illuminate, I believe, these essential themes.

EIGHT

Differing Views of the Mountain: Understanding How Siblings Respond to Disability

His younger brother Peter had been silent for thirty-nine years. Then, through the sometimes controversial technique of facilitated communication, a breakthrough occurred when he spoke his first words to his older brother

Jeffrey, I'm not stupid, he typed with the aid of his facilitator.

Jeffrey, I love you so much sometimes it hurts.

Those were Peter's first words to his brother, Jeffrey Lurie, the current owner of the Philadelphia Eagles. For hours on a day in early January 1992, Peter "talked" to his brother about their family life together. He remembered being at a residential school at the time of their father's death thirty years before, when Jeffrey, the oldest of three, was nine years old. Peter said that he had wanted to share his grief with the rest of the family, and now finally he could.

Jeffrey Lurie's grandfather, father, and uncle had built a four-billion-dollar movie house and publishing business embodied in General Cinema and Harcourt Brace. Seemingly, Jeffrey had all the comforts in life, but he didn't have a father or a normal brother. Jeffrey related his family's story to a spellbound audience of several hundred people at the Small Miracles Award Dinner sponsored yearly by the Center for Autistic Children in Philadelphia. Before and after his speech he was friendly and available, and as other community groups in the city have noticed, he didn't act like he was doing the world a favor by being there.

Jeffrey's brother's silence and his father's death had taught him how fragile life can be. As Lurie told Sal Paolantonio, a sports writer for the Philadelphia Inquirer,

> Every day, it's like having a friend inside your head....It makes me want to really make the most of every day, month, and year, in terms of the people I am with. The relationships. The family that you have. The work that you do. It makes you want it to be the most intense experience possible, eliminate all kinds of mediocrity. If I'm going to have a relationship with my daughter, let's say, I want it to be as great a relationship as I can make it, because I don't know how long it's going to last.

The Imprints of Birth Order and Gender

The view of family life that Jeffrey Lurie expressed that evening was similar to that of other siblings with disability in their families. We are not only parents; we are siblings all our lives with one foot back in the world of our own childhood and one foot in the world of adulthood and parenting. Facing a disability in the family heightens a parent's challenge to be fair to all. In this quest, grasping the lessons of our family of origin can help to understand the dilemmas of the family that we procreate.

Historically, primogeniture meant that the firstborn son received the inheritance as well as a key position. At times, the "natural" order was reversed in religion and mythology when a later-born son overtook the elder. When such a reversal occurs, it threatens the self-concept of the older child and can leave the younger one feeling chronically guilty. Even today, most parents long for a son to carry on the family name. Despite recent social advances in the realm of gender equality, a son born after a daughter represents a reversal of the traditional social order, and daughters are not valued equally. On the positive side, having a sibling of the opposite sex, when both are valued equally, can be a great advantage throughout life in learning how to get along with the opposite gender.

Same-sex siblings have a special kind of identification with each other. Since they may be so alike, they can have a special challenge to establish individuality. Two women who grew up together tend to be more intimate and sometimes more jealous. Two male siblings tend to be more competitive. The greatest power struggles are between siblings of the same sex. This is especially true when there are only two children and there is no one else to dilute or buffer the struggle.

Breakfast With My Brother

I had known him all his life, and if nature is kind to us, I will know him the rest of my life. I got a warm feeling going to meet him for breakfast. He is one of my younger brothers, and on this brisk October morning, fallen leaves crackled under my feet as I walked to the train station. It was still dark as I waited for the 6:05 train. I was leaving early to meet Paul before I started seeing my patients at the office. The Phillies had just won the National League Championship Series. As the train rumbled along the tracks, I read the sports page and thought of my grandfather and how he would have enjoyed this time if he was alive, especially since the Phillies of 1993 had gone from last to first. They were the collective Rocky of this town, and with their scruffy image of a band of biker types, some overweight, some chewing tobacco and drinking beer, they had captured the imagination. They had charisma, sex appeal, and watchability.

I remembered all those summer nights on my grandparents' back porch listening to the Phillies whether they were winning or losing. Pop was a real fan....I wondered if Paul was having the same thoughts. My reminiscence was punctuated as the train lurched to a stop at my station. It was getting lighter outside as I emerged from the underground station. I always enjoyed the walk to my office through the historic section. Passing Independence Hall, I remembered my father taking all of us as children to see the Liberty Bell. We had taken turns putting our fingers in the crack. My brother Don was there with us then, but his image was now frozen in time. His loss was premature; he is not forgotten. There is always a space for him in those family images stored in my memory.

Recalling those memories brought back a whole world of warm, compassionate, loving feelings mixed with the inevitable rivalry and jealousy that exists among siblings. This morning rendezvous with my brother brought up the complexity and richness of the family life that we share. Since we are ten years apart, we were not in direct competition with each other, and I reflected on how this had helped our relationship.

As I approached the little deli where we had agreed to meet, I saw my brother's car parked outside on South Street. He's always on time. As I entered the eatery, I saw that Paul was reading the sports page. He looked up, and our eyes met. It was a little like looking at myself in the mirror. I look more like my mother, and he looks more like my father, but everyone always knows that we are brothers. I like how it feels when people say that. Of course, it is the same feeling that I have with my other siblings and to a lesser extent with my cousins and others in the extended family.

As I sat down across from Paul in the booth, we exchanged greetings, and our talk initially centered on the Phillies. He sat with his head cocked slightly to the right—his good ear pointed toward me. He lost all hearing in one ear after a severe infection damaged his eardrum as a young child. He compensates well, and most times I forget about his hearing loss. The server brought us steaming hot coffee, reminding me how much Paul always liked coffee and how as a small boy he would drink what was left in the cups when my mother and father had left the table. Then my mind came back to the present.

"I was thinking of Pop. He would have loved this series."

"Me too," he responded with a knowing smile. "I remember one time when I took him to a Phillies game at Veterans' Stadium. He wasn't comfortable; he kept asking when we would be leaving. He would have preferred to listen to it on the radio."

We laughed, and it was the special kind of laughter that you can enjoy with a brother or sister. There were so many memories, so many mixed feelings, that we shared growing up in the same family. There was also the love and loyalty that is easy to talk about. On the other hand, the darker, more difficult side of our emotional lives is easy to ignore. Overemphasizing sibling rivalry tends to accentuate the negative, while ignoring it denies an integral part of the reality that bonds siblings.

Every time I have an involved conversation with one of my siblings, it seems that our similarities and differences come up. Fortunately, our differences naturally have a wide span through age, sex, temperament, and abilities. Affirming our differences helps to control rivalry and serves as a way of expressing it constructively. Am I as accomplished a psychologist as my brothers are in their careers? Am I as far along my career path as I am supposed to be by virtue of my age? Have I been a good big brother?

In the Bible, the first murder was a fratricide; Cain killed his brother, Abel. It's a story about that murky area in the consciousness— the wish to get rid of a sibling and be the sole beneficiary of the parents' affection. There is a certain amount of shame in seeing oneself as competitive or as having angry murderous impulses. After all, aren't we supposed to love and respect our brothers and sisters unconditionally? What are we doing comparing achievements? Most people long for a balanced view of these emotions that can emerge in adulthood. In *The Sibling Bond*, psychologists Stephen Bank and Michael Kahn discuss the positive aspects of aggression and rivalry. Two brothers wrestling, for example, can represent contact, warmth, and presence.

This point reminds me of the endless wrestling matches between my brother Al and me. Al is two years my junior and was my constant companion until I left home for college. In a fight, a child is alive and real and noticed. In these power struggles and interactions, siblings can learn how to resolve conflicts. Yet I always felt some guilt for winning, even though I was supposed to by virtue of being older and putting myself under tremendous pressure to do so. Certainly this was the downside of feeling responsible to lead and achieve.

When Al and I discussed this as adults, it was a relief to know that he had not held it against me, but I still could never feel good about having completed so roughly and consistently winning. Now we eat breakfast together on occasion and take a walk in the woods where our grandmother took us as little boys. Sometimes I follow his lead when we climb rocky trails, and I get a hint of the feeling of what it was like for him to follow in my footsteps during those early years. As he has pointed out to me, our roads diverged so long ago that it's very different now since we relate from different vantage points, and each of us has hair that has begun to gray. Our bonds have truly passed the test of time.

For parents, the fantasy of a close, cozy set of siblings is part of the image of a perfect family. Squabbles among brothers and sisters sometimes crush that dream. There can be a dilemma over when to let children work out their differences and when to intervene. Too much intervention keeps children from learning for themselves how to resolve conflict. The key is to be able to express negative feelings without doing damage. The goal is for children to work out their own solutions whenever possible. It takes parental patience and wisdom to give up an element of control and facilitate this process for children. Sometimes it just means waiting a moment or two.

One of the ways that siblings can help each other as children and as adults is to validate their shared reality about parents and relatives. My conversation with my brother Paul about our grandfather did that for us on that particular morning, and it reaffirmed the length and strength of our bond. Sometimes a different perspective can be helpful and comforting. Paul saw my relationship with Al differently since he primarily remembered the closeness of his two oldest brothers. On the other hand, there may be a difference in perspective that can breed conflict and ill will.

As the oldest in our family, I had grown up always helping my parents to take care of the younger ones. The feeling of being so responsible at a young age is very common among eldest children. The pressure to set a good example is a burden at times but naturally develops leadership ability. As for most eldest children, my role was always clear, and that has been a blessing. Since my teen years, I have found myself in leadership positions in sports, union activities, professional groups, and now speaking to and for parents of children with disabilities.

My brother Paul was the sixth of eight. He was a younger brother to three brothers and two sisters and an older brother to two younger ones. Middle children like Paul tend to have a hazy role in most families and to be pressured from all sides. They have no clearly defined place, but their experience tends to produce people who are friendly, diplomatic, and good negotiators. They are usually blessed with a moderate sense of responsibility, connect strongly with older siblings, and are very protective of younger siblings.

I remember teaching my younger brothers how to play baseball and being proud of their accomplishments in Little League. I remember how, at one point, they thought I could do anything. There was a certain competition among the older group of siblings for the attention and admiration of the younger ones. This is another frequently cited form of rivalry mentioned in the literature on this topic. Nonetheless, it is hard to admit and carries a twinge of embarrassment along with it. The oldest is by nature bigger, stronger, and knows more, so he or she is expected to win out. There's a lot of pressure, and the oldest may also feel guilty for winning at the expense of a younger sibling who is also loved. No wonder so many siblings report strained relationships in adulthood.

The youngest, like the oldest, has a unique position and is never displaced. The child in this position feels chosen for special protection by older siblings as well as parents. On the other hand, the youngest is often regarded as spoiled or as the favorite whether that is true or not. While the oldest is usually expected to help in parenting, the youngest is often expected to take care of the parents as they age.

In *Mixed Feelings: Love, Hate, Rivalry, and Reconciliation*

Among Brothers and Sisters, writer Francine Klagsbrun explores the unique perspective of each position in the birth order. There is such a wide range of factors that make up the building blocks of our personalities that these generalizations about birth order don't always hold up. Nonetheless, many of them can be used to better understand ourselves and others. In every case, sibling bonds leave special imprints that affect the way we parent our children whether our experience fits the norms or not.

In a workshop I conducted I met a man who was the second child in his family, but he was the first son. He was treated as if he was the oldest child, and that always felt weird to him. Of course, it also strained his relationship with his older sister, who was never treated in accord with her natural position. His dilemma is full of meaning in reference to how gender affects the birth order.

Our Family Matters

Paul asked me how Tariq was doing. It was an uneasy moment. There wasn't much to say, but I wanted to answer because I didn't want Paul to stop asking me. Some people never ask, so that he asks me regularly and listens to the answer is comforting.

"He's getting whiskers. He'll need to be shaved soon. I doubt he'll ever be able to safely handle a razor...."

There was an awkward pause; Paul didn't know what to say. He didn't really want to think about this, and I didn't really blame him, nor did I really want to talk about it. I'd rather avoid the pain of those thoughts, and I didn't want him to feel too uneasy or inadequate, so I shifted the subject.

"How's Sam doing? What's his latest accomplishment?"

My brother's eyes lit up. This was the sort of thing that parents of normal children can easily talk about. Fortunately I could join him in this. Sam was almost two at the time, a few months younger than my daughter Kara, and it was always fun to talk about them. There are the inevitable comparisons, and I wonder if this reflects our own rivalry. I'm glad I have a daughter since the competition will never be as direct as if these toddler cousins were of the same sex. They are supposed to be different by virtue of their biology. On the other hand, I am both glad for Paul and somewhat jealous that he has a healthy son.

Sometimes we talk about the movies we have seen recently. Our conversation on this particular morning reminded me of the television movie *Family Pictures* which we talked about briefly and related to our family's experiences. Based on the novel by Sue Miller, it is about a man and a woman struggling to raise five children including a son with autism. It is about relationships and forgiving.

The story is told through the eyes of Nina, the oldest child, giving it a different and much needed perspective. Randall, the child with autism, strains everyone's patience, and the viewer can feel the tension. Lainie, the mother, tries to treat him as normally as possible, devotes most of her time to his care, and seems inseparable from Randall. David, the father, and the other children all feel neglected at times. This is a major dilemma for all families with a child who isn't "normal."

One day the family receives the devastating news that Randall has wandered away on a field trip at his school and has been killed by a car. I shuddered. This is still my worst fear for Tariq, and I could imagine a funeral like the one in the movie. What made this film special to me is the confrontation and the subsequent reconciliation that occurs between Nina and her mother at the end. There had been much friction between mother and daughter. They had argued bitterly for years, and at this point Nina is married and pregnant with her first child.

Nina starts with a shrill voice asking why her mother divorced her father after Randall's death. Lainie explains in a firm tone that they had both worked hard to stay together.

Nina counters, from her perspective, that it seemed like their marriage was only for Randall's sake since when he died her parents broke up. She feels that her mother's love is conditional and summarizes it in her tearful statement: "It's be quiet, be good, be happy, be well. Most of all, be well. Be all of those things, and I'll love you. I'll love you, my perfect baby."

Lainie responds by explaining that she wishes she could have loved Randall the way she loved her other children. She explains that it would have been a gift if she could have asked the same from him as from her other children. She acknowledges that she wasn't a good mother to Nina because she yelled and hit. She makes no excuses as she admits that perhaps Randall did keep the family together. Lainie concludes that her love for Nina and her other "typical" children held her to the earth.

The reconciliation that results is possible between a parent and an adult child when both can speak honestly and openly. It takes courage to have this kind of dialogue, but it can liberate its participants from so many dark feelings.

In speaking her mind and in hearing her mother's response, Nina begins to make sense out of her life. As the film ends, Nina reflects on a portrait of a large extended family and sees it as a portrait of courage. From this perspective, every child who is born represents an immense risk on the part of the parents. There is so much potential for pain and tragedy that any child's existence is a miracle.

I reflected on the risks my parents had taken to have and raise eight children—only to lose one of us in a car accident. I thought of my grandparents and their courage. My grandfather came over alone on a boat from Italy when he was twelve years old to meet his father who was already here in America. He never knew his mother, who had died when he was only two. During the Depression, my grandparents raised five children to adulthood. They lost a two-year-old daughter to illness, which wasn't uncommon in those days. In fact, around the turn of the century as many as 20 percent of all children died before their first birthday.

I wasn't the only or the first in my family tree who had rolled the dice and lost. I thought of Cindy and her parents, because she, too, had lost a brother—he was only seventeen—in a bus accident in Israel. He was buried on the kibbutz while her family sat *shiva* half a world away in Philadelphia. Every family has its share of tragedy. Nina's words from the movie keep echoing inside me. Love is such a risk, but who would want to live without love, without connection to others?

I wondered what Antoinette would make of Tariq when she was grown. All parents want to be fair, and we want our normal, healthy children to grow up loving us as parents and loving their siblings who are less fortunate in some ways. Recently, one night when everyone else was out, Antoinette and I were having dinner together, and she asked me if I would rather have one healthy son than three daughters. What a heavy question for her! But I was glad for her sake that she was able to ask it. I told her that I would be overjoyed if Tariq were normal, but not in place of any of my daughters. She seemed relieved by my answer.

Veteran Parents Speak Out

Recently I addressed a unique group of parents—Vietnam veterans who had been exposed to Agent Orange. One of the tragic consequences of their exposure to that chemical compound is that their children have a much higher incidence of all sorts of disabilities, especially those of a neurological nature. The class action court case that had awarded damages to these veterans and their families also established funds for parent training for those whose children had a disability.

The topic of my presentation was the issues facing parents in raising siblings of children with disabilities. The timing seemed perfect. Since I had videotaped *Family Pictures*, I decided to show the ending to stimulate a discussion. There was some risk involved because the movie was so intense, and these fathers' genes had been damaged by chemicals in southeast Asia. Did I dare uncover that pain? I knew the parents who had come had difficult lives and wanted all the help they could get. About fifty people were present, two-thirds of them women. After a brief introduction about myself and the movie, I showed the last ten minutes of the film, which began with Nina confronting her mother.

There was a heavy silence when I turned off the VCR. I asked if anyone would start the group off for the evening by sharing what had opened inside of them as they watched the film clip.

Almost instantly a woman in the front row spoke up. "I felt very sad," she said. "I'm always yelling at my child who doesn't have the problem. I expect so much from her, and she's not even four. I know I have to change."

Another woman in the front said, "I'm always running around trying to keep up with my son who has ADHD (attention deficit hyperactivity disorder). I'm never sure what I'll find around the next corner. My nerves are shot. My other children are really on their own. I don't know what to do."

Another woman said, "My child just developed juvenile diabetes. Now that he's insulin-dependent, it's like his whole personality is changing. He feels so different. My daughter is losing the healthy brother she used to have. I'm not sure how to help her. I'm a school social worker, but I'm at a loss for how to handle this."

"My two-and-a-half year old has a hearing impairment and neurological damage," said a woman in the back. "My four year old looked at her the other day and said, 'Why won't you talk to me? Why?' I don't know what to tell her. I told her that her sister's ears were broken, and she will have to learn to talk with her hands. Did I do the right thing?"

Of course, it was right—information liberates us all, parents and children, from some of our darkest worries. Getting reliable information can be like having your electricity restored after a storm has knocked out your power. The pain is still there, however, and that is one thing that makes it so difficult to know if we are doing the right thing as parents.

In 1972, researcher Frances Grossman reported on the first large-scale study involving college-age siblings in *Brothers and Sisters of Retarded Children*. These brothers and sisters reported that talking to their parents about the disabilities of their brothers and sisters was as difficult as talking to them about sex. One of Grossman's conclusions was that the feelings and attitudes of the brothers and sisters to a large extent mirrored the way the parents had handled the disability. Parents who can speak freely help their children to understand their own emotions.

A hand went up right in front of me. There was an urgency to the gesture, and the woman's voice trembled as she spoke. "I think I talk to my healthy daughter too much. My husband doesn't want to talk about our child's problems. For years I've confided in my other daughter, who is now a teenager. I know this isn't right, and I feel horrible about it, but I haven't known where to turn."

We all need to share with other adults. It doesn't make things "all better," but it helps. Sometimes we get isolated from other people, but this meeting was an opportunity to connect and maybe go back refreshed to the important people in their lives.

So far none of the men had spoken, which was not unusual in these meetings. A simple intervention often can change that. I opened the door by asking if any of the men wanted to share.

After an awkward pause, a man seated near the center of the room with his arms crossed came through. "Our three year old has just been diagnosed with PDD (pervasive developmental disorder)," he said clearly and directly. "We don't know what to think. My wife is really worried about the effect on our two older children, and I am too. That's why I'm here tonight."

He had no sooner finished when another man raised his hand. He was a slightly built man with glasses and spoke timidly. "My wife tells me I don't talk about this enough, but I don't know what to do, and that's why I have nothing to say. It really makes me feel like a nothing as a father. I want to go home with something to say."

The man seated beside him patted him on the back to comfort him. Many men and women nodded around the room. It was a signal to move on. Stressing how many answers to these questions were already within the group, I asked everyone to imagine that they had a sibling with a disability or chronic illness. What would they want from their parents?

What Siblings Want

There is the clear simple voice of the child in all of us. Everyone who grew up with siblings can access those deep mixed feelings. Most, if not all, parents aspire to have a perfect family with warm unconditional love between brothers and sisters.

The first thing that came up at the Agent Orange gathering was that siblings would want a fair distribution of attention from their parents. This could be in the form of taking their problems just as seriously as those of the child with the "special needs." Recognition of the positive in each child without having the pressure of being "the star" of the family was mentioned.

"So much gets taken for granted when you're normal," said another speaker. "As parents we make such a big deal out of the accomplishments of our special child. If I was a sibling, I would really resent it if my parents didn't notice my struggles and accomplishments."

That comment, like Nina's in *Family Pictures*, reflected the realty that the child with the disability does not have to compete for the parents' attention. From the siblings' perspective that child always wins.

"I'd want my own life!" said the man who had been the first male to speak up earlier.

Other parents followed up talking about time alone without any responsibilities and time with their friends. Because they are always expected to help out their exhausted, bereaved parents, siblings often feel like junior parents and yet find it hard to express their negative feelings about this role. They may feel inconsiderate or disloyal to their struggling parents.

Looking for solutions within the group made ideas flow freely; I wrote them on a newsprint tablet in the front of the room. The mood of the group was shifting. Energy was beginning to flow out of the heavy thoughts that had dominated the evening so far. People were eagerly copying down the ideas.

"I would want to be treated as an individual, and I would absolutely hate it if my parents always reminded me how lucky I was. That would drive me up the wall," added a woman who hadn't spoken previously.

A man who had listened intently so far spoke next. "I would want information about the disability," he said. "I'm sure I would have a lot of questions, and I would want answers."

Just as parents need information, so do siblings, on their level. Information helps siblings to answer the questions that come from their peers or even from adults who are too uncomfortable to ask the parents directly.

The woman whose child had ADHD shared next. "That makes me think that I would want my parents to be concerned about my feelings. I would want them to ask me how I felt."

Like their parents, brothers and sisters have a host of feelings that run the gamut from confusion, to fear, to anger, to sadness, to embarrassment. Sometimes their shame is so acute that siblings wish they didn't even know their brother or sister who acts or looks unusual. This can be especially true if there is a strong physical resemblance between the two. While it may be hard to express these thoughts, most siblings long to have their feelings described or confirmed in some way. It helps to relieve their guilt about having negative feelings toward a brother or sister.

Let's take the anger that a sibling might feel toward a sister who keeps messing up his things like his video games, for example, including pulling out the plug when he is playing with it and forcing him to start over again. The anger makes him want to get rid of, or even beat up, his sister, who is being a pest. Then there is the guilt that may be felt when he thinks it over and remembers that she just wants to play, doesn't understand how to play that game, and wants him to do something different. Surely this is an understandable cycle of emotions, but very difficult to deal with internally.

Parents who have come to terms with the darker side of their own feelings about their child's disability and their own feelings as siblings are in the best position to help their other children feel whole and lovable. Research on the adjustment of siblings of children with disabilities consistently shows this.

"I would want a normal family life," commented the man whose child had PDD. "That would mean doing things together as a family as well as time alone with my parents to do things or just talk."

"Privacy would really matter to me; I'd be sick of a kid who didn't understand any better constantly getting into my things," declared the woman whose child was deaf.

A man who had listened with a somber expression all night stated firmly, "I would want a break once in a while from all the worries and responsibilities. It would be great if there was a sense of humor in the family."

Another woman who had been listening intently spoke up next. "My nine-year-old daughter has a learning disability. The other day when I was serving breakfast, I spilled some orange juice. I started joking that I had a spilling disability...."

She was interrupted by a hearty round of laughter, and then she told us that her joke had caught on with the whole family. There were many nods and smiles around the room. There was a resurgence of hope following the open expression of the group's feelings. They had captured the essence of what siblings themselves say in interviews and what is recommended by professionals. It was time to move the group forward another step. Given that everyone wants to be a good parent to all their children, and we get a sense of their needs when we meet together and talk, then why is it hard to do?

The room got quiet briefly, and then the woman whose child had ADHD spoke up. "So much of the time I'm out of breath chasing the special one—watching out for what might happen next. I find myself calling my daughter for help when my husband isn't home. It's hard for me to hear my daughter's concerns. I feel like a broken record. I'm so wound up...."

It got quiet again. It can be really, really hard, and sometimes we run out of gas. People always tell me, and I'm sure other parents get this a lot, that they don't know how I've survived. Sometimes that makes people angry, but I think people are saying that they admire the strength and courage and love exhibited in such quantity by the parents of children with special needs.

As Shakespeare wrote in *Hamlet*, "There is nothing either good or bad, but thinking makes it so." Talking about these things is one way that parents can find the good side, take care of themselves, and replenish their energy. And they can take better care of their children by learning to take care of themselves. That sounds simple, but there's something more to take into account. Disability can disrupt normal occurrences in the family life of brothers and sisters.

Recently I met a man who was very concerned about the unsettling outlook of his three-year-old daughter. She kept calling her older sister who was six "the baby." The six year old was visually impaired and developmentally disabled. Although it seemed weird to this father, in this case, the younger daughter functioned at a much higher level than her older sister. Her way of looking at things was in accordance with the reality she experienced.

Disability had reversed the natural order. Her father had explained the disability to his younger daughter, but she still called her older sister the baby. That will stop when the younger girl develops the capacity to understand the abstract concepts involved. She will nevertheless probably be uncomfortable at times. This younger child, like my own daughter Antoinette, feels like she is the older child. In a functional way, what is chronologically false is actually true in terms of the role that the children play in the family. The younger, "normal" child loses both a "normal" playmate and a role model and, moreover, the attention she would have naturally gotten as the baby of the family. When parents are sensitive to this, they can help their children understand.

When the normal child is born second, parents are quite naturally thrilled with the healthy child's development. However, this is a two-edged sword. Every achievement can remind parents of the limits of their special child. Without warning, the inner confusion and turmoil may be reignited. In this way chronic grief can reverberate through a family.

Physical resemblance is another tricky area. As Antoinette moved toward adolescence, I noticed that she got uncomfortable when people commented on her resemblance to Tariq. That bothered me at first. I wanted her to have the warm feeling I had when people told me that I looked like my siblings.

Indeed, I still want that for her. I realize that Antoinette was responding partly from her own fear that something might be wrong with her—a fear revealed by every sibling of a disabled child I have interviewed. When the disability is invisible, such as with a learning disability, autism, and mental disorders or deficiencies, this worry seems even more prominent.

The Meaning of *Rain Man*

A certain level of mystery shrouds sibling bonds. The 1988 movie *Rain Man* provided a compelling illustration of this theme. Dustin Hoffman's masterful protrayal of Raymond, an autistic savant, focused attention on children with autism. At the time the movie was released near Christmas of 1988, I was interviewed about autism from a parent's perspective for a local television station. Tariq had just turned nine and was home for the holidays. We didn't own a VCR at the time, so I asked my sister Marilyn to tape the interview for us. When you are lucky, siblings are always there for you, as Marilyn has been time and again, calling me regularly to ask about Tariq's progress and always making Tariq welcome in her home.

My son and I appeared on the evening news together. Antoinette was only seven at the time and was too shy to be interviewed, but she showed up in the background. At the end of the interview, Tariq hugged me and then gave the reporter a high five. It was a warm and memorable moment that I am happy to have preserved on tape as one of our "family pictures."

Unlike Raymond, Tariq, and most children with autism, cannot read and write or memorize the phone book. Nonetheless, this movie depicts a character transformation in Raymond's brother that has meaning and relevance for siblings of children with various kinds of disabilities. Raymond's brother, Charlie, is an angry hustler who is callous and self-centered. His mother died when he was two. He is estranged from his father and does not at first even know he has a brother.

"My father has stuck it to me all my life," Charlie complains. He feels that nothing he does is good enough. When his father dies, Charlie discovers that he has been excluded from a three-million-dollar inheritance. In his quest to find out about it, he discovers that he has a brother in an institution. Charlie kidnaps his own brother in order to bargain for his fair share of the inheritance. As a result of his disability, Raymond lives in a world without normal perception and human relationships and unwittingly provides his brother with someone he cannot con. Charlie is forced to confront his own stunted emotional development.

Ironically, Charlie begins to find himself and his feelings as he struggles to relate to Raymond, who cannot connect emotionally with another person. Since Raymond doesn't crave or accept attention or affection, he is not inherently lovable. On their long car trip together from the Midwest to Los Angeles where Charlie lives, Charlie begins to appreiciate his brother.

When Charlie was little and got scared, he thought someone called the rain man could save him. During the trip, Charlie calls Raymond Rain Man and inadvertently discovers that the *rain man* in his fantasy was his brother *Raymond*, who remembers singing to Charlie. Eventually Charlie comes to love Raymond for the unique person he is, and then he wants the best for him. As he tells Raymond's guardian, "I'm not pissed off at my dad any more. It's not about the money anymore. Why didn't he tell me? Why didn't you tell me? It would have been nice to know him for more than the past six days."

By making a genuine connection with his brother, Charlie is transformed. Raymond cannot be normal, but Charlie proves to himself that he can have genuine relationships.

I hope that someday my daughters find a meaning for themselves in Tariq's existence, and I trust that they will. Sometimes when we confront our own limitations, we realize just how fragile life can be. This can lead to a deeper appreciation of our own talents and abilities and a fuller sense of self.

All of Us Are Fragile

Tragedy can visit any family. In 1987 I was teaching a graduate seminar in special education at Antioch University in Philadelphia. One night after class, one of my students approached me. Emily Simon was always serious and intense about her studies and her job teaching students with hearing impairments. When everyone else had left the room, she shared with me that her younger brother had died from leukemia several years before. Her parents wanted to be interviewed for my research.

I was invited to spend a day with the family. They lived in a fashionable neighborhood in Delaware. Emily's father was a physician in general practice; her mother was a physical therapist. Her brother, Brad, was an undergraduate special-education student. They were a family of survivors. Emily admired the way her parents had handled their situation, and I hoped that this family could tell me something about how they coped. As I pulled into the driveway, I noticed a basketball backboard and imagined how the boys in the neighborhood must have gathered here. Part of me wished I could play ball that day instead of having to talk to a family about death, but I was honored that they trusted me enough to share their deepest emotions.

As I rang the doorbell, I hoped that I could avoid any mistakes—asking uncomfortable questions or probing too far. Emily's mother, Helen, offered me tea and invited me to sit in the living room to talk. Helen began her story in a slow, deliberate voice. Pictures of the family were all around, and from them I could see that Danny had been a very attractive child. She explained that Danny had leukemia since he was three years old and was constantly in and out of hospitals, but in every possible respect, he was treated the same as her other children. His IQ was in the normal range, although his development had been somewhat slow. He was small for his age and couldn't keep up physically with his classmates, but he enjoyed school and socializing with other children. He needed special education classes because of a mild learning problem, and a tutor was necessary when he had to be hospitalized or stay home for extended periods of time.

The Simons believed that life was lived one day at a time and, although they worried about how long Danny would live, they treated their son as normally as possible. I was drawn in as I listened to Helen's account. She told her story with flair, a sense of drama, and suspense. I shared the hope this family had for the survival of their baby.

Brad and Emily always watched out for their younger brother. When the neighborhood children were playing baseball or kickball, his big brother or sister made sure Danny was on their team. People in the neighborhood knew Danny and were very kind to him. If he began to feel dizzy or weak while riding his bike, he could always rest at someone's house or use the phone to call home.

Unexpectedly, in his ninth year, Danny had died in his sleep. Emily had been away at college. My mother's phone call to me about my brother ran through my mind as I pictured the phone in Emily's dorm. I recollected going to the hospital with my dad to see my brother's body—but there was no way I could imagine the horror of finding a child of mine in his own bed, never to wake up again.

It was time for a break, so Helen invited me into the kitchen and began to put out a spread of cold cuts on the table for her husband, David, who would soon be home from the office for lunch. He greeted me warmly with a firm handshake, and once we began to talk, he reflected on how hard it must have been for his son and daughter to live with bereaved parents. I thought this was his way of saying he wasn't the perfect dad. Helen excused herself, leaving David and me alone. He encouraged my questions as he prepared a sandwich.

I asked how he and his wife had treated Brad and Emily throughout the period of Danny's illness. He said they had tried to keep family life as normal as they could. For example, they always vacationed together even though the uncertainties of Danny's illness made planning difficult. They all helped in his care, but Brad and Emily were always encouraged and helped to maintain their normal activities.

David believed that Danny's illness had not disrupted the family from functioning. In fact, he said, "We rallied around him when he was ill." David had to spend extra time with Danny, attending him at home with intravenous fluids and other medical necessities. Still, he always found time for Brad and Emily. In commenting on what his painful experience had taught him, he said, "Everyone's mortality became much more on my mind. I thank God every day that my surviving children are alive and healthy, but I now realize how quickly that can change. Life is truly fragile, and health is something I give thanks for every day."

Another View of the Mountain

A mountain looks different from every direction. It could be a slow-rising chain of hills from the north and a granite wall from the south. There might be a creek on the east. The rocks, the trees, and the soil may be different depending on the approach. None of the views may match, yet they are all views of the same mountain. The same is true of families; what any member sees is determined by his vantage point. The challenge of a disability or chronic illness fits this metaphor, which was originally developed to describe how groups appear to their members by Temple University professor Vytautas Cernius. Age, place in the birth order, gender, native abilities, emotional temperament, parents' attitudes, and individual history all make each person's position unique.

After lunch, I spent the rest of the day talking to Emily and her brother, Brad. From her vantage point as the oldest, Emily had not at first been aware that there was anything radically different about her little brother other than his frequent hospitalizations—although she knew he didn't run as fast as the others his age and his coordination was not as good. She and Brad were athletic, and Danny wanted to participate in athletics at their level, but he couldn't. When she entered high school, she began to worry more about Danny.

Emily was always encouraged to ask questions, and there was open discussion about whatever issues she raised. She recalled how everything always led her to one question, "As Danny gets older, will he get better?" Her parents only said that they hoped so. Her best friends had known Danny since birth and accepted him, but sometimes Emily was embarrassed to tell other people about Danny's condition. She didn't tell anyone she didn't have to. When necessary, she would just explain what had been explained to her.

As far as discipline was concerned, both Brad and Emily told me that their parents were very fair. They had been praised for everything they accomplished and disciplined when they did something wrong. Danny had been encouraged to do everything he could "until the last day of his life," and his accomplishments were considered as praiseworthy as were hers and Brad's. The virulent resentment depicted in *Family Pictures* was not present in this family.

At the end of our conversation, I asked Emily if there was anything else that was important about being a sibling of a child with a disability. She told me something that virtually every sibling I have met since has confirmed. She said she knows that other people her age rarely think about it, but she wonders about having a child with a disability. Her worry will not stop her from having children, but it is a heavy weight to carry up the mountain.

Brad told me his first memories of Danny were of medical problems. He recalled beginning to ask his parents questions when he was about five. At first his parents explained that his brother was not as strong as other children. As Brad got older and asked more detailed questions, he got more detailed answers. Brad would get annoyed when other children at school would ask "Is he bald or something?" and became embarrassed when people asked too many questions. When he got older and could verbalize his answers better, it was easier for him to deal with the questions.

Brad thought that he had not missed out on anything because of his brother. He never had to stay home when Danny was sick. He realized that other children his age didn't have the same experiences. At first Danny was like two different people to him. He was loud and noisy and wanted his way when he was healthy, and yet could be very sick at other times. Like his sister, Brad wondered whether his brother would get better.

Emily and Brad both believed that Danny had brought their family close together—he had been part of the bond of love and compassion that linked them. Having a physician for a father had made Brad feel secure. As a child, he thought his father could fix anything. If anything seemed wrong, Brad thought, "Call Dad at work—he'll know whether to worry or not." He knows now that his father did not feel that way about his own abilities.

As Brad spoke, it struck me that he was describing the parents' task, disability or not, to carry the brunt of the worries and the responsibility. Parents lead the way up the rocky mountain trail. That's the only fair way—as hard as it might be. When there is a disability in the family, the trail is steeper, more treacherous. More than ever, the children in the family look to their mother and father for direction in how to handle the practical obstacles as well as their mixed emotions.

What sustains parents as well as siblings is a special kind of pride that develops. Brad and Emily had that special pride in their younger brother. They knew how much effort it took for him to accomplish some things that others took for granted—like riding a bike or learning long division. They were proud of their parents for how they handled the problems and made each of them feel special. They were proud of their own accomplishments and grateful for their health— both physical and mental.

For myself, I hope and trust that my daughters will be able to look back as young women and feel the same way. Love and hate, rivalry and reconciliation, grief and joy, embarrassment and pride. We are really all in this together—parents and siblings of special children—it is only our views of the mountain that differ.

NINE

The Trouble With Elephants: Finding and Building Circles of Support

A friend is one to
whom one may pour out
all the contents of one's
heart, chaff and grain
together, knowing that
the gentlest of hands
will take and sift it,
keep what is worth keeping
and
with the breath of kindness
blow the rest away.

—ARABIAN PROVERB

While sorrow sends us inward to be alone and lick our wounds, we can heal those hurts by opening up and confiding in others. True friendship, as the proverb above states, divides the grief and makes it more bearable. It is indeed a special friend to whom we can turn in our darkest moments for solace. Some people already have such friends while others have to find some—either among their acquaintances or elsewhere.

When someone you are close to dies, relatives, friends, and even acquaintances rally around to offer help. But after a short time, perhaps not knowing what to say or how to respond to the bereaved

153

person, they seem to avoid broaching the subject of death. The same is true when you are worried that something is wrong with your child's development or after your child has been diagnosed with a disability or chronic illness. The topic may be horrifying or psychologically threatening to talk about.

One of the things that we are the least prepared for is the kind of social isolation that comes with grief. As several people have said to me, and as I have experienced myself, it is as if there were a giant elephant in the living room. It fills the room and is hard to get around. It is difficult to communicate honestly when you are bereaved. People say, "How are you?" and we respond, "I'm fine." We talk, about work, the weather, the news, the economy, and everything else but the obvious—the elephant in the room that is unavoidably on our minds.

Maybe the trivial chatter is just a way of saying that no one wants to be alone with the elephant and an attempt, however awkward, to acknowledge connection and express concern about a shared sorrow.

As John Donne wrote:

No man is an island entire of itself; every man is a piece of the continent, a part of the main…any man's death diminishes me, because I am involved in mankind; and therefore never send to know for whom the bell tolls; It tolls for thee.

When I look back over my own experiences searching for help and support in the early days of worrying about Tariq, I see that much of what I went through was fairly typical. At first, as I mentioned earlier, I believed that if he could just start talking again then everything would work out from there. When something is wrong with your child, you often feel like a little child yourself and you want your mom and dad to help you—to rescue you—and protect you from the hurt you are feeling.

My mother and father would counsel me to be patient, that things would work out. My mother would tell me that she was praying. They would ask me how Tariq was doing, as if he had the flu and was expected to get better each day. I would describe any little changes I had noticed. Our conversations lessened the tension I felt, helped me to get through another day, and kept me working with Tariq to help him develop. They couldn't, however, wipe away the tears or bandage the wounds, and that has been hard for them as well as for me.

My grandparents, who were still alive when Tariq was younger, would reassure me too. I have a cousin my own age, who has mild mental retardation and whose speech came late, and they had helped my aunt and uncle a lot when Gregory was a little boy. They reassured me, based on how my cousin had developed. Even though he still stutters, he learned to read and write a little bit. He has a driver's license and holds a civil service job as a janitor. All in all, he has done very well for someone with his ability. My grandparents seemed confident that Tariq would be like Gregory. Because of their direct experience and their love for me, I trusted their wisdom and hoped desperately that they were right.

I remember how my grandfather would put Tariq on his lap and recite Italian nursery rhymes, the same ones he had recited to me when I was a small boy. He would take Tariq's hands within his strong palms, as he had taken mine, and rub them on his coarse beard until it tickled. Tariq would smile and then squirm to get away because he didn't like to be held for long. My grandmother, too, would try to hold Tariq, and she would sing the lullabies that she had sung to me and my siblings and cousins when we were little.

So many people never tried to hold my son, perhaps shying away from what they could not understand and what was uncomfortable. They would just make small talk, and I would withdraw in the embarrassment of the moment, always remaining outwardly calm. That's why I get such a warm feeling recalling those moments that my grandparents tried to hold Tariq, despite his squirming and wriggling away. Of course I wished that he would sit still and cuddle with them, but nonetheless, I felt myself held by them because they never stopped trying with him.

I know I am not alone. Many parents have told me how isolated and abandoned they have felt in their hour of greatest need. There is a longing for someone to reach out and take a special interest in your child and therefore in you. When you finally do find that kind of support—a gentle hand to touch you and your child and a kind heart to ask how things are—that's when you know for sure that you are not alone.

Intergenerational Grief

Recently a young father who had come to me for help with his grief told the familiar story of looking to his parents for help. His father had died when he was seven, and he had rarely visited the gravesite. When his son was diagnosed as profoundly deaf, he went to the cemetery, stood by the grave, and told his dad what was going on with his grandson. He cried and asked for help and for strength to carry on. He cried as he told me about this, saying that he had found an emotional relief and has thought about his father and missed him more ever since that day in the cemetery. Certainly my own father must have missed his parents as he went through the normal trials and tribulations of childrearing; who else would you naturally turn to for guidance, whether your child was "normal" or not?

As time passed, and Tariq didn't speak, my parents, my grandparents, my siblings, and my other relatives all kept saying basically the same thing—that Tariq would outgrow this. Instead of being comforted, I felt frustrated and terrified to think about how I would handle it if he never spoke again. Tariq was different from what they expected, so when he was eventually diagnosed with autism, they didn't know what else to say—understandable enough, but it made me feel very alone, and I would just want to be by myself—to withdraw.

I believed that I was the only person who had ever felt this way. No one could help me, I thought, because no one else had ever experienced what I was going through. I believed that it was all my responsibility and that I should be able to handle it. I didn't want to burden others, but sometimes I felt like I was in a land beyond tears and beyond comfort. Everything—toys, playgrounds, clothes, healthy children—reminded me of the little boy I had dreamed of and the sorrow that Tariq's silence presented to me.

There's still more to this set of beliefs that many parents of children with disabilities get into. You start to think that others don't want to hear your problems because they have enough of their own. It's so easy to get tangled up in a web of distorted beliefs as you grieve the loss of your "normal" child. You might even believe that it's too hard to find support and that it takes too much energy to explain your situation, so therefore it will be easier to just hold it in and do everything yourself.

Many parents report that their relatives bring up the same ideas over and over again. The grandparents of one child with a rare terminal illness, for example, kept bring up their idea that perhaps the illness had been caused by Agent Orange since their son had served in Vietnam. The disease was, in fact, genetic and could not have been caused by Agent Orange, so the grandparents' response brought their son and his wife only frustration and provided no comfort. Perhaps it was just too painful for them to face the idea that they might have transmitted the deadly gene that skipped their generation.

Fortunately, in most cases, the passage of time brings a gift of perspective. It becomes clear that grandparents can have as hard a time accepting a disability as parents do, or even a harder one, and their acceptance can take longer. They face the double grief of their grandchild's disability and their own child's pain. The grandmother of a child who was killed in the bombing of the federal office building in Oklahoma City put it this way, "I've lost my grandchild, and I have to watch my baby suffer for the rest of my life."

This second level of grief often renders the grandparents powerless to offer the support that their son or daughter longs for. They may despair that they could not protect their child from this fate; they may worry that they have passed on a defective gene and that it could appear again in another grandchild. They may also feel overwhelmed and guilty that they cannot help more.

Another couple whom I counseled had a problem with their child's grandparents. Jennifer's parents could not grasp why their grandson had so many peculiar repetitive behaviors and why his speech was so limited. They were simple, uneducated folks, who had never heard that neurological damage could cause such problems. They kept asking Jennifer if she had had Tommy tested for lead poisoning. No matter how much Jennifer, who is a registered nurse, disclaimed the possibility of lead poisoning, her parents wouldn't give up. She was close to her parents, who watched Tommy when she was at work, so she really wanted them to understand and agree with her. That they apparently could not was causing a lot of friction.

I suggested that more information and direct involvement in Tommy's professional care might be helpful for his grandparents and asked Jennifer to bring them to her next therapy session with me. After introducing myself and explaining my role with the family, I asked Jennifer's parents if they had any questions about Tommy. Of course they brought up lead poisoning right away, and Jennifer sighed. Jennifer's mother commented that it was getting hard to talk about this issue between them. It was clear, nonetheless, that these grandparents wanted to help, and that their help was needed and wanted.

In my most dignified and authoritative manner, I explained that the cause of Tommy's limitations was unknown. From reviewing his records, I knew that he had received excellent care at some of the best medical facilities in our area and that there were no indications of lead poisoning. I patiently explained that bringing this up repeatedly was frustrating Jennifer and recommended that they avoid doing it. Knowing that they were trying in their own way to understand, I suggested that they visit their grandson's classroom and meet and talk to his teachers. I also recommended that they take a look at the books and articles that their daughter had collected related to Tommy's speech and language development.

Hearing this firsthand from a doctor made a difference. I wasn't a part of their family system and was considered an objective source of information and guidance, and they could tell I cared about their grandson. Therefore, they couldn't write off my comments as they might have if they heard them through their daughter. Jennifer told me at her next session that her parents had stopped talking about lead poisoning. She felt relieved and was much more comfortable when she was around them. They were reading and getting a better understanding of Tommy's condition and his present limitations.

Looking forward to a warm, indulging role with their grandchildren, grandparents may naturally expect to have pleasure without the responsibilities of being an authority figure that they had with their own children. Being involved with the new generation can be a source of special pride and satisfaction, but when they are confronted by disability, they find their role is not what they expected. And if they go into some form of denial, they can add to the parents' burden.

The grandparents lose their dreamed-for grandchild who was to be their legacy to future generations just as the parents have lost their dream-child. Getting to know their actual grandchild can be more difficult because they are often removed from the child's everyday life and also because they have the burden of providing support to their adult child in a time of tremendous need. In these ways, grandparents are affected by what happens in the nuclear family, and they also affect the rest of the family members. Because they see and hold the child less often, it takes proportionately longer to bond with that child. They need help from their children to understand their grandchild's disability, but it takes time for parents to be ready to lead the way.

Once grandparents understand the problem, they can be a great asset. With the experience and wisdom gained from raising their own children, they may have much to offer in sharing coping strategies and in discerning which issues are linked to the disability and which ones are the normal challenges of childrearing. They may also have time to help with many of the practical demands of caring for a grandchild with special needs.

The Mind-Body Connection

While many people temporarily conclude that it is easier to hold in their feelings and do everything themselves, in reality nothing could be further from the truth. Even Hippocrates, the father of medicine, stressed that emotional factors could be a contributing cause in disease as well as a factor in recovery. In more recent times, research psychologist James Pennebaker and his students found a mountain of evidence that demonstrates that disclosing our pain when we're suffering through a major upheaval can greatly improve our physical and mental health. Conversely, holding it in can lead to recurrent health problems such as colds, flu, high blood pressure, ulcers, and even cancer.

Having a child with a disability certainly qualifies as a "major upheaval." Keeping our upsetting thoughts and feelings bottled up is tough physical work, the burden of which can lead to long-term health problems. People who can open up in a group situation generally report that they enjoy it and learn from it. In addition, their health notably improves—which incidentally provides the scientific basis for the rapid increase of self-help groups for all sorts of problems.

In *Healing and the Mind*, Bill Moyers interviewed psychiatrist David Speigel of Stanford University Medical School about a groundbreaking study on the mind-body connection. Spiegel's patients were women with metastatic breast cancer, which kills most women within two years. Speigel set out to test the hypothesis that women who received group therapy in addition to standard medical care would show an improved quality of life, and they did. The women in the group reported less anxiety, depression, and pain than those who did not take part in group psychotherapy. What startled Speigel some years later when he was reviewing the data was the discovery that those who took part in the group psychotherapy had also lived twice as long after they entered the study as those who received only standard medical care. Social isolation is painful and dangerous to physical and mental health, while connection and support is healing and promotes physical and mental health. The group therapy was indeed powerful medicine.

According to Pennebaker, writing about our inner turmoil can also be therapeutic. Writing helps us to organize and understand our thoughts and feelings. Keeping a journal that we write in with some regularity can thus be extremely helpful for our physical and emotional well-being. By translating our feelings about events into words, we can gain perspective and understanding about ourselves and what has happened.

When we confront upsetting circumstances by talking or in writing, we are often relieved when we find out we are not alone and this helps us gain insight into how we feel. Since the federal government estimates that there are as many as forty-five to fifty million people with a disability or chronic illness, there must logically be others not far from us who could view us with empathy and understanding. We need a place to connect and talk freely. Then, with this kind of support, we can see ourselves as just ordinary people who happen to be going through a difficult ordeal, and this can be a great consolation.

Part of the journey to get to the other side of sorrow is to find the people, whether related to us by blood or not, who really want to listen. Brett Webb-Mitchell is a Presbyterian minister who has worked for many years with children with disabilities. In his book *God Plays Piano, Too: The Spiritual Lives of Disabled Children*, he points out that when someone listens to a story that you tell, the listener takes the essential first step in acknowledging your existence. Through telling our stories, we make meaning out of what may seem chaotic. Storytelling reinforces the notion that life can be best understood as an ongoing narrative. It is clear that telling and listening to stories is crucial to human caring and interconnection.

Alas, telling and listening is not always easy. Some people want to avoid adversity, and they avoid others who are going through it. They may not want to be reminded of how fragile life and health can be, or they may not have enough physical or emotional resources to share. There is a true burden in listening to other people's pain and even a possible health risk, as Pennebaker documented, for the listener may not know how to handle internally what she is hearing. One place to find people who can listen is in support groups. These groups are often organized in local school districts to include interested parents of children with various disabilities, or they may cover larger geographical areas and be limited to specific conditions such as learning disabilities, autism, hyperactivity, or Down syndrome.

Finding Support in Groups

A special kind of camaraderie exists among parents of children with disabilities. Although we are not related by blood, we are deeply related by our circumstances and can offer each other much comfort and understanding. There is one support group for parents of disabled children near the central New Jersey shore that usually asks me to facilitate a meeting each spring. Last year many in the group had children who were graduating from a half-day preschool program and moving into a full-day kindergarten program. The subject of this particular meeting was the parents' worries and concerns about their young children moving on to another educational setting.

The meeting was held in the morning, so I expected mostly mothers, but a fair number of fathers came and participated actively. The group had agreed to videotape the session for some people who couldn't attend. The description that follows is based on the complete video record of what happened. What transpired in ninety minutes illustrates the power and potential of parent groups to provide a type of support available nowhere else. When the meeting began, I asked people to speak out about their worries. What part of those worries did they think would be the same for any young child, with or without disability? What part of the worries had to do with special needs? I knew that thinking about these questions and sorting them out can have a calming effect.

A young mother in her mid-twenties, her red hair pulled back in a ponytail, spoke first. "My child started a full-time program this past fall. I was so worried. I didn't think anyone else could care for her properly. I remember standing with my husband and looking in the one-way window of her classroom and crying. I knew I would miss her, and I did. She's my first child, so I didn't know what to expect. What really helped, though, was that she came home happy every day. That told me she was well cared for. I felt truly liberated. That feeling washed over the whole house...."

With that comment, the meeting was off to a good start. People know they are cared for when their stories are appreciated and taken seriously. The next person to speak was a mother in her thirties, obviously more experienced, but no less expressive. She recounted, "This little one in special education was the hardest for me to let go of; I think because he is my youngest. I'm not sure what life holds for me now without a child home all day. I'm not sure I can be as free as I could if he was 'normal.' Is this the beginning of the empty nest?"

A mother who worked outside the home spoke next, adding a somewhat different perspective. "What's really hard for me," she explained, "is how my children have their alert, fun time with another person. My time is care-giving like fixing breakfast and dinner, giving baths, and getting them dressed. There's not much play. I mostly get to discipline them. That hurts. There are more hassles over behavior with the 'special' one, and that pains me even more."

A burly man spoke next. He had been staring so blankly that I had the impression his eyes were turned inward. "We're glad to be here," he began, apparently speaking also for his wife who was seated beside him. "When our baby turned one, he showed us how really far behind our three year old was. I'm really broken up inside...."

As his last words trailed off, his wife continued, taking up where he had left off, "He was really slow speaking, and we were devastated, but it's picking up now that he's in a special class. His teacher thinks he's doing really well."

It sounded like her husband was still reeling from his broken dreams. Somehow this man's expression of emotion seemed like the "go ahead" signal for the group to start talking about the harder, darker side of their experiences. The open and direct male expression of emotion often has that effect in a group. Perhaps the women hold back, fearing that the men may shut down and withdraw leaving them alone to do the group's work. Next, the mother of a child born prematurely told some of her story.

"My child was a preemie—only three pounds. I knew right away there were problems. It was difficult for her to see. The doctors in the hospital thought she was mentally retarded. She wasn't just behind because she was born too soon. She developed very slowly. She got all the early intervention therapies. Still, she didn't walk until two months after her second birthday. Even that was sooner than expected. It's been so hard; I never thought I would make it this far. Now she's five, and she's not mentally retarded. She won't always be a child, which is what I was told when she was born. It's a great relief; sometimes I cry over it. I'm glad she survived those first months in the intensive care nursery. I'm ready for her to go to school full time. I need a break...."

Her voice trailed off. There were tears in her eyes, so she reached for a tissue and looked away from the many eyes looking tenderly upon her. At this point, I asked to hear from some more of the men. They had been quiet up until now. There was a pause until some laughter broke the silence. A man who identified himself as a carpenter and said he'd been home for the winter because work was slow took the ball: "I didn't know how hard it was day in and day out until now. My son is a real handful. Every time it seems that we have things figured out, he goes to the next stage. He doesn't wait for us to catch our breath or anything. It hasn't been easy being out of work, but I am glad that I've gotten to learn all about him at this early age. I never really imagined that. I had thought I would get more involved as he got older, and we would play ball, and go fishing, and work on little projects around the house. You know, the typical father-and-son stuff. I think this has made me a better father and a better husband. I understand firsthand what my wife goes through. Right now she's at work, and I'm bringing home the information from school. She's bringing home the bread. What a switch!"

"I wish I was in her shoes," said Julie, who'd been the first speaker during the meeting. "Sometimes as soon as my husband gets home, I say 'I'm outta here,' and I'm off to the mall. He's not thrilled, but I just need a break."

A single mom with frosted hair and a somber expression said she had twins with hyperactivity and language delays. She sounded overwhelmed and her voice was pained. "When we are all home together, I can never sit down. I can't get babysitters. I'm almost forty; my mother is in her seventies, so she can't keep up with them even though she wants to help out. Other people just see my little boys as wild. It's so sad. That's where my frustrations are....It's a luxury just to sit and read the paper for ten minutes when you're a single parent. I'm worn out all the time, so I don't feel guilty sending them to school for a longer day."

Another father told his story. "There's some kind of miracle happening to my daughter," he began. As people looked more intense in response to the idea of a miracle, the explained that his daughter had congenital heart problems and had needed three major surgeries in her first three years. She had learned to walk at two and had begun to talk at three. "She still has speech problems, but now we can understand her. My wife is her stepmom; I couldn't have done it without her. We're a real team. I'm a happy man now—I'm no longer discouraged. We're having a baby."

Several people smiled, sharing his elation. Others looked rather sober, perhaps contemplating the risks of having another child.

The oldest woman in the room spoke next. "I thought I was done raising children, but now I'm starting all over again. My son's wife had multiple sclerosis, and when she passed away, he and my grandson came to live with us. Fortunately, my husband is retired, and he's home now, so he can help out. He's amazed. He keeps asking me, 'Was it that hard to raise the children?' And for the most part, as I tell him each time he asks, it was. Their speech was normal, but everything else was the same."

The wisdom implicit in this woman's experience lent a helpful perspective to the group. Many different living situations were represented in the room; the group was a microcosm for the outside world. After the grandmother spoke, I intervened to ask what was going on in the room and what direction the group wanted the rest of the meeting to take.

Julie spoke again. "It has been so good hearing from others, especially about the normal parts of this kind of life with a special child. This helps me to feel more normal."

"Let's get a list with names," suggested a woman who had been silent up until now.

"What will we do with the list?" I asked.

"My son doesn't have any friends in our neighborhood," answered the woman who had suggested the list. "I wouldn't mind going over with him and being with the twins for a few hours, so Mary can get a break. I know her children from school, and I can relate to them. If they run around with my Billie and scream and play, that would be fine with me, and Billie would love it."

"What else do we want for ourselves from each other?" I inquired, to keep this trend going.

"Just a couple of hours for ourselves once in a while, maybe at someone's home with coffee and doughnuts. I'll volunteer my house," said Sallie, the grandmother who had spoken earlier.

"That would be great to do without the kids," said Julie. "We could also have a play group at my house with the kids. I have a big fenced-in backyard with swings and a sandbox. We could drink lemonade and relax a little on a nice day while the kids have fun."

"Some of us guys might want to get together and do something like hit a few golf balls or shoot a few baskets," added Dan, the carpenter. His suggestion reflected the typically male mode of being together in an activity as opposed to just getting together to talk and share experiences, a more female style.

With time running out, I asked for someone to sum up the meeting.

Sallie took the floor, cómmenting, "When we can get together and talk like this, it's pretty clear that we're just ordinary people. That feels really, really good."

Many parents don't find their way to a group like this until it seems that there is no place to go. When relatives and friends don't know what to say, other parents of children with disabilities can provide a perspective and support that is available nowhere else. It is calming to share your fears and insecurities without having to do a lot of explaining. You don't have to worry about appearing weak or asking for pity.

There is also the practical benefit of learning from each other's experience. Talking to people with older children who have survived, shows that having a child with a disability is not the end of the world. Parents of children even a year or two older can give a preview of what lies ahead. You can get positive but realistic ideas about what the future holds. It can also be easier to talk to a fellow parent than to a professional, who, while knowledgeable, has not lived with a child with special needs and has not experienced the emotional roller coaster of everyday life with such a child.

Another wonderful aspect of participating in a parent support group is being able to experience giving as well as receiving help. There are moments when you need help and moments when you may be the person with the answer or a helpful comment. A parent who can give as well as receive is stronger and more self-confident. He or she can reach out to others in a way that was not possible before. It used to be commonly accepted that the blind couldn't lead the blind, but the self-help movement has taught us otherwise.

Support in Cyberspace

The current explosion of on-line services has exponentially increased the possibilities for connecting with other parents of special-needs children. Computer prices have come down making it easier to begin "surfing the net." Unfortunately, we still live in a society where equal access to resources of all sorts is very much an issue. The Internet has an ability, however, to be an equalizer. While many parents don't have the ability to spend the time or money to utilize this service, it only takes one interested person to share information with a group. As more and more public libraries and schools provide access to the

Internet, more and more communities will be able to take full advantage of what it can offer.

A woman I know through the local chapter of the Autism Society has made me more aware of just how dynamic the Internet can be. She asked her friends in cyberspace to comment for this book on how the Internet has been helpful in their role as parents. Here is a sampling of their E mail responses:

Emily wrote that the Internet disabilities lists have been great for her because they are available when she needs them, twenty-four hours a day, seven days a week. She doesn't have to find a babysitter in order to attend her support group meeting because her meeting is at home. She can use those precious hours when a sitter is available to go out with her husband, for example. Another plus for Emily is that much recent information is not available in her local library, and most of what is there is written for a professional audience. The information on the Internet lists is by parents for parents on "the real nuts and bolts of dealing with a disabled child that is often not an area that schools or doctors are much help with."

Emily also felt a large part of her frustration and anger diminishing as she realized how many other people were in the same boat. As she put it, "I stopped feeling as weird, or as if I was to blame, and became empowered to try things that worked for other kids. Even if the tips don't work (they don't always work, darn it), the helpless feelings I used to be plagued by have largely gone away." The Internet provided Emily with the kind of information and support that she needed most. She is now more self-confident because she knows more about her son's disability—autism—than do most of the professionals she deals with. She reports that she is far less depressed and has even stopped taking Prozac, replacing it with a "holistic antidepressant"— getting and giving help on the Internet.

Janette responded from a fairly remote part of the English-speaking world—Perth, Australia. Computer-aided communication has helped her to learn about the alternative therapies for children with autism that professionals in her area were reluctant to suggest or even tell her about, such as auditory training, epsom salts, diet, etc. Janette also commented that the Internet "is also a place to make friends through the shared common thread of autism....What else are friendships made from if not common beliefs, common ideas, shared experiences?"

In this vein, Tammy, another woman who responded, noted that when her child shows some improvement, she can share it with all of her friends on the Net who get really excited at the news, unlike others who may not understand their joy in seeing even the smallest steps forward by their child as a miracle.

Rosita wrote about how much brighter and more meaningful her son's future looks thanks to the Internet. Through the real, caring friends she has met in cyberspace, she has learned everything from how to stand up to her school system to how to enjoy her child and get him to hug her. With this confidence, she has become the best advocate for her son and has learned to speak effectively for him since he couldn't do it for himself.

Getting Help From Others

You can get more support when you are strong enough to ask for it, and when you can make the first move. Although most parents feel abandoned while they isolate themselves from others with the wall of their sorrow, more often than not there are kind people nearby waiting for a cue as to how to help.

In *The Lost Art of Listening*, psychologist Michael Nichols explores how to listen and be listened to. The heart of the problem, according to Nichols, is reactive emotions that trigger hurt, anger, or fear in the listener, which in turn triggers defensiveness and blocks understanding and concern. Furthermore, when we talk to people we are close to about what upsets us, they may feel implicated and tell us not to feel that way, thus creating misunderstanding and conflict. An empathic, accepting response, on the other hand, would be for a supportive person to say "Tell me more about how you feel," or "What's that like for you?"

Once we understand our own grief and our child's disability then we can explain it to others. This frequently ends the awkwardness described earlier, particularly when we are at a loss for words when asked about our child's problem.

We can often get what we want by asking for it. We can tell people, for example, that we just need to talk and need them to just listen. Likewise, we can explain that we have a problem that we need to discuss but that we're not expecting them to come up with a solution. This approach releases the listener from responsibility for solving the problem or making the pain go away.

Support groups as well as professional guidance can help us learn how to reach out to others. A therapist or fellow parent isn't responsible for your problems and therefore is unlikely to get defensive when told of them. After you learn to listen and be listened to, you can practice these skills almost anywhere with great results.

For example, the parents of a child with a disability often have friends with children of the same age. It may become difficult for them to ask them how their friends' little boy or girl is doing because it brings up their pain. The friends, in turn, may back off a little, worrying that hearing about their child's accomplishments may make the parents of the disabled child feel worse. Bridging these gaps whenever possible is a hurdle to get over in regaining normalcy for the parents of children with disabilities.

After Tariq was diagnosed and was attending the Center for Autistic Children, I came across some old baby pictures of Tariq and Leo, my friend Charley's son. I realized then what had held me back from calling my friend for the past four years, so I picked up the phone, somewhat unsure of what response I would get. My ambivalence subsided when I heard Charley's voice. It was as if he had been there all along, just waiting. Resuming our friendship, we caught up on each other's lives: Tariq's diagnosis, Leo's interests, Antoinette's development, my divorce, his two other sons who were born in the interim, our careers, and the baby born too soon that he and Michelle had lost. Grief had divided us, and now sharing it had reunited us.

My friend Dave, on the other hand, who I met in graduate school, does not have children, and perhaps that made it easier for me to maintain our friendship throughout the years since Tariq was born. Dave has a wonderful ability to listen and reflect without backing off. (As David Speigel tells his medical students at Stanford: "If you see someone crying, don't just do something, stand there. Be with them a few minutes, and let them know that you're open to their discomfort. It doesn't take a lot of sophistication. It just takes knowing what to do in a difficult situation.")

Dave was always just there when I called. When Tariq was four, Dave helped me make a video of me working with Tariq to use as a baseline to measure Tariq's progress. Dave's keen memory for the sequence of events also served as a point of reference for me over the years. When he called, he was never intrusive. Several years ago, when his mother died unexpectedly, he sent word to me through a mutual friend. I was glad that he had remembered me in his hour of grief. I had learned by then that there was nothing better than just being there for a friend. Sharing our losses cemented the bond of our friendship.

When *Family Pictures* was on television, Dave called to tell me about it. "I'm not sure if you'll be watching it," he said, "but I thought you would want to know about it." The door was always open, and he was very perceptive—for there were times that I wouldn't have been up for watching a movie about a family with an autistic child.

The passing of time and contact with Tariq helped my family to understand in whatever way they can. I remember vividly getting a phone call from my youngest brother, Greg, who wanted to meet me for dinner and offer whatever help he could for Tariq. We shared dinner in a Chinese restaurant while Greg insisted that I accept his financial help to get Tariq to the Option Institute. What a reversal of roles that was. Greg is fifteen years my junior, and I was used to looking out for him. When I went out with him while I was in college, people sometimes took him for my son. The money he had offered was sorely needed, but his sentiment was the invaluable jewel of that occasion that will always glisten in my memory.

My sister Luci also made a perceptive overture that stands out in my memory. When Tariq was little, and I was exhausted and beat up from living in the survival mode from day to day, she offered to watch him and Antoinette for an afternoon or an evening so that I could get a break and just do something that I wanted. What a welcome respite that was! It was one of the most thoughtful gifts I have ever received.

When Tariq entered the residential program at Devereux, my grandfather asked if we could visit together so he could see what it was like. This was how I discovered firsthand how seeing a child's school can help relatives to understand. Pop was old and frail. We sat on a picnic bench in the fenced-in yard behind Tariq's unit. My grandfather watched the other children intensely; many looked outwardly more impaired than Tariq.

Pop turned, looked at me intently, and stated his conclusion of many years of observation; "Robert, you have had a hard life." I nodded, feeling a lump in my throat and a twitch in my eyes. From that day forward, my grandfather never talked about Tariq outgrowing his condition. He understood something at Devereux that words could never have accomplished. I realized that I should also take my parents to see Tariq there. When the next Family Day was held, they came to the picnic with the other families and children at Devereux. That encounter helped them, too, to understand in a way that they hadn't previously. Being able to bring my family to Devereux and benefiting from the experience showed that I was getting stronger.

Connecting With Laughter

In their camaraderie, parents of children with special needs can share a special kind of laughter. That laughter can serve as an antidote to the sorrow sometimes caused by everyday events. Those who can relate to your sorrow can understand your laughter. Over the years many parents have told me that developing a sense of humor about their situation has been a key to finding the strength to get through the hard times.

R. Wayne Gilpin, the father of a child with autism and the former president of the Autism Society of America, has collected a volume of stories entitled *Laughing and Loving With Autism*. The stories are about his son, Alex, as well as about many other children and adults with autism. These accounts are based on the literal interpretations of things that children with autism make. They see things exactly as they are presented, and in so doing, highlight the humor in how seriously "normal" people often view the same words or deeds. The incidents described, like real life, are simultaneously funny and touching.

The logic of a child with a mental disability, such as autism, can be hard to refute. One example in Gilpin's book involves his son coming to dinner with no socks on. When asked to put on some socks before dinner, Alex responded, "But, Dad, if I drop food, I'll get my socks dirty!" Another instance was described by the parent of a young boy struggling to find the right word to express himself. When his dad told him, "Spit it out, son!" the boy stopped talking and spit; then he continued trying to find the right word.

In my own life, even the lack of speech did not stop Tariq from developing a sense of humor. Soon after he was toilet trained at around four years of age, Tariq began to signal that he needed to use the bathroom by tugging at his pants and sometimes pulling them partway or all the way down. I would rush him to the bathroom before he could have an "accident." Sometimes while I was trying to get him to bed, he would do the same thing. When we got to the bathroom and he didn't have to go, he would laugh—deep and hearty from the belly—the joke was on me.

Often I have heard parents spontaneously sharing funny stories or situations at meetings and conferences. One woman I know always gets a kick out of telling how she finds time to vacuum. Parents of young children can't do this when the children are napping because it will wake them up, and when they are awake it will scare them. Her son has severe hearing loss, so she runs the vacuum while he's napping. "I have the cleanest floors of any of my friends," she always likes to remark with a smile. What she seems to enjoy even more is how much other parents in similar situations understand and enjoy her sense of humor.

Another mother told me about how she was rushing one evening to get her family ready to go to the movies together. "Hurry up," she told them, "so that we can get good seats." Her nine-year-old son, who needed a wheelchair because he had cerebral palsy, spoke up, "That doesn't bother me, Mom. I'm bringing my own seat."

Laughter like this in your everyday life has a practical value. In *Head First: The Biology of Hope*, Norman Cousins described how ten minutes of solid belly laughter would give him two hours of pain-free sleep when he was suffering from severe inflammation of the spine and joints that caused great difficulty in sleeping. Cousins's experience has been corroborated by medical research, which shows that laughter helps the body to produce brain chemicals called endorphins—with benefits including lower blood pressure, enhanced respiration, relaxed muscles, and increased production of disease-fighting immune cells.

Cousins regarded laughter as a metaphor for the full range of positive emotions including hope, love, determination, purpose, and a strong will to live. These promote physiological well-being as much as the negative inhibited emotions can damage our health. I highly recommend Cousins's book, which also includes a list of humorous books and movies used as a resource by the Duke University Comprehensive Cancer Center.

Donald Nathanson suggests that the pain associated with withdrawing from distressing or embarrassing situations can be relieved by comedy. According to the affect theory of psychologist Silvan Tomkins, anything that causes a rapid reduction in whatever is going on in the central nervous system will stimulate laughter. Comedian Buddy Hackett said in an interview reported in Nathanson's book *Shame and Pride* that whenever he creates laughter he releases people from pain. In the joy of the moment, whatever is causing physical or emotional pain is released. What a blessing from our inborn nature!

As attested by famous examples such as Christy Brown, Helen Keller, and Kathy Buckley, a positive outlook can help a child to develop as fully as possible. Even if a child doesn't accomplish as much as these role models, the quality of family life is always greatly improved by a hearty sense of the comedy in everyday life. In fact, this was one of the common characteristics that I found in my doctoral study of families who had coped successfully with disability. Each and every family told me that a sense of humor had helped them to survive and even prevail through the problems they faced. As Goethe observed long ago, "A joy shared is a joy doubled."

THERE are many lessons on this journey for connection and support as we are drawn together by our similarities, meeting through tears and laughter. It takes courage to acknowledge the hurt or grief and loneliness and to risk being hurt again. But that risk is necessary to get to the other side of sorrow. Whether we are related by chance or choice, we must learn to accept and honor our differences. When we do this, we can then divide our sorrow, multiply our joys, and make connections to support us through a lifetime.

TEN

Parents and Professionals:
A Perilous Partnership

What we really need from professionals is empathy for our situation and good services for our children. When we don't get one or the other, we tend to doubt them and ourselves and usually get angry in the process. From my own experience as well as from the testimonies of countless other parents, professionals lacking in feeling and hope, who seem to be just doing their jobs, provoke sharp resentment. It is rare to meet a parent who doesn't have a horror story or two about a doctor or the educational system. On the other hand, professionals who are compassionate and hopeful and who take a special interest in the family are remembered kindly and effusively praised.

The anger and anxiety experienced when parents seek help can be simultaneously intense, confusing, and energizing. As many parents can testify, it would be next to impossible to get over the hurdles and through the maze of obtaining the proper services for their child without the tremendous energy and determination that comes from uncomfortable but motivating feelings.

Anger is difficult to decipher, but doing so is part of "emotional intelligence." Psychologist Daniel Goleman quotes no older an authority than Aristotle on this subject: "Anyone can become angry—that is easy. But to be angry with the right person, to the right degree, at the right time, for the right purpose, and in the right way—this is not easy." While Aristotle understood the dilemma, modern mandated policies on children with disabilities and their parents' rights along with the psychological concept of assertiveness give us the tools today to be angry in the "right way."

The outcomes for children and families are best when parents and professionals work as partners with mutual respect and shared decision-making power. Parents, by virtue of their bond with their child, are true authorities in their own right, with information to contribute that no one else has access to. Professionals, on the other hand, through training and experience can often offer expertise and a broad perspective that parents alone don't have. Each has only partial knowledge, with complete expertise possible only in the partnership. Their combined viewpoint is the best upon which to base decisions, plans, and goals.

Parents' relationships with professionals are born of necessity and desperation during a time of grief and are therefore rife with opportunities for misunderstanding and conflict. You don't want to be there in the first place. No one wants to spend countless hours having his or her baby diagnosed and treated in offices, clinics, hospitals, and special schools by doctors, therapists, psychologists, teachers, social workers, et al. You simply want someone to fix your child and your dream—to take your pain away.

The denial, anxiety, guilt, shame, depression, and anger of the grief process (as discussed in earlier chapters) occur repeatedly, and sometimes several of these feelings arise simultaneously. You don't want teams of professionals peeking over your shoulders asking questions. After all, parenting is very personal and many of the questions professionals ask may lead parents to doubt themselves and wonder whether they are to blame for their child's problem. These are understandably difficult waters to navigate, and parents are understandably impatient with professionals who don't seem to grasp the intricacies of the situation.

Professionals, on the other hand, have their own stresses in handling administrative pressures, paperwork, large caseloads, upset parents, and their own professional goals and ideals. Professionals are human, too, and they have emotional reactions of their own while diagnosing and treating children they care about. As they bond with the children in their care and work for their development, they experience many of the same emotions as the parents—from excitement with a child's new achievement, to discouragement at a child's lack of progress, or to anger when they are powerless to provide services they really want to.

Unfortunately, most professionals who work with children have had little formal training in how to understand parents' natural reactions to disability and are unsure about how to work with the parents and the child as a unit. When a parent is visibly anxious or depressed, professional observers quite naturally speculate about what effect this might have upon the child's development and want the parent to "calm down" and "cheer up." What is often missing is the realization that accepting those feelings helps to facilitate the parents' grief, and therefore also helps the child as the parents learn how to face the future more hopefully and how to enjoy being with their child.

As the parent of a child with spina bifida, professional writer Gilbert Gaul, in *Giant Steps: The Story of One Boy's Struggle to Walk*, helps us to understand why these early experiences with professionals are so intense. Gaul writes about how parents don't readily give up the heroic image of the physician. We want it to be true that doctors are next to God so that they can make our children whole and healed. If our expectations weren't so high, it might be easier to change them, and there might then be less anger, which routinely accompanies unmet expectations. While easier said than done, we have no choice but to accept the limitations of medical science and its practitioners in order to be able to function as partners over the long haul for our children.

As we try to implement this principle, we discover the barriers on both sides of the partnership when dealing with today's dominant medical model of providing services in many public and private agencies. In this system, services are provided from the top down, and primary expertise and decision-making power is squarely with the professional partner. Some parents have had negative experiences with professionals or authority figures. These can be carried over to the new situation, contributing to parents' justifiable anger and making trust and collaboration difficult. Parents who are also professionals have a special view of this dilemma that can be helpful for others on both sides of it.

A Unique Perspective

No matter who you are before your child is diagnosed with a disability or chronic illness, you can never be prepared for what is to come. It can help to hear from people you think know how to handle things—perhaps with less anger, worry, and frustration than you. In 1992 at a family conference for parents and professionals entitled From Mental Health Professionals to Special Needs Parents, Paul and Penny LeBuffe collaborated in a presentation about their personal experience as parents of a preschool-age child with a rare condition.

Before they had a child with a disability, the LeBuffes worked at the Devereux Foundation, a residential facility in West Chester, Pennsylvania, for children with severe disabilities who cannot be cared for at home or in public school settings. Tariq has been a student there since 1988. Penny LeBuffe had been a residential counselor and supervisor and then served as an admissions representative. Paul was employed as a research psychologist. They found that they were not as prepared as they had imagined for parenting a child with special needs, but that having hundreds of people listen to their story had helped them find meaning and purpose in their family life. As Penny credited Ann Turnbull, a well known parent-professional from the University of Kansas, for pointing out that academic degrees can sometimes be a hindrance.

Penny's first conversation with a caseworker about her daughter, Katie, was seared into her memory, and like so many parents, myself included, she could recall exactly what was said. "It was like being run over by a truck," Penny said.

Until Katie's sixteenth month, the LeBuffes thought they had a Gerber baby, but then her vocabulary stopped developing. Katie kept using the same five or six words and was still cruising around holding on to the furniture without walking independently. In their search for confirmation that something was wrong, Paul and Penny were told that they were overanxious. While this is not unusual, these parents in particular *knew* something was wrong. Katie's pediatrician had guaranteed that she would walk and was alarmed when she didn't because he had predicted it.

After two years of tests, Katie was found to have a rare, progressive, degenerative neurological disorder. It was likely to be a terminal condition, and what had occurred was that she was losing the skills that she had developed prior to sixteen months of age. The people in the audience gasped when they heard this. "I didn't know what to say to make Penny feel better," Paul commented. Their grief had to take its course and wash over them, as they contemplated whether their daughter would be happy, whether she would have friends, and whether she would ever live outside their home. These concerns are common to parents and come with them to every interaction with professionals, and in the short run, there are no answers that make you feel better.

Geneticists told the LeBuffes that there was a one in four chance that they would have another child with the same disorder. In a stroke of good fortune that they surely deserved, the couple had already conceived their second child, Denise, by the time they found out what was wrong with Katie. Paul told the audience that day that the new baby kept them "sane." Many couples, have had a similar experience. Their pain and anguish are healed when they conceive a "typical" child. Would that it were always so simple and miraculous. Unfortunately, others in similar situations are terrified, with good reason, to try again for a normal child for fear they are tempting fate and will lose the genetic lottery for a second time and have a second child with special needs.

It's a shame that so many professionals seem to be unaware of the intensity of the emotions parents feel despite the fact that the couple may be holding hands and wiping tears as they sit through a meeting. Perhaps the couple is being asked for the tenth or twentieth time to recount their child's early development. While professionals may indeed be so overloaded and swamped with paper, that they cannot read every report, this all too common experience is infuriatingly unacceptable. Penny and Paul went through having to recount their daughter's history three times during the same visit to a well-known medical center for an operation for the child. No matter what your education or prior experience, there is no way to bypass the pain. It can even be harder for professionals, who may expect themselves to have an easier time getting through it because of their education and experience.

Paul and Penny concluded their presentation by challenging a current practice of "professionalizing" parents by asking them to serve as cotherapists and coteachers. This approach often leaves parents with little time to hold and cuddle their children and each other. It is part of the parents' job to obtain services for their child, but above all to love and nurture that child. This is where floor time, described in previous chapters, is so valuable in guiding parents into loving, satisfying, growth-inducing relationships with their children, whether specially challenged or developmentally typical. "We're parents, and that's enough," as Paul and Penny said in this conclusion.

The story that they told was reminiscent of the collection of essays entitled *Parents Speak Out*, edited by Rud and Ann Turnbull. It is a unique book about disabilities because the editors and contributors are all professionals in the field and are all parents or relatives of someone with a disability. Their perspectives highlight the tremendous challenges of living normally while relating to and caring for a person with a disability. Even competent, loving, and well-trained parents who work in the field sometimes feel overwhelmed when dealing with the "system."

David, a physician and the father of a boy with leukemia, spoke to me frankly on this theme. As he put it, "When you're dealing with your own child, things suddenly hit home....No matter how much training you have, you don't appreciate what someone else in this circumstance goes through until you experience it yourself. In a way, being a physician was a disadvantage. As a lay person, you tend to attribute more abilities to doctors than they actually have. The limits of medicine are far greater than most people realize. As a doctor, I knew that, and I knew that everything isn't curable. Someone who is not a doctor is better off because it is easier to have faith in the medical establishment when you are not a member of that establishment. As a doctor, I knew the limits all too well."

From Birth to Diagnosis: The Medical Perspective

Let's take a closer look at how misunderstandings arise between parents and professionals so that we can see how to close the gap and develop a working alliance. Many children with special needs present a complex clinical picture for doctors. The obstetrician presides at the birth, and the pediatrician is on the front line thereafter as the child is seen for immunizations and checkups throughout the early years. But unless the child is diagnosed at birth, or even before (as in the case of Down syndrome, for example), parents usually suspect a problem before anyone else. Because every child is unique and development is often uneven, the doctor, like the parents, may have no choice but to "wait and see." Likewise, both parents and doctor may unconsciously minimize the problem because neither party wants it to exist.

When there is fear and worry, parents are hungry for reassurance, and doctors may be reluctant to confront them with the negative possibilities or even the bleak truth. Doctors, like parents, can deny their observations or the implications and conclusions of those observations in order to avoid the pain of the ensuing helplessness if there is no easy cure, and the pain of having to tell the parents. A good physician knows all too well the limits of medical science.

As Norman Cousins has pointed out, the physician-patient relationship is a powerful medicine in its own right. Parents worried about disability or chronic illness long for a closer link to their child's doctor, which can help them to manage their fears while waiting for answers that only come with time.

Any child's developmental problems and the parents' ensuing pain touches doctors and may provoke anxiety in them that can make communication awkward. Parent and professional Helen Featherstone reported on her interviews of several physicians who clearly saw themselves as lightning rods for parents' denial, anger, and anxiety. Since no one wants to be in this position, this may explain why many parents are referred to specialists and shuffled around until they finally get answers to their hard questions and a straightforward diagnosis.

Even in the most clear-cut diagnostic workup, some form of parental denial usually arises as part of the spontaneous outflowing of grief. As psychologist and parent Ken Moses explains, the loss is so personal and elusive that few are aware at the time of what they are experiencing. Physicians may take this denial personally when they have to convince parents of what is best for their child. But along with the doctors' "truth," parents also need validation from the doctors of *their* "truth"—that life at that moment has been changed forever and that the loss of their perfect child is momentarily unacceptable. Imagine being asked to trust and believe someone who is telling you that one of your worst nightmares has come true!

The complexity of many developmental problems usually does require assessments by various specialists, so evaluation at a children's hospital or university medical center by a multidisciplinary team is probably the best way to get the expertise needed without the frustration of feeling you're getting a runaround. The primary care doctor may be slow to make this kind of referral, believing that the parents aren't ready for it, or she may be reluctant to give up control to specialists.

Doctors are understandably cautious in the diagnostic process and generally would rather go slowly and "wait and see," not wanting to err in such a serious matter. Proper treatment depends on accurate diagnosis, of course, but parents are eager to find out what's wrong and move on to cure their child. No one enjoys being in the dark, so these two very different perspectives unavoidably generate conflict and uneasiness on both sides.

Parents' anxieties can be further heightened when doctors use medical jargon instead of everyday language to explain their concerns and uncertainties, although this language may be one way to hide real feelings. Being rushed in and out of the examining room can also compound the problem.

Many of the horror stories that parents tell have a recurring theme: an overly negative prognosis. The doctor in the hospital said "that my child would never walk," "would be a vegetable," "would never live independently," "will need to be institutionalized." Even if a doctor hasn't given such a prognosis, a parent may assume it in the dark, devastating moments that immediately follow getting the horrible news. Pediatrician T. Berry Brazelton recommends that physicians first help the parents find the child's strengths and delay a realistic discussion of prognosis until a postdiagnostic conference, giving parents time to absorb the diagnosis.

I discovered inadvertently how radically my perceptions of professionals had changed over time. Readers may recall that when Tariq was finally diagnosed with pervasive developmental disorder at four years of age at the hospital where he was born, I was furious with the multidisciplinary team. I vividly remember how I wanted to reach across the table and strangle the people who were telling me that my little boy would never be normal. When I returned with Tariq for a reevaluation four years later, they seemed like kind, caring people. I could see the concern in their eyes as I contemplated why they looked so different from the first time, when they had seemed so cold, distant, and aloof. The main difference was in me: I was over the shock that came with hearing that my son would never be normal—not to mention that Tariq and they and I were all four years older and presumably wiser.

Many of those who tell the angriest stories have never confronted or revisited the personnel who inspired their anger. They may unconsciously need their anger as an exterior focus, a means of protecting their spouse and their child and themselves from their grief. In my case, I revisited the scene only because my lawyer recommended a reevaluation by the same team as evidence for a due process hearing before a impartial arbitrator. The reevaluation turned out to be serendipitous; it helped me to turn off an angry tape that had been playing in my head. My anger hadn't been wrong or bad, for it was part of my grief, but it wasn't healthy to displace it onto others or to hold a grudge. I was relieved when I was able to let it go and breathe normally again.

Some readers may find my outlook on the medical profession too forgiving. This may be true in some cases, but doctors are people too, and they can be good, bad, or mediocre; moreover, even the best can make mistakes and have weaknesses. I recommend that readers who are dissatisfied with their child's doctor discuss their problems with him or her and try to resolve them. You can ask for an "extended consultation" so that your doctor will have plenty of time for your discussion, and you won't feel rushed in and out.

If a discussion does not resolve your problems and the negative feelings that accompany it, then seek out another doctor whom you can trust and rely on. You need that kind of relationship with your child's pediatrician for yourself as well as for your child. Other parents of children with disabilities are a fine source of referrals in your search for an understanding physician. The books by Mark Batsaw listed in the bibliography may also be helpful as a source of medical information about various disabilities. Dr. Batsaw, physician-in-chief of Children's Seashore House in Philadelphia, was developmentally delayed and had learning disabilities and attention deficit disorders himself. He credits his mother's devotion to his development as the motivation for his eventual success—and he became a developmental pediatrician because of his desire to help other children like him.

Early Intervention: The Educational Perspective

Day by day, after diagnosis, parents live with their children and learn to love them as they are. While grief can be prolonged over a matter of years and throughout the life cycle, the most intense and immobilizing initial reactions are usually short-lived, lasting at most a few months. After that time, most parents are strongly motivated to find the best program they can to maximize their child's achievements. Once goals have been readjusted, parents usually will find meaning and joy in their child's accomplishments, no matter how small.

Just as parents have no control over the problem, they also have no control over the services available to resolve it—even though these services have recently become more accessible with the enactment of Public Law 94–142, which was championed through by parent organizations such as Pennsylvania ARC (formerly the Association for Retarded Citizens, but now known simply as ARC). Many parents report having to conduct long searches to find information about their child's disability, early intervention, preschool programs, speech and physical therapies, and other community resources, such as respite care. When a child has an uncommon problem, such as pervasive developmental disorder, deaf-blindness, or an even rarer chronic illness, the search for services can be even longer and more torturous, particularly in rural areas where shortages of experienced service professionals are common.

Because early-intervention services are now federally mandated, some parents fortunately find adequate services easily; others may still find them only with persistence, advocacy, and sometimes legal representation.

Take the example of Cynthia and Eric, whose three year old, Jessica, is deaf and has cerebral palsy. Jessica was assigned by the local school district to a preschool classroom for children with multiple disabilities in a wheelchair accessible building—which was fine, but there were two major problems. First, every other child in the class was mentally retarded, while Jessica's intelligence was above average according to specialized testing she had received. Second, her teacher did not know sign language and had no experience with children with hearing impairments. The school district adamantly refused to change Jessica's placement, maintaining that it was "appropriate." Did they think her parents were retarded? Fortunately for Jessica, her parents filed for due process and retained an attorney.

Prior to a hearing, the school district conceded and offered a placement in a specialized setting where the teacher was trained in sign language and other techniques for educating children with hearing impairments and where there were children with various IQ levels plus accommodations for physical disabilities. Is it any wonder that there are embittered parents?

Mary's five-year-old son, Pete, who was diagnosed with pervasive developmental disorder, autistic spectrum, also had a poor initial placement. In her quest for information, Mary had read about the breakthroughs sometimes possible through facilitated communication. When she requested this kind of help for her child through her local early-intervention program, she was told that it was too expensive and that no one in the region knew how to do it. Unfortunately, Mary hadn't been told the truth. The department of education in her state provided assistive technology and technical assistance to local programs under a federal grant that was well publicized to early-intervention programs and schools. Fortunately for Pete, his mom didn't accept what she was first told and called a parent advocate who gave her the information she needed to get her request taken seriously. Consequently, Pete got specialized help as well as facilitated communication and is benefiting from them.

While instances like those cited here are far too common, they are more the exception than the rule. But these injustices should not occur at all, and parent groups can help keep them to a minimum. Exchanging information helps parents to be more assertive in advocating for their children's rights.

Fortunately, the struggle, however involved, is worth it; those who refuse to give up, like Christy Brown's mother, are often rewarded. Study after study has shown that when children receive early-intervention services, they progress more rapidly and further than children who do not receive such services. Generally parents can see this progress during the preschool years, prior to age five, and are heartened and relieved to witness their child's growth.

Once a child has found a suitable placement, strong bonds often develop between parents and their child's therapists and teachers. These bonds are often closer than those with the child's physicians. The doctors were the messengers for the bad news and got caught in the crossfire, and it may be hard for parents to think of them as kind, caring professionals. On the other hand, teachers and therapists in early-intervention services are usually seen as allies as parents come to a realistic acceptance of their child's disability and limitations.

Tariq's primary therapist once arrived on our doorstep on Christmas Eve with a present for him as well as one for my daughter Antoinette—a sensitive gesture that I will never forget.

School Years: Entering the Mainstream

Most parents have come to terms with their child's disabilities, have realistic goals and expectations, and are attempting to live as normal a life as possible by the beginning of the school years. Our educational system, however, is structured to meet the needs of typical children and doesn't always meet the needs of those who are exceptional. Parents and educators often disagree on what is best for the child. When placements are made for the convenience of the school system instead of being made to meet the needs of the child, conflict results. There may also be disagreements over related services, such as speech, occupational, or physical therapies the schools must provide. Another area of disagreement concerns the inclusion of children with disabilities with their same-age peers as much as possible, which is mandated by current federal legislation. It is more likely to hear educators say that parents are unrealistic, while parents in turn complain that educators' expectations for their children are too low. These differences in expectations are a frequent sore point in the parent-professional relationship. But if your child's needs cannot be met in a normal classroom with added special-education support staff, he or she may be better served in what is called a "self-contained" special-education classroom.

Conflict between parents and educators is common, and I'd like to offer some suggestions on how to bridge the gap. Unfortunately, criticism of parents is common within the culture of schools. Just like parents, however, teachers are rewarded and encouraged by children's successes. Problems in learning and behavior, on the other hand, leave them frustrated, sad, and unsure of their competence. Since no one wants to feel inadequate, is it any wonder that parents and teachers spend so much time and energy blaming each other for a child's difficulties? This dynamic is, of course, intensified in special education.

The Feelings Checklist explained in chapter 2 has been used in sensitivity training with groups comprised of parents and professionals by the New Jersey Department of Education's Division of Special Education. When responses are compared, parents and educators have remarkably similar responses when asked to check off the feelings that they experienced during a typical day either with their own child or one of their students. In the ensuing discussion, the walls come down as each party gains an appreciation for the other's role and perspective. This type of dialogue can facilitate making collaborative decisions.

It is not uncommon to hear professionals say that it is a relief to go home to typical children. One teacher remarked in a group that every afternoon when she picks her own children up from day care, she hugs them with tears in her eyes and gives thanks that they are still healthy and growing normally. Parents who hear comments like that are likewise thankful and relieved to lessen the emotional distance between themselves and those who serve their children. While educators have been trained and expected to be affectively neutral, that is a myth that undermines partnership. It is not possible to work diligently with a child and not develop an emotional bond, and parents should appreciate this attachment.

Upon learning how much educators really care, parents frequently remark that they are impressed with how many children and their very unique needs are taken care of in an average professional workday along with paperwork and other bureaucratic duties. In addition, they wonder how professionals "have enough left" at home for their own families. Responses like this in the dialogue that follows doing the Feelings Checklist encourage professionals to keep on giving, because their caring is appreciated. Burnout is much more common for professionals who are not recognized for their caring.

Likewise in these discussions, when educators hear about parents' grief and frustrations directly, they are often moved to be more understanding and less concerned with issues like "realistic goals" and parents' denial. When professionals contemplate what it would be like to go home to a child who does not sleep through the night, or who is not completely toilet trained, or who is medically fragile, a different attitude and tone pervades the dialogue. Parents are often impressed with how difficult it would be to deal with so many angry, frustrated, and desperate people who want answers that are beyond the professionals' control and have trouble hearing and understanding the answers that they do get. One lesson of this type of training activity is that professionals as well as parents need to share memories, dilemmas, and insights as they learn to listen better.

Outside of a structured situation with an experienced facilitator, the kind of dialogue described here may be difficult to begin in everyday life. As Seligman and Darling explain in *Ordinary Families, Special Children*, the schools, where parents and professionals meet, are the "turf" of the professionals, and therefore parents often find them intimidating. Not to mention the fact that in team meetings to plan a child's program and goals the parent or parents are outnumbered by teachers, psychologists, social workers, learning consultants, and various therapists. Such a setup does not promote the equal valuation of parents' input, and without serious effort the professional views will dominate—not necessarily to the best interests of the child. This is where all parents are called upon to develop some skills in advocacy and assertiveness as an extension of their role.

Developing Assertiveness

Fortunately modern psychology offers a concept that can give us a handle on how to channel anger into effective assertion in the case of obtaining services for a child with special needs. There is a continuum from passive to assertive to aggressive problem-solving styles. The characteristics of each of the various styles are described by Robert Alberti and Michael Emmons in *Your Perfect Right*, a classic self-help book.

Passive problem-solving allows other people to treat you; your ideas, your feelings; and most important, your child, in this situation when you are trying to obtain services, in whatever way they think best, without challenge. You do what others want, and not what you think is best. By being passive you may avoid the conflict necessary to solve the problem, but you will have given up your rights and established a pattern of allowing others to dominate you. The other person is left to guess how you think and feel, and resentment and anger can accumulte. A person who uses this style talks to others with a great deal of respect, but with little confidence, and therefore merely waits and hopes for the best services for his or her child.

Aggressive problem-solvers stand up for what they want without regard to the rights, thoughts, or feelings of others. Through aggression, they claim their rights by attacking, viewing their rights as superior, and establishing a pattern of fear and avoidance on the part their "opponent." Aggressive problem solvers talk to others without respect and often come across as cocky and hostile while demanding what they want. The goal is to be neither passive nor aggressive, but rather to strongly, clearly, and considerately express your point of view.

Assertive problem-solvers, when they are the parents of a child with special needs, think and act in ways that back up the child's legitimate rights. An assertive parent can express strong thoughts and feelings without putting down the thoughts and feelings of another. She can attack a problem with respect for a professional's knowledge and establish a pattern of respect, thus avoiding the buildup of anger often caused by miscommunication. The assertive parent is both respectful and self-confident while requesting the services his or her child needs.

One mother told me how angry she gets when professionals don't hear and understand her. The problem reminds her of difficulties she had with her mother while she was growing up. Once she can refocus on the love and dedication of the professionals who work with her daughter every day, she is able to calmly and clearly express her thoughts, and this usually resolves the problem.

A parent is the most effective case manager for his child because he knows the child the best. Although it might not seem fair that the parent is thrust into this position, accepting this responsibility is a key to getting the best program and services possible for your child. A child whose parents are involved in his or her education and treatment every step of the way, despite occasional frustration, generally gets more than the child whose parents get discouraged by the difficulty of navigating the service system. Involved, informed parents who communicate assertively can readily build and maintain good working relationships with professionals. As your child grows and his needs evolve over time, these relationships become invaluable.

Unfortunately, there are many occasions where merely being assertive is not enough, and it becomes necessary to acquire an advocate for your child. Of course, parents must learn as much as possible about their child's disability and how to work through the maze of available services.

Here are some tips if you are having trouble resolving a problem with an agency or school system:

Gather information. It is vital to know all you can about your child's problem, both as you see it and as others see it. Become familiar with the treatments and educational programs available to children with similar conditions in your area as well as in other geographical areas. It is also wise to learn about your rights and those of your child under federal laws and the laws governing special education in your state. A sixties slogan "knowledge is freedom" applies here: The more you know, the less likely it is that you or your child will get lost in the shuffle. The appendixes to this book list many sources of information from books, organizations, and the Internet.

Make a plan. When working with the system, keep in mind what you really want to get for your family and any outstanding issues. It is a good idea to prepare notes before a meeting or phone call. Think through several options, so that you are ready to discuss whatever might work in the event that it is offered to you. Contact parent organizations and advocacy groups for support and consider the possibility of taking an advocate with you to a meeting to help you stay objective as well as to let the person you are dealing with know you are serious.

Take action. Have your notes in front of you when you call schools or service agencies and take additional notes on every contact you make and the date you make it. If you cannot reach the person you need to talk to, leave a brief message. Do not assume that you will get a call back. Be prepared to call persistently every few days until you get results. When you do reach the person you need to talk to, state your ideas simply, directly, and assertively. If the person needs to get back to you, then ask when you might expect to hear from him or her. If you have not heard by the agreed upon date, call back. The person you talked to may be overworked or may be avoiding you, so be persistent, firm, and assertive for as long as it takes. It is not just, but it is often true that the squeaky wheel gets the grease, so let the individual and the system know that you won't go away until your problem is resolved.

Take it further. If you do not get satisfaction, ask to talk to a supervisor. If that doesn't work, then take your problem to the director of the agency or the school district's director of special education. If that fails, then call a legal rights or advocacy group to represent you. Your notes about the problem, including the dates of all contacts and the names of the people you spoke to and what you were told will be extremely helpful if you have to go this far. However, most problems can be resolved before legal proceedings are necessary if you follow the steps outlined above.

LIKE all long-term relationships, the link between parents of children with special needs and the professionals who serve them, either as physicians or as representatives of agencies and school systems, is vital and yet challenging.

The anger that can energize you is often as hard to let go of as the dream for the perfect child, yet carrying it for too long can make one weary. When we first encounter these professionals in the midst of our grief for our child, we are challenged to relive and rework our own childhood experiences with our parents and other authority figures. There is an added benefit to learning to be assertive, knowledgeable authorities. When we do this, we can work in partnership with other authorities, which will help to resolve our childhood experiences and will also carry over into many other areas of life at the same time that it sets the stage for our special children to grow into all they can be.

Epilogue

October 28, 1996

Dear Tariq,

After a wet summer, the fall foliage is as brilliant and iridescent as ever. As fallen leaves crackle under foot, the book that I began writing in the winter of 1990 is finally done. This relationship of ours has truly been "a road less traveled," in the words of the poet Robert Frost. It wasn't a road I wished for or chose, but rather one I was shoved down by the hand of fate. Ever since you were a toddler and stopped talking, I (like many other parents of children with communication disorders) have been having this dialogue inside my head with you.

When I first thought about writing this book, I imagined quite a different ending. I wanted to change you, so that you could talk and do all the things that I dreamed of for you and me. I even hoped that someday you would read the book and be grateful to me for my efforts to rescue you from autism. It turned out, however, that through the journey you changed me in a way that I could never have foreseen.

In order to understand you, I had to tune in to all of the little clues about your needs and wants and feelings. To do that, I had to work on understanding myself so that I could accept and love you for who you are—not for who I wanted you to be or what I wanted you to achieve. This whole process chronicled in these pages is an abridged version of what made me who I am today. The truth of it is, that if you were any other way, you wouldn't be my Tariq, and I wouldn't be the same Bob. I wouldn't want another son. Even though this didn't turn out to be a book about a miraculous recovery from autism, it did turn out to be a story about what Faulkner calls "the human heart in conflict with itself" and about surviving and prevailing.

Our family has grown and changed quite a bit during the time these pages were written. After living with Cindy and me for several years, Antoinette is in her second year of high school and is living with your mother now, having the ups and downs of teen life. Like many children whose parents are divorced, she has needed to spend time living in both households. Her artwork was displayed last month at the Please Touch Museum, and she is thinking about college. She is in the graduating class of 1999, the last high school graduating class of this century. When you were a toddler, you had a T-shirt that said CLASS OF 1997. It brings back a lot of memories when I see a photo of you in that shirt. It was a time of innocence for you as well as me. Now there has been a coming of age.

Kara is five. She loves art, too, and is talking about opening a bookstore when she is grown up. Zoë will be three soon. She follows Kara everywhere she can, carrying her Minnie Mouse dolls, and wants to be read to all of the time.

Antoinette gets tears in her eyes when she reads parts of this book. She has missed not having you as "the older brother," although you are no less a brother and no less important to her. Kara is thrilled to see her name in print and asked whether the book would be in the bookstores we go to. Zoë can now recognize her name and will be no less excited by the time the book appears on the shelves. I will be glad when they are all older, although I hope the time goes slowly, and they read these pages and know who I am, how much I have loved them, and how Cindy and I have piloted the family boat together.

That road we were shoved down together, Tariq, diverged so long ago that I have no idea who I would be today if you had been a typical child. Frost talked about how "way leads to way" and doubted if he would ever come back. Our whole experience together transformed me and became a part of me, a part of my character; a part I hold in high esteem and a part that I wouldn't want to be without. I accept you the way you are in my heart, but still I wish we could sit and talk. While that will never happen, it is just as true that no other son could have done for me what you have. You are in the very fiber of my being, in my every moment, and I wouldn't want to change that.

As I have learned through you, there are many ways to talk, many ways to listen, many ways to see, to move. The term *differently abled* actually does make sense, and as other parents confirm from their experiences, having a special child can make the parents special too. I am grateful to you for that, and in that way also I couldn't have had a better son. In our modern world, many people search for angels. For all you have shown me, you qualify as my guardian angel, my ever-present spirit guide.

When things are tough, I talk to you more, so it is fitting to both begin and end this book with letters to you. It's been a long time since I expected you to talk back, so really I look for the answers in my own head or through other people or in my writing. Still sometimes I wonder what could have been. Some people say they get over that, but so far I have not. Helen Keller wrote an essay called "Three Days to See," in which she described how she would spend her time if she could have but three sighted days. It relieves me to read that from a person who made everything she could have of herself but still wondered what it would be like to have what she was missing. I can see you struggle to make yourself understood at times, so it's not that farfetched to wonder what you would say if you could.

In the past year, your running away from the people who take care of you has become a bigger problem than ever. Sometimes they can't catch you, and other times you manage to elude them and get away for a few moments unnoticed. Two of the incidents were very serious. Once, you ran out, or "eloped," as the behavioral terminology goes, from the school building. You were found running the water in someone's bathtub about a half mile away. Fortunately, the man who lives there called the police, who knew they should call Devereux right away. A few months later, you eloped around midnight in your pajamas and turned up at the local convenience store about three quarters of a mile away. There was no shoulder or sidewalk on the road that led there, making your journey there even more perilous. Perhaps an angel watched over you.

All this occurred despite the highest level of supervision. One of your abilities is to make an advantage of the slightest distraction. Often I have longed that you could use those powers of observation for a different purpose. After these incidents, concerned and worried staff members informed me of what had occurred. When we met soon after that, their faces reflected the gravest worry. Their fears for your life awakened those I have had since you were very little with a fury that I'd rather not have recalled. I was visualizing myself at your funeral and feeling the deep hole that your loss would be. This has long been my greatest fear: No parents want to outlive their offspring.

It was difficult to come to the shared conclusion with the professionals that you would need a more secure facility than might be available in our state. After all that has occurred and the struggles to get you the best care, there is more to come. As if that isn't enough, an incident occurred that reminded me once again how frightening the future remains. A parent's job is never done.

∽ ∾

Journal Entry, March 25, 1995

We went to see Tariq, and it was a hard visit. After ordering our food in a fast food restaurant, we sat down, but Tariq was hungry and couldn't understand the wait. He grabbed my arm and pressed his chin into my biceps as hard as he could. It hurt right down to the bone as the pain shot up and down my arm. I was furious. I could feel the blood rush to my head and face.

I got up to take him for a walk outside in the shopping center while the food was being prepared. We walked down the sidewalk. He was calmer now, and I held his hand. We were walking at the brisk pace that is average for Tariq, and it didn't dawn on me that he might bolt. And then in the twinkle of an eye, he yanked his arm away from me and took off into the parking lot running all out.

I froze for a second in disbelief. I had been trying to chill out my anger from the restaurant scene. I took off after him. I'm not sure if I checked for cars, but I think I didn't—my parental instincts took over.

"Tariq! Tariq!" I yelled. He didn't slow, didn't turn, as he often did. I dug down for strength.

By now he was ten or twelve yards in front of me. My mind was racing. Scenes from my life were flashing before me as I ran as hard as I could through the lane that divided the long rows of cars. It looked to be about a hundred yards to the crossway where cars were entering and leaving the parking lot.

Now eight yards separated us. Was this how it was to end? Tariq running. Me chasing. It was like a scene from *Forest Gump*, but this was real life.

Six yards. Then Tariq turned and looked, saw where I was, and kept going. The moving cars were less than fifty yards away. It reminded me of when I was seventeen and racing the one-mile run entering the home stretch. The city champion was in front of me and wanted to expend as little energy as possible in beating me, and I was going all out, with far less talent, to catch him anyway. But now Tariq didn't laugh, which would have been a sure sign that he would slow up. He still had that intense look that he had had in the restaurant.

Damn! Why couldn't he run this way in the Special Olympics? He would win there in safety. Now I could see the cars ahead in the crossroad. I couldn't tell how fast they were going, or if they noticed a tall, thin teenager streaking forward out of control and unaware of danger with his middle-aged father in pursuit.

Now only four yards separated me from Tariq. If he were killed, I would be free of the burden. Often I had longed for that weight to be lifted. But not this way! I didn't want him to die. I didn't know how I could go on living.

My heart was pounding. My chest was heaving. Three yards separated us. And then he slowed. I lunged forward and grabbed him. He stopped almost as suddenly as he had started, offering no resistance.

I hugged him tightly, panting heavily. Then I looked him in the eye. He seemed to have no sense of what had happened.

I was furious. I yelled. I could feel the blood rushing to my head and a new wave of adrenaline surging through me.

I held his arm tightly now, walking back the way we had come from the restaurant. I hadn't been vigilant enough. I had been trying to cool off and wasn't completely present in the instant that he bolted. Back in the restaurant, the rest of the family was waiting for us. I sat down, visibly shaken, and Cindy asked me what was wrong. I responded that we would talk later....

ᘓ ᘔ

THERE are moments like those described in this journal entry full of fear and anger, and then peaceful moments when it seems like "all's right with the world." Those are times walking or running in the woods together or riding in the car. You gaze contentedly at the trees, the clouds, the snow-covered fields, just as anyone else would. Once again I come to terms with the grief, with who you are and who I am. In my journal I find the words to describe it.

ᘓ ᘔ

Journal Entry, May 1, 1995

I fall asleep thinking about Tariq, and then I wake up with him on my mind. Where will he wind up in order to be safe? If not in Pennsylvania, will it be New Jersey? Delaware? Rhode Island?

Massachusetts? Georgia? Florida? My little boy—but he isn't
little. Still, he'll always be my little boy.

It feels the same as long ago—right in my gut, like my stomach
is separated from my ribs, a hollow space has formed there again
with this new crisis. Sure, I've thought about this chronic grief
before, written about it, talked about it, and experienced it at a
milder intensity.

As I reflect, there is a difference now. The frantic cognition is
gone, the shock is absent—I know this is it—I know I can't change
it.

The fear, the anguish, and the incredibly dark sadness wash
over me. Somehow the tears of last night make me stronger and
deeper, but a little more worn.

Ꮧ Ꮧ

THE WRITING brings up the pain all over again. So why bring it up?
Because it also brings a certain serenity to understand what has
occurred in the light of your essential peace and unspoiled innocence,
Tariq. Last winter we lived through the Blizzard of 1996, as over thirty
inches of snow fell in the Philadelphia area. Everything came to a stop
and for a few days life was simpler. No one was expected to get out
and do anything. People stopped rushing, "smelled the roses," and
talked to each other as they walked in the streets and helped each
other dig out.

Life was much fuller, richer, warmer. The city felt like an old-time
village. It reminded me of the warmth that can be found whenever
people, like the parents of children with disabilities, connect on
common ground.

If your disability were less severe and you lived at home, I doubt
that I could have mustered the time or the energy to write this book.
While this is but another of those bittersweet realizations, perhaps it
is more than that. Maybe the voice developed in these pages can add to
the symphony of voices of the parents and professionals who have
gone before me in this work.

It is a symphony that represents a host of others who may not have
the time or the inclination or the ability to articulate what they know
in written words. While you, Tariq, will not produce offspring, this
book is a living legacy that will touch others. In the Talmud it speaks
of this theme when it states, "Have a child, plant a tree, write a book."

൜ ൚

Journal Entry, July 27, 1996

After exploring all the options, it's been decided that there is no alternative that offers substantially more safety than Devereux. Even more precautions have been taken to protect Tariq, and the Cheltenham School District has provided funds for one-to-one supervision during more dangerous times and to attempt to teach more communication skills to avert the problem. I am relieved because I like Tariq nearby, yet the worries are never far.

On this bright, clear Saturday morning, Tariq and I got a canoe at Marsh Creek. The water was still and clear, and the morning sun gripped us gently in its warmth. The attendant remembered Tariq, so he gave me a life jacket but no second paddle, since Tariq can't use one. It's always easier when I don't have to explain....

As our canoe moved out from the shore, I could see the rich plant life teeming below us, a sign of the lake's health and vibrance. I felt it inside me too. Tariq put his right hand in the water enjoying its coolness and the feeling of the plants. When we got to the other side, there were wildflowers and cattails growing at the water's edge. An iridescent blue dragonfly hovered around the bow of our boat. Some Canadian geese perched calmly on a rotting tree trunk in the shallow water. An egret took flight as we approached. Perhaps the stillness within me helped me to take in the beauty.

And then in the next moment, Tariq got restless and began shifting his weight back and forth, rocking the canoe and signaling that he had had enough. I went with the flow, turning the canoe and heading back to the boat house, so Tariq became calmer.

When we got back, we were both thirsty, so we shared a Sprite while sitting on a bench looking out at the lake. Tariq leaned his head gently on my shoulder for a moment. I wished for more of these moments. I had hoped to stay out on the water longer, but I was pleasantly satisfied with how it worked out.

൜ ൚

I KNOW a number of fathers of boys with autism, and occasionally we meet over dinner or lunch. When the video of *Pinocchio* was selling two years ago, a number of the men mentioned that they identified with Geppetto. I must admit that your disability evoked the same longing in me for "a real boy." Gregory Burns, the father of a child with a rare chromosomal disorder, wrote on the same theme in the October 1995 issue of *Exceptional Parent,* he said that "knock on wood," his daughter made him real. *The Velveteen Rabbit* also pivots around the idea that living, taking your knocks, and showing the wear makes you real and lovable.

So the lesson, Tariq—would that I had learned it sooner—is that I've had a real boy all along. The road to this realization has been the one less traveled by, "and that has made all the difference." Your disability deprived us both of a certain "normalcy" but gave us other gifts that are just as valuable, just as natural as the snow. You can read the book, after all, for I know you can feel the stillness within me as I rest my pen today.

I love you for that,
Dad

Acknowledgments

This book is the product of a journey in which one person was indispensable. She is my best friend, my colleague, my lover, my wife, my coparent, and my first editor. In these many roles, Cindy Ariel is the sine qua non (without which nothing) of this book. Perhaps this public recognition can make her sacrifices on my behalf a bit more worthwhile.

There are many others whom I want to thank for their patient listening, reading, feedback, and support along this long and winding path: Emmanuel Ahia, Jerry Allender, Joyce Boose, Jack Doren, Gilbert Gaul, Skip Genuardi, Bert Kauffman, Paul and Penny LeBuffe, Sue Levine, Joe Lichtman, Sal Lucca, James May, Phyllis Morgan, Dave Murphy, Ted Narden, Claire Punda, Merrill Purdom, Evelyn Rispo, Paquita Roberts, Mel Silberman, David Smith, Emil Soucar, Sue Wheelan, Michelle White, and Roberta Wohle.

Countless parents and professionals whose lives have intersected with mine have inspired and supported this effort with their shared experiences full of hope, tears, and laughter. To all of you, I hope that this work gives voice to your lives.

At the Center for Autistic Children, Jean Ruttenberg directs a staff of tireless therapists and teachers who loved Tariq, accepted him as he was, and helped me to learn to love him just as he is at any given moment. I am especially grateful to Susan Kramer, Louise Lucreta, Trish Miron, Carol Morris, Joyce Scott, and Corliss Walker. Likewise, I appreciate the board of directors for their strenuous efforts and personal warmth behind the scenes to keep this unique little place alive for the families of children like mine.

At the Devereux Foundation campus in West Chester, Pennsylvania, where Tariq has resided since 1988, there is an equally special group of people. Their round-the-clock commitment to Tariq's safety and happiness has been unflinching and has given his life and mine a stability that I needed in order to write. Their loving efforts bury the notion that a residential school is a place for children who are "put away." Mialee Anderson, Meredith Babin, Buff Bates, Debbie Cordery, Pattie Giroult, Jim Hamilton, Mary Ann Tazi, Carolanne McNellis, Lori Rhoades, and Laurie Ann Tomsho are the names who come to mind, but there are many others whose kind words and warm hearts never go unnoticed. Carol Giersch, the liaison from Cheltenham School District, has also been a kind and steady support.

To the New Jersey Department of Education, Division of Special Education, let me express my gratitude for the privilege of spending a few years there as a trainer and for what I learned about the "system" and myself, working on the inside. I especially appreciated the dedication shown by my peers and superiors to making parent-professional partnerships a reality.

Also those parents who have sought my counsel as a psychologist are due my humblest gratitude. Their confidence in my ability to guide them helped to sustain the dream of this book, and helped us all to learn—how to meet the challenges and reap the rewards.

Margaret Wolf, my editor at Carol Publishing, really got the feel of this book. Her efforts served to highlight the heart and soul of the message, and her enthusiasm sustained me through the final hurdles. Also thanks are due to Marcy Swingle; Renata Somogyi, my production editor; and Ellen Jaffe, my copy editor; whose questions served to further polish the manuscript.

From my parents and grandparents came the confidence that I could achieve what I put my mind to and persevered through. For imparting this they deserve a special credit for a priceless gift.

Lastly, I am indebted to my daughters for their love and patience in awaiting their turn at our home computer.

A Final Note

I welcome reactions to this book. I am also available to conduct workshops and training sessions for parent and professional organizations as well as schools and human service organizations. If you are so inclined, please write and let me know about your story. I will pass along what you tell me to other parents:

Robert Naseef, Ph.D.
514 South 4th Street
Philadelphia, PA 19147
www.alternativechoices.com
rnaseef@alternativechoices.com

APPENDIX A

National Resources

Aid to Adoption of Special Kids	800–232–2751
AIDS Hotline	800–342–2437
American Brain Tumor Association	800–886–2282
American Cancer Society	800–227–2345
American Council of the Blind	800–424–8666
American Heart Association	800–242–8721
American Juvenile Arthritis Foundation	800–283–7800
American Society for Deaf Children	800–942–2732
Amyotropic Lateral Sclerosis Association	800–782–4747
The Arc (formerly Association for Retarded Children)	800–433–5255
Association for Persons With Severe Handicaps	206–361–8870
Asthma and Allergy Foundation of America	800–727–8462
Association for Children and Adults With Learning Disabilities	412–341–1515
Attention Deficit Information Network	617–455–9895
Autism Society of America	800–3–AUTISM
Captioned Films and Videos for the Deaf	800–237–6213
Center for Rehabilitation Technology	800–726–9119
Center for Special Education Technology	800–873–8255
CHADD: Children and Adults With Attention Deficit Disorders	800–233–4050
Children's Hospice International	800–242–5338

Cystic Fibrosis Foundation	800–344–4823
DB-Link: National Information Clearinghouse on Children Who Are Deaf-Blind	800–438–9376
Epilepsy Foundation of America	800–332–1000
FACES—National Association for the Craniofacially Handicapped	800–332–2373
Family Empowerment Network: Supporting Families Affected by Fetal Alcohol Syndrome/FAE	800–462–5254
Higher Education and Adult Training for People With Handicaps Resource Center	800–544–3284
Job Accomodation Network	800–526–7245
Juvenile Diabetes Foundation	800–533–2873
Little People of America	800–243–9273
Lupus Foundation of America	800–558–0121
Magic Foundation for Children's Growth	800–362–4423
National Aphasia Association	800–922–4622
National Association of the Dually Diagnosed	800–331–5362
National Association of Developmental Disabilities Councils	800–562–6265
National Association for Parents of the Visually Impaired	800–562–6265
National Center for Learning Disabilities	212–687–7211
National Center for Stuttering	800–221–2483
National Down Syndrome Congress	800–232–6372
National Down Syndrome Society	800–221–4602
National Easter Seal Society	800–221–6827
National Family Association for the Deaf-Blind	800–255–0411, ext 275
National Head Injury Foundation	800–444–6443
National Hemophilia Foundation	800–424–2639
National Information Center for Children and Youth With Disabilities	202–416–0300
National Mental Health Association	800–969–6642
National Multiple Sclerosis Society	800–624–8236

National Network of Learning Disabled Adults   602–941–5112

National Association for Rare Disorders   800–999–6673

National Pediatric HIV Resource Center   800–362–0071

National Spinal Cord Injury Association   800–962–9629

Orton Dyslexia Society   800–222–3123

Pregnancy and Infant Loss Center   612–473–9372

Recording for the Blind and Dyslexic   609–452–0606

Sickle Cell Disease Association of America   800–421–8453

Spina Bifida Association   800–526–3456

Sudden Infant Death Syndrome Alliance   800–221–2483

Technical Aids and Assistance for the Disabled   800–346–2939

United Cerebral Palsy Associations   800–872–5827

Note: This list was as accurate as possible at the time of publication, but there are often changes and moves due to factors such as consolidation and funding changes. *Exceptional Parent*, 209 Harvard Street, Suite 303, Brookline, MA 02146-5005 publishes a yearly comprehensive Resource Guide that is an excellent source of further information and listings.

APPENDIX B

On-Line Resources

Note: For those readers who are familiar with the Internet, these listings are self-explanatory. For those who haven't yet begun to explore this exciting resource, a book such as *The Internet For Dummies* by Margaret Levine Young and John Levine (Foster City, CA: IDG Books, 1996) will get you started. More and more public schools and libraries are on-line every day. At the time of publication "WebTV" is available for about three hundred dollars. With a television and a phone line, one of these devices can bring your home on-line, even if you don't own an expensive personal computer. (Remember, these addresses are subject to change, and new ones appear frequently.)

Ability On-line Support Network

Connects young people with disabilities and chronic illnesses to peers and mentors with and without disabilities.

http://www.ablelink.org/

Attention Deficit Disorder Archive

Information about ADD including diagnosis, articles, and other resources.

http://www.seas.upenn.edu/~mengwong/add/

Autism List

Information and discussion for the families of children with autism.

List Name: Autism
Subscription Address by e-mail: listserv@sjuvm.stjohns.edu

Autism Resources

Long lists of information and resources.

http://web.syr.edu/~jmwobus/autism

Blind Children's Center
For blind and partially sighted children and their families.

http://www.primenet.com/bcc

Blind News Digest
This is a digest of information posted on the Blind News list for the partially or totally blind. Covers personal experiences, medical, and technical matters.

Usenet:
Newsgroup: bit.listserv.blindnws

CHATBACK Trust
For children to have dialogues with others through e-mail.

http://www.tcns.co.uk/chatback/

Children's Defense Fund
A voice for children with particular attention to poor, minority, and disabled children.

http://www.tmn.com/cdf/index.html

ChronicIll Net
An on-line library about chronic illness.

http://www.calypte.com

Deaf Magazine
A weekly magazine for the deaf.

List Name: deaf-magazine
Subscription Address by e-mail: listserv@deaf-magazine.org

Deaf-Blind Discussion List
Devoted to the topic of dual sensory impairment. For professionals, individuals with deaf-blindness, and their families.

List Name: deafblind
Subscription Address by e-mail: listserv@ukcc.uky.edu

Disability Resources
Legal, medical, and rehabilitation resources along with announcements, articles, and newsletters on all kinds of disabilities.

http://www.eskimo.com/~dempt/disability.html

Disabled Data Link and Chatback for Children

Involves 100 schools supporting children with special needs and links
the children in discussion with each other.

Subscription Address by e-mail: Cliff.Jones@f71.n254.z2.fidonet.org.

Down Syndrome www Page

Information and links to parent support groups and other resources.
A web nexus for individuals with Down syndrome and their families.

http://www.nas.com/downsyn

Emotional Support Guide

Information and links to on-line support and discussion groups.

http://asa.ugl.umich.edu/chdocs/support/emotion.html

Family Village

A relatively new site with a wealth of information as well as ways to
get in touch with other families with similar disability issues.

http://www.familyvillage.wisc.edu/

Fathers of Children With Disabilities

Fathers as well as professionals are welcome to join this list which
shares information, ideas, and opinions.

List Name: dadvocat
Subscription Address by e-mail: listserv@ukcc.uky.edu

Father's Network

The www page for the National Fathers' Network. Includes many
articles from *Exceptional Parent* and other journals.

http://www.fathernetwork.org

Sibling Support Project

Support groups, workshops, and newsletters for brothers and sisters
of children with disabilities.

http://www.chmc.org/departmt/sibsupp

Special Education

Networking for teachers, therapists, and researchers.

List Name: spedtalk
Subscription Address by e-mail: majordomo@virginia.edu

For more information

Many thousands of listings cam be found for the families of children with disabilities. Go to one of the www search engines:

http:///www.altavista.digital.com

http:///www.webcrawler.com

http:///www.yahoo.com

From Harley Haken, *The Internet Yellow Pages*, 3rd ed. New York: McGraw Hill, 1996.

Bibliography

Alberti, Robert, and Michael Emmons. *Your Perfect Right*. San Luis Obispo, Cal.: Impact, 1982.

Albrecht, Donna. *Raising a Child Who Has a Physical Disability*. New York: John Wiley, 1995.

Bank, Stephen P., and Michael Kahn. *The Sibling Bond*. New York: Basic Books, 1982.

Barkley, Russell. *Taking Charge of ADHD: The Complete, Authoritative Guide for Parents*. New York: Guilford, 1995.

Batshaw, Mark, L. *Your Child Has a Disability: A Complete Sourcebook of Daily and Medical Care*. Boston: Little Brown, 1991.

———. *Children With Disabilities: A Medical Primer* (3rd edition). Baltimore: Paul H. Brookes, 1992.

Beck, Aaron T. *Love Is Never Enough: How Couples Can Overcome Misunderstandings, Resolve Conflicts, and Solve Relationship Problems Through Cognitive Therapy*. New York: Harper & Row, 1988.

Bly, Robert. *Iron John: A Book About Men*. New York: Addison-Wesley, 1990.

Brown, Christy. *My Left Foot*. London: Mandarin Paperbacks, 1990.

Brazelton, T. Berry. *Infants and Mothers: Differences in Development*, (Revised edition). New York: Dell, 1983.

Brazelton, T. Berry, and Bertrand G. Cramer. *The Earliest Relationship: Parents, Infants, and the Drama of Early Atachment*. New York: Addison-Wesley, 1990.

———. *Touchpoints: Your Child's Emotional and Behavioral Development*. New York: Addison-Wesley, 1992.

Buck, Pearl. *The Child Who Never Grew*. Rockville, MD: Woodbine, 1992.

Callahan, Charles. *Since Owen: A Parent-to-Parent Guide for the Care of the Disabled Child*. Baltimore: The Johns Hopkins University Press, 1990.

Chess, Stella, and Alexander Thomas. *Know Your Child: An Authoritative Guide for Today's Parents*. New York: Basic Books, 1987.

Christopher, William and Barbara. *Mixed Blessings*. Nashville: Abingdon Press, 1989.

Cousins, Norman. *Head First: The Biology of Hope*. New York: E. P. Dutton, 1989.

Darling, Rosalyn Benjamin. "Parent-Professional Interaction: The Roots of Misunderstanding". In *The Family With a Handicapped Child: Understanding and Treatment*, edited by Milton Seligman. New York: Grune and Stratton, 1983.

Dickman, Irving, with Sol Gordon. *One Miracle at a Time: How to Get Help for Your Disabled Child—From the Experience of Other Parents*. New York: Simon and Schuster, 1985.

Dorris, Michael. *The Broken Cord*. New York: HarperCollins, 1990.

Faber, Adele, and Elaine Mazlish. *Siblings Without Rivalry: How to Help Your Children Live Together*. New York: W. W. Norton, 1987.

Featherstone, Helen. *A Difference in the Family: Life With a Disabled Child*. New York: Basic Books, 1980.

Farrell, Warren. *Why Men Are the Way They Are: The Male-Female Dynamic*. New York: Berkeley, 1986.

Fowler, M. C. *Maybe You Know My Kid: A Parent's Guide to Identifying, Understanding, and Helping Your Child With ADHD*. New York: Birch Lane Press, 1990.

Gallinsky, Ellen. *The Six Stages of Parenthood*. New York: Addison-Wesley, 1987.

Geralis, Elaine, ed. *Children with Cerebral Palsy: A Parents' Guide*. Rockville, Md.: Woodbine, 1991.

Gaul, Gilbert M. *Giant Steps: The Story of One Boy's Struggle to Walk*. New York: St. Martin's, 1993.

Gibson, William. *The Miracle Worker*. New York: Bantam, 1962.

Gilligan, Carol. *In a Different Voice: Psychological Theory and Women's Development*. Cambridge, Mass.: Harvard University Press, 1982.

Gilpin, R. Wayne. *Laughing and Loving With Autism—A Collection of "Real Life" Warm and Humorous Stories*. Arlington, Tex.: Future Education, 1993.

Ginott, Haim. *Between Parent and Child*. New York: Avon, 1969.

Goffman, Erving. *Stigma: Notes on the Management of Spoiled Identity*. Englewood Cliffs, N.J.: Prentice-Hall, 1963.

Goleman, Daniel. *Emotional Intelligence: Why It Can Matter More Than IQ*. New York: Bantam, 1995.

Goodman, Joan F. *When Slow Is Fast Enough: Educating the Slow Preschool Child*. New York: Guilford, 1992.

Goodman, Joan F., and Susan Hoban. *Around the Clock: Parenting the Delayed ADHD Child*. New York: Guilford, 1994.

Gottlieb, Daniel. *Voices in the Family: A Therapist Talks About Listening, Openness, and Healing*. New York: Penguin, 1991.

Greenfield, Josh. *A Child Called Noah*. New York: Washington Square, 1970.

Greenspan, Stanley, and Nancy Thorndike Greenspan. *First Feelings: Milestones in the Emotional Development of Your Baby and Child*. New York: Penguin, 1985.

Greenspan, Stanley, and Jacqueline Salman. *Playground Politics: Understanding the Emotional Life of Your School-Age Child*. Reading, Mass.: Addison-Wesley, 1993.

The Challenging Child: Understanding, Raising, and Enjoying the Five "Difficult" Types of Children. Reading, Mass.: Addison-Wesley, 1996.

Grossman, Frances Kaplan. *Brothers and Sisters of Retarded Children*. Syracuse, N.Y.: Syracuse University Press, 1972.

Hallowell, Edward, and John Ratey. *Driven to Distraction: Recognizing and Coping With Attention Deficit Disorder From Childhood Through Adulthood*. New York: Simon and Schuster, 1994.

Hartmann, Thom. *Attention Deficit Disorder: A Different Perception*. Grass Valley, Cal.: Underwood Books, 1993.

Hendrix, Harville. *Getting the Love You Want: The Guide for Couples*. New York: Harper and Row, 1988.

Kaufman, Sandra. *Retarded Isn't Stupid, Mom!* Baltimore: Brookes, 1988.

Keen, Sam. *Fire in the Belly: On Being a Man*. New York: Bantam, 1991.

Kingsley, Jason, and Mitchell Levitz. *Count Us In: Growing Up With Down Syndrome*. New York: Harcourt Brace, 1994.

Klagsbrun, Francine. *Mixed Feelings: Love, Hate, Rivalry, and Reconciliation Among Brothers and Sisters*. New York: Bantam, 1992.

Klein, Stanley, and Maxwell Schleifer. *It ISN'T Fair: Siblings of Children With Disabilities*. Westport, Conn.: Bergin and Garvey, 1993.

Kubler-Ross, Elisabeth. *On Death and Dying*. New York: Collier, 1969.

Kushner, Harold S. *When Bad Things Happen to Good People*. New York: Avon, 1981.

When All You've Ever Wanted Isn't Enough. New York: Simon and Schuster, 1986.

Lamb, Michael. "Fathers of Exceptional Children." In *The Family With a Handicapped Child: Understanding and Treatment*, edited by Milton Seligman. New York: Grune and Stratton, 1983.

Levine, James, Dennis Murphy, and Sherill Wilson. *Getting Men Involved: Strategies for Early Childhood Programs*. New York: Scholastic, 1993.

Mackey, Wade C. *Fathering Behaviors: The Dynamics of the Man-Child Bond*. New York: Plenum, 1985.

Mehren, Elizabeth. *Born Too Soon*. New York: Pinnacle, 1991.

McKay, Matthew, Peter D. Rogers, and Judith McKay. *When Anger Hurts: Quieting the Storm Within*. Oakland, Cal.: New Harbinger, 1989.

Miller, Sue. *Family Pictures*. New York: Harper and Row, 1990.

Miller, Stuart. *Men and Friendship*. San Leandro, Cal.: Gateway Books, 1983.

Monette, Paul. *Borrowed Time: An AIDS Memoir*. New York: Avon, 1988.

Moyers, Bill. *Healing and the Mind*. New York: Doubleday, 1993.

Moses, Kenneth L. *Not Me! Not My Child!: Dealing With Parental Denial and Anxiety* (audio tapes). Chicago: Resource Networks, 1985.

Meyer, Donald, ed. *Uncommon Fathers: Reflections on Raising a Child With a Disability*. Bethesada, Md.: Woodbine House, 1995.

Meyer, Donald, and Patricia Vadasy. *Grandparent Workshops: How to Organize Workshops for Grandparents of Children with Handicaps*. Seattle: University of Washington Press, 1985.

———. *Sibshops: Workshops for Siblings of Children With Special Needs*. Baltimore: Brookes, 1994.

Miller, Nancy, with "The Moms": Susie Burmester, Diane Callahan, Janet Dieterle, and Stephanie Neidermeyer. *Nobody's Perfect: Living and Growing With Children Who Have Special Needs*. Baltimore: Brookes, 1994.

Mulick, James, and Sigfried Pueschel. *Parent-Professional Partnerships in Developmental Disability Services*. Cambridge, Mass.: Academic Guild, 1983.

Nathanson, Donald, ed. *The Many Faces of Shame*. New York: Guilford, 1987.

Shame and Pride: Affect, Sex, and the Birth of the Self. New York: W. W. Norton, 1992.

Oe, Kenzaburo. *A Personal Matter*. New York: Grove Press, 1970.

———. *The Silent Cry*. Tokyo: Kodansha International, 1974.

———. *Teach Us to Outgrow Our Madness*. New York: Grove Press, 1977.

Osherson, Samuel. *Finding Our Fathers: The Unfinished Business of Manhood*. New York: Free Press, 1986.

———. *Wrestling With Love: How Men Struggle With Intimacy With Women, Children, Parents, and Each Other*. New York: Fawcett Columbine, 1992.

———. *The Passions of Fatherhood*. New York: Fawcett Columbine, 1995.

Osman, Betty B. *No One to Play With: The Social Side of Learning Disabilities*. New York: Random House, 1982.

Park, Clara, C. *The Seige: The First Eight Years With an Autistic Child With an Epilogue, Fifteen Years After*. Boston: Little Brown, 1988.

Pennebaker, James, W. *Opening Up: The Healing Power of Confiding in Others*. New York: Avon, 1990.

Powell, Thomas H., and Peggy Ahrenhold Ogle. *Brothers and Sisters: A Special Part of Exceptional Families*. Baltimore: Brookes, 1985.

Powers, Michael. *Children With Autism: A Parent's Guide.* Rockville, Md.: Woodbine, 1989.

Pueschel, Sigfried, ed. *A Parent's Guide to Down Syndrome: Toward a Brighter Future.* Baltimore: Brookes, 1990.

Rapport, Judith. *The Boy Who Couldn't Stop Washing: The Experience and Treatment of Obsessive-Compulsive Disorder.* New York: Penguin, 1989.

Reit, Seymour. *Sibling Rivalry.* New York: Ballantine, 1985.

Robinson, Bryan E., and Robert L. Barret. *The Developing Father.* New York: Guilford, 1986.

Sachs, Oliver. *Seeing Voices: A Journey Into the World of the Deaf.* New York: HarperCollins, 1990.

Scarf, Maggie. *Intimate Partners: Patterns in Love and Marriage.* New York: Random House, 1987.

Schaeffer, Charles, and Theresa Foy DiGeronimo. *Winning Bedtime Battles: How to Help Your Child Develop Good Sleep Habits.* New York: Citadel Press, 1992.

Schiff, Harriet Sarnoff. *The Bereaved Parent.* New York: Crown, 1977.

Schwartz, S., ed. *Choices in Deafness: A Parent's Guide.* Rockville, Md.: Woodbine, 1987.

Seligman, Martin E. P. *Learned Optimism.* New York: Alfred A. Knopf, 1991.

Seligman, Milton, ed. *The Family With a Handicapped Child: Understanding and Treatment.* Orlando, Fla.: Brune and Stratton, 1983.

Seligman, Milton, and Rosalyn Benjamin Darling. *Ordinary Families, Special Children: A Systems Approach to Childhood Disability.* New York: Guilford, 1989.

Sifford, Darrel. *The Only Child: Being One, Loving One, Understanding One, Raising One.* New York: Harper and Row, 1989.

Silberman, Mel. *Confident Parenting: Solve Your Toughest Child Raising Problems With a Four-Step Plan That Works!* New York: Warner, 1988.

Silberman, Mel, and Susan A. Wheelan. *How to Discipline Without Feeling Guilty: Assertive Relationships With Children.* New York: Hawthorn, 1980.

Simons, Robin. *After the Tears: Parents Talk About Raising a Child With a Disability.* New York: Harcourt Brace Jovanovich, 1985.

Smith, Romanye. *Children With Mental Retardation: A Parent's Guide.* Rockville, Md.: Woodbine, 1993.

Smith, Sally. *No Easy Answers: The Learning Disabled Child.* New York: Bantam, 1981.

Staudacher, Carol. *Men and Grief: A Guide for Men Surviving the Death of a Loved One.* Oakland, Cal.: New Harbinger, 1991.

Steinman, Marion. *A Parent's Guide to Allergies and Asthma*. New York: Delta, 1992.

Stern, Daniel N. *Diary of a Baby*. New York: Basic Books, 1990.

Styron, William. *Darkness Visible: A Memoir of Madness*. New York: Random House, 1990.

Taffel, Ron. *Parenting by Heart: How to Be in Charge, Stay Connected, and Instill Your Values When It Feels Like You've Got Only Fifteen Minutes a Day*. New York: Addison-Wesley, 1991.

Tannen Deborah. *You Just Don't Understand: Women and Men in Conversation*. New York: Ballantine, 1990.

Thompson, Keith, ed. *To Be a Man: In Search of the Deep Masculine*. Los Angeles, Jeremy P. Tarcher, 1991.

Toman, Walter. *Family Constellation: Its Effect on Personality and Social Behavior*. New York: Springer, 1993.

Turecki, Stanley. *The Difficult Child*. New York: Bantam, 1985.

Turnbull, H. R. III, and Ann P. Turnbull. *Parents Speak Out: Then and Now*. Columbus, Oh.: Charles E. Merrill, 1985.

Veninga, Robert L. *A Gift of Hope: How We Survive Our Tragedies*. New York: Ballantine, 1985.

Viorst, Judith. *Necessary Losses: The Loves, Illusions, Dependencies, and Impossible Expectations That All of Us Have to Give Up in Order to Grow*. New York: Simon and Schuster, 1986.

Webb-Mitchell, Brett. *God Plays Piano, Too: The Spiritual Lives of Disabled Children*. New York: Crossroad, 1993.

Weiss, Elizabeth. *Mothers Talk About Learning Disabilities: Personal feelings, Practical Advice*. New York: Prentice Hall, 1989.

Weiss, Gabrielle, and Lily Trokenberg Hechtman. *Hyperactive Children Grown Up: ADHD in Children, Adolescents, and Adults*. New York: Guilford, 1993.

Wender, Paul H. *The Hyperactive Child, Adolescent, and Adult: Attention Deficit Disorder Through the Lifespan*. New York: Oxford University, 1987.

Williams, Donna. *Nobody Nowhere: The Extraordinary Autobiography of an Autistic*. New York: Times Books, 1992.

Worden, J. William. *Grief Counseling and Grief Therapy: A Handbook for the Mental Health Practitioner*. New York: Springer, 1982.

Wright, Beatrice A. *Physical Disability: A Psychosocial Approach* (2nd edition). New York: Harper and Row, 1983.

Wyckoff, Jerry, and Barbara C. Unell. *Discipline Without Shouting or Spanking*. New York: Meadowbrook, 1984.

Books for Children About Disabilities
and Chronic Illness

This bibliography for children was compiled and annotated with the assistance of Susan Levine at Family Resource Associates, 35 Haddon Avenue, Shrewsbury, NJ 07702, (908) 747–5310. Susan also edits two newsletters for siblings: *For Siblings Only*, for young children, and *Sibling Forum*, for preteens and teens. Both are available through Family Resource Associates.

Amenda, Charles. *Russell Is Extra Special*. New York: Bruner Mazel, 1992. About a child with autism and his family.

Asetine, Lorraine, Evelyn Mueller, and Nancy Tait. *I'm Deaf and It's Okay*. Morton Grove, Ill.: Albert Whitman, 1986.

Abbott, Deborah, and Henry Kisor. *One TV Blasting* and A *Pig Outdoors*. Morton Grove, Ill.: Albert Whitman, 1986.

Bergman, Thomas. *Finding Common Lauguage: Children Living With Deafness*. Milwaukee: Gareth Stevens, 1989.

———. *On Our Team: Children Living With Physical Disabilities*. Milwaukee: Gareth Stevens, 1989.

———. *One Day at a Time: Children Living With Leukemia*. Milwaukee: Gareth Stevens, 1989.

Bernstein, Joanne, and Bryna Fireside. *Special Parents, Special Children*. Morton Grove, Ill.: Albert Whitman, 1991. About children who have parents with disabilities.

Betschart, Jean. *A Magic Ride in Foozbah-Land: An Inside Look at Diabetes*. Minneapolis: Chronimed Publishing, 1995.

Brandenburg, Aliki. *Feelings*. New York: William Morrow, 1984.

Brown, Tina. *Someone Special, Just Like You*. New York: Henry Holt, 1984. A photo essay about young children witha range of disabilities.

Bunnett, Rochelle. *Friends in the Park*. New York: Checkerboard, 1992. Shows children with disabilities included in the community.

Corman, Clifford, and Esther Trevino. *Eukee, the Jumpy, Jumpy Elephant*. Plantation, Fla.: Specialty Press, 1994. About and for children with ADHA.

Duncan, Debbie. *When Molly Was in the Hospital: A Book for Brothers and Sisters of Hospitalized Children*. Windsor: Cal.: Rayve Productions, 1994.

Dwight, Laura. *We Can Do It!* New York: Checkerboard, 1992. About children with spina bifida, Down syndrome, and cerebral palsy.

Dwyer, Kathleen. *What Do You Mean I Have a Learning Disability?* New York: Walker and Company, 1991.

Elder, Vicci. *Cardiac Kids: A Book for Families Who Have a Child With Heart Disease*. Dayton, Oh.: Dayton Area Heart and Cancer Association, 1994.

Fassler, Joan. *Howie Helps Himself*. Morton Grove, Ill.: Albert Whitman, 1975.

A small child who struggles to master his wheelchair world.

Gehret, Jean. *Eagle Eyes: A Child's Guide to Paying Attention*. Fairport, N.Y.: Verbal Images Press, 1990.

———. *The Don't Give Up Kid and Learning Differences*. Fairport, N.Y.: Verbal Images Press, 1990.

Girard, Linda. *Alex, the Kid With Aids*. Morton Grove, Ill.: Albert Whitman, 1991.

Gross, Ruth Belov. *You Don't Need Words: A Book About Ways People Talk Without Words*. New York: Scholastic, 1991.

Hafer, Jan, and Robert Wilson. *Come Sign With Us: Sign Language Activities for Children*. Washington, D.C.: Gallaudet University Press, 1990.

Helfman, Elizabeth. *On Being Sarah*. Morton Grove, Ill.: Albert Whitman, 1993.

Sarah has cerebral palsy, moves about in a wheelchair, and communicates with a symbol board. She has the same dreams as other twelve-year-olds.

Herzig, Mali. *A Season of Secrets*. Boston, Mass.: Little Brown, 1982.

A teenage girl struggles to understand her brother's epilepsy.

Katz, Illana, and Edward Ritvo. *Joey and Sam*. Northridge, Cal.: Real Life Story Books, 1993.

About a boy with autism and his family

Kova, Sara Jean. *My Journey of Hope: A Child's Guidebook for Living With Cancer*. Grand Rapids, Mich.: Zondervan Publishing House, 1993.

Written by an eleven-year-old.

Lasker, Joe. *He's My Brother*. Morton Grove, Ill.: Albert Whitman, 1974.

About a child with the invisible differences of slow learning.

Litchfield, Ada. *A Cane in Her Hand*. Morton Grove, Ill.: Albert Whitman, 1977.

———. *A Button in Her Ear*. Morton Grove, Ill.: Albert Whitman, 1976.

———. *Words in Our Hand*. Morton Grove, Ill.: Albert Whitman, 1980.

———. *Making Room for Uncle Joe*. Morton Grove, Ill.: Albert Whitman, 1984.

Uncle Joe has Down syndrome.

London, Jonathan. *The Lion Who Had Asthma*. Morton Grove, Ill.: Albert Whitman, 1993.

Marcus, Irene and Paul. *Scary Night Visitors: A Story for Children With Bedtime Fears*. New York: Magination Press, 1990.

Martin, Bill and Archambault. *Knots on a Counting Rope.* New York: Henry Holt, 1987.
A Native American boy who is blind and his special relationship with his grandfather.

Mellonie, Bryan and Robert Ingpen. *Lifetimes: The Beautiful Way to Explain Death to Children.* New York: Bantam, 1983.

Meyer, Donald, Patricia Vadasy, and Rebecca Fewell. *Living With a Brother or Sister With Special Needs: A Book for Sibs.* Seattle: University of Washington Press, 1985.

Moss, Deborah. *Lee, The Rabbit With Epilepsy.* Rockville, MD: Woodbine, 1989.

Muldoon, Kathleen. *Princess Pooh.* Morton Grove, Ill.: Albert Whitman, 1989.
A child with a physical disability who needs help every day seems like a princess to her sister.

Ostrow, William and Vivian. *All About Asthma.* Morton Grove, Ill.: Albert Whitman, 1989.

Peterson, Jean. *I Have a Sister, My Sister Is Deaf.* New York: Harper-Collins, 1977.

Pirner, Connie White. *Even Little Kids Get Diabetes.* Morton Grove, Ill.: Albert Whitman, 1991.

Powers, Mary Ellen. *Our Teacher's in a Wheelchair.* Morton Grove, Ill.: Albert Whitman, 1991.

Quinn, Patricia, and Judith Stern. *Putting on the Brakes: Young People's Guide to Understanding Attention Deficit Hyperactivity Disorder.* New York: Magination Press, 1991.

Rabe, Berniece. *Where's Chimpy?* Morton Grove, Ill.: Albert Whitman, 1988.
About a child with Down syndrome.

Sesame Street Sign Language Book. New York: Random House, 1980.

Simon, Norma. *I Was So Mad!* Morton Grove, Ill.: Albert Whitman, 1974.

Why Am I Different? Morton Grove, Ill.: Albert Whitman, 1976.
A book for children who are different and feel left out.

Shapiro, Lawrence. *Jumpin Jake Settles Down: A Workbook to Help Impulsive Children Think Before They Act.* King of Prussia, Penn.: Center for Applied Psychology, 1994.

Sobol, Harriet. *My Brother Steve Is Retarded.* New York: Macmillan, 1977.

Wolf, Bernard. *Connie's New Eyes.* Philadelphia: Lippincott, 1976.
Raising and training a seeing-eye dog and the dog's relationship with the child.

———. *Anna's Silent World.* Philadelphia: Lippincott, 1977.

Index

217